FAKE
MISSED
CONNECTIONS

FAKE
MISSED
CONNECTIONS

Divorce, Online Dating, and Other Failures

A MEMOIR BY
BRETT FLETCHER LAUER

SOFT SKULL PRESS • AN IMPRINT OF COUNTERPOINT / BERKELEY

This is a work of nonfiction. In some cases events have been compressed. Names of individuals have been changed to protect their privacy. Dialogue in the work has been reconstructed to the best of the author's recollection.

Library of Congress Cataloging-in-Publication Data is available.

ISBN 978-1-59376-632-0

Cover design by Kelly Winton
Interior design by Elyse Strongin, Neuwirth & Associates

SOFT SKULL PRESS
An imprint of COUNTERPOINT
2560 Ninth Street, Suite 318
Berkeley, CA 94710
www.softskull.com

Printed in the United States of America
Distributed by Publishers Group West

10 9 8 7 6 5 4 3 2 1

FOR MY MOTHER
AND FOR GRETCHEN

Passing stranger! you do not know how longingly I look
upon you,
You must be he I was seeking, or she I was seeking, (it comes
to me, as of a dream,)
I have somewhere surely lived a life of joy with you,
All is recall'd as we flit by each other, fluid, affectionate,
chaste, matured,
You grew up with me, were a boy with me, or a girl with me,
I ate with you, and slept with you—your body has become not
yours only, nor left my body mine only,
You give me the pleasure of your eyes, face, flesh, as we pass—
you take of my beard, breast, hands, in return,
I am not to speak to you—I am to think of you when I sit
alone, or wake at night alone,
I am to wait—I do not doubt I am to meet you again,
I am to see to it that I do not lose you.

—WALT WHITMAN,
"To a Stranger," *Leaves of Grass*

1

This is what I am trying to say: I was in no condition to have paid closer attention to plot development. There were no flashbulb memories pausing time, creating a mental photograph of how sunlight fell in a pattern on the parquet floor, individual facial expressions, what I was wearing, or the particular geometry of where bodies were located in the apartment's floor plan. I've requested all the mental and visual impressions in the library of my brain, like an interlibrary loan—*The Book of Devastating Phone Calls & Their Aftermath* (153.1BFL)—only to learn the book has been pulled from the shelf and remaindered. I have only the fragments of conversations, the scrapbooks, the digital debris, and the patchwork of letters saved. I revisit and reread them. I look at them over and over, hoping if I stare at them long enough it becomes something like being there again, like remembering, and thus, once relived innumerable times, becomes solidly the stuff of a past. The phone was ringing. The phone rang. I answered it.

We were living in Oakland, on the border of Berkeley, where the neighborhood began its shift from bungalows carefully crafted in a shabby chic aesthetic to buildings run down by economic factors. I was depressed and could barely leave our apartment. If we were out of milk, I drank my coffee black, spooned the dry breakfast flakes into my mouth. If I managed to leave I checked the front door ten times, knowing each time it would be securely locked. The outside world was oppressive, the streets populated with the unfamiliar eyes of others looking through me and sensing my fears. Fear wasn't my best friend, rather my only friend. Halfway to the train, I'd turn back to check the lock an eleventh time.

I opened the door, inspected each knob on the gas stove, waved my hand before the outlet to ensure the coffeepot was unplugged, and pointed a finger at each cat, an obsessive compulsion manifested to create order, as if the physical gesture could trick my mind into acknowledging the cats hadn't slipped past me and out the front door. I said aloud, "One cat, two cats." I closed the door. I opened it again; there they were as I pointed. "One cat, two cats." If I made it to the train, I put on my earphones and pressed play. Or I put on my earphones to appear preoccupied enough to avoid commuter small talk, the obligation to provide the wayward stranger with directions. I averted my eyes. I looked sideways. I wore a nondescript neutral colored sweatshirt, the hood up in order to appear more menacing from a distance. Anything to get moving properly, rise with enough gusto to get out of the house and order a sandwich, rent a movie, and have a conversation with the cashier at the coffee shop, but one brief enough not to give the wrong impression.

My wife Nina and I sat in our living room. It was less than a week before we left to visit her parents and then embark on the annual Christmas cruise to Mexico with my in-laws. Indistinguishable days at sea, the hours of each day to be marked by meals—a breakfast buffet of wet eggs and burnt bacon, a midday snack of nachos or grilled hot dogs and French fries, a five-course dinner (formal attire required), and a 24-hour self-service soft ice cream machine—all said, on average, to add a pound a day to each traveler. Somewhere onboard, I was told, there would be a gym, not that I would use it. A trip filled with indifferent shuffleboard, karaoke with grandparents in the "community" lounge that at 11 PM promptly transformed, assisted by strobe lights and a fog machine, into a "club" named something like The Cove. Teenagers, twentysomethings with glow-in-the-dark drinking-age wristbands, and inevitably me crowded in and dancing to Nelly's "Hot in Herre." I'd taken a version of this cruise before. It advertised exactly three port destinations in which one could pay an additional fee to swim with dolphins or scuba dive. We wouldn't. We would wander the historic section of town or sit for half of a day on a crowded beach where I'd have to disguise my pale skin in a T-shirt.

We had waited until the last minute to secure a pet-sitter and had to forego comparison shopping. And so we found ourselves slightly annoyed and embarrassed to be paying $125 a day for a stranger to collect the few bills and catalogs from our mailbox, deposit them on the coffee table, then perform the required task of petting our cats. There was nothing to be done about it. A middle-aged woman sat across from us. I want to say she wore Crocs and a polar fleece, but this is how I've come to describe everyone in the Bay Area: a blur of stock footage reduced to fair-trade granola, a breezy disposition, and a yoga mat. I'm not positive, but I don't believe she maintained eye contact when I interrupted to confess we didn't feed our cats grain-free food. I can say with certainty I observed the cat-sitter's mouth twist with disapproval when I admitted we left a bowl of kibble out at all times, rather than providing a structured meal schedule.

Everything I did in California inspired this feeling of being judged—the look of a cashier when I packed our groceries with a brown bag, or when, instead of carrying my wife's box of tampons two blocks home, I asked for a plastic bag. My friends left piss to brew in my toilet under the conservationist theory "If it's yellow, let it mellow." I double-bagged groceries from spite and allowed myself guilt-free extra-long showers in which, well after the last lather of soap was rinsed off, I did nothing but lean my forehead against the cool tile while hot water slid down the drain. Once, I plucked a dead leaf from the jade on the windowsill, placed it in the toilet, and flushed twice.

So it was then in our living room, prompted by this Californian condescension and not necessarily by an overprotective love towards my cats, that I took the liberty to articulate my every whim to our sitter: "Here is the leopard printed carrying case. Here is the catnip cigar. Hold your hand exactly two feet from the ground as I'm demonstrating to you now, so Ruby, the black–and-white cat, can rub her head against your opened palm. Here is the laser pointer; please take care that the beam should never touch their body, their paws, as it may confuse their limited notions regarding the physical world."

Two hours later, the cat-sitter long gone, the phone was ringing in our kitchen. I answered it.

"You don't know me. My name is Sophie Reynolds. What I have to tell you is difficult." Her voice reminded me of a nurse's, a professional stranger, and I imagined my mother in a hospital across the country, imagined this nurse in a white hallway with gray doors, wearing white Keds on a linoleum floor, surrounded by fluorescent lights, calling to inform me my mother had died in a drunk driving accident or she was in a coma, and it was uncertain if and when she would wake.

That was what I anticipated, what my family history had prepared for me. Not this: "Your wife is having an affair with my husband. It's caused some trouble in my marriage and I thought you should know." What can one say? Dumbfounded. A lump expanding somewhere in the throat, I managed "Thanks" and hung up the phone.

"Who was that?" Nina was on the couch as I walked across the room to the closet. "Sophie Reynolds." I opened the closet. "Do you have anything you want to tell me?" Silence. I grabbed a coat, or sweater, or sweatshirt. "Do you have anything you want to tell me?" More silence. I closed the closet door and casually put on the garment to maintain a sense of composure as I moved towards the front door. "She said you were having an affair with her husband." I paused; I opened the door, walked out into the morning. It happened that suddenly. I opened the door. I walked out into the sun.

I went straight to the market for a pack of cigarettes, my first in a year. The first cigarette was a task needing completion: confused and in shock, light-headed and slightly ill, the influx of toxins to my bloodstream added to the mixture of psychological stimulants circulating through my body. My body adjusted, began to compensate, the initial spike to the system leveled out, and I began to feel more normal. I remembered to exhale, the aura of bright light closing in on my field of vision receded; I looked at my hand and there it was, shaking. The cloud of shapes in the distance came into focus and there was a man on the corner wearing a multicolored poncho and a faded Santa Claus hat ringing a bell. I felt his eyes watching me. The bell rang like a metronome marking a normal heart rate. I chain-smoked four cigarettes before I called my brother Simon. Sitting on the stoop of the Oakland Public Library, the fucking sun absurdly shining, I could only speak the most necessary words: "Nina cheated on me."

The day after our wedding, in Nina's parents' living room, Nina cried uncontrollably on the couch. I wanted to believe it was a fit, a state that would arrive and depart, a curse bewitching her that I could outwit, kissing her forehead and reversing the effects. There were piles of gifts wrapped in silver and gold with light blue bows, stuffed in multicolored bags with congratulatory fonts announcing "Best of Luck." I held up a stainless steel rice maker, a polished stockpot, waved a fan of checks and hundred-dollar bills to make her laugh, to break the crying spell. I conducted a fake conversation with an iridescent knock-off Tiffany lamp shaped like a turtle, a gift from her aunt. "Hello, Mr. Turtle. Welcome to the family."

She couldn't stop crying. Her mother rubbed her back, stroked her hair. Nina's anxiety never seemed to manifest itself as a dull dread in the bones, as a momentary pulling of the duvet over her head as the morning alarm rang. It was always inconsolable, always crash-and-smolder for days. Her mother seemed to be the only one who could comfort her, since forever, or at least college. In Nina's first semester at junior college, she was overcome with such a degree of uneasiness that her mother attended classes with her. I imagine they sat in the back, both taking notes, fulfilling their requirements. I unwrapped the cellophane around a Williams-Sonoma gift basket from Ted Danson and Mary Steenburgen. Nina had gone to school with Mary's daughter. I licked my lips. "We'll be eating famous pancakes in no time."

Between gasps, Nina explained she was experiencing a delayed reaction to the pressure of the wedding. I wanted to believe her. Post-Matrimony Depression. The day had come and gone. She had been eerily matter-of-fact through the various stages and negotiations of the wedding. There were no pre-wedding jitters, freak-outs over seating arrangements, favors, or obsessively tracking storm patterns to predict the day's weather. What did I know—this could be an unspoken initiation for newlyweds.

Maybe similar episodes happened to everyone and simply weren't spoken of in polite company. It wasn't until my friends began having children that I learned about a mother's hair falling out after birth, shoe sizes changing, the release of feces and fluids during labor. That wasn't discussed in my health classes. I wanted to believe I was being initiated into marriage. For better or for worse. I believed her.

We were scheduled to fly to Dublin in a few hours and it was unclear if we would make the flight, or depart for a honeymoon at all. I'm sure I said things like: "Europe's not going anywhere—we can cancel reservations, postpone for a month, a year; could go to Paris for our five-year anniversary. People do that all the time. We'll have something to look forward to."

Nina called her doctor. A prescription would be sent to her mother, filled by her mother, and sent to us at our hotel in Dublin. A small majority of the honeymoon was then spent calling FedEx offices, navigating languages and procedures to track the pharmaceutical package. In between, we ducked into Irish doorways so Nina could cry. She remained outside of a bookshop while I browsed the aisles—she pleaded for me to go off on my own while she stayed in the hotel room. "You can't do anything to help me." We went to the natural history museum filled with taxidermy animals in large glass vitrines, a claustrophobic collection recalling a nineteenth-century cabinet of wonders. Polar bears stood on hind legs next to ferrets. There was no discernable logic. I waited in line to witness a page of the *Book of Kells* and examined it for too long—the anxious rustle of purses and guidebooks behind me becoming more and more aggressive. I didn't care. I was alone even when I wasn't. I had nowhere to be. I looked at all things stuffed, ancient, and illuminated. I walked on without her.

Her meds arrived in Dublin the day after we had left for Prague. The room in Prague had us sleeping in separate beds. I stretched out and stayed up late rereading Kafka, and Hrabal's *Closely Observed Trains*. Each morning we crossed the Charles Bridge—past gold objects adorning the bodies of saints. I walked as slowly as possible, the Baroque statuary staring back as they had through beheadings, floods, resistance, the hands and hammers of bygone craftsmen. Reading the guidebook in the airport waiting for our departing flight, I discovered the statues were fakes—the originals long ago shipped to museums for proper tourist admissions and safekeeping. Nina's medication arrived in Prague the day after we arrived in Paris. By the time we reached Paris, we were almost enjoying ourselves, and stopped at an Internet café to translate the phrase: "Cancel shipment."

I went home. There was nowhere else to go. Nina wasn't there. I waited. I lay on the shiny tiled kitchen floor blowing smoke out the screen door of our smoke-free building. I ashed into an orange coffee saucer. I waited. Nina didn't sleep at home that night. I don't know where she slept; rather, I know only where she said she slept. A friend's. The nights she did arrive home after work she went directly into the bathroom to change. She closed and locked the door. I was a stranger now, or actually, something worse—she undressed in front of strangers at the gym.

After *The Phone Call*, as I came to call it, Nina told me she had driven over to Sophie Reynolds's house to confront her, yelled at her through the screen door, "How could you do this to Brett?" I was further humiliated. "Don't you understand she did nothing wrong? You were fucking her husband?" Nina told me Sophie had no right to hurt me. "You understand *she* didn't hurt me, *you* did."

There were a few nights leading up to the cruise in which Nina and I stopped arguing long enough to watch a movie, and as the credits scrolled across the screen, we promptly resumed where we left off. "Why are you crying?" Nothing. "Why are you crying? You can't tell me?" I tried to initiate sex. I placed my hand on her inner thigh. *Take pity.* I thought, *this is how people make up, express forgiveness, mark their territory, alleviate the pain.* She insisted on sleeping on the couch, as if at that point the little gestures of penance could set things right. *Fuck you.* At the same time, I didn't want to rest side by side like two acquaintances sharing a motel bed on a business trip, straining not to touch each other.

This was all before Nina avoided seeing me in person, before she avoided speaking with me on the phone, before she requested all communication travel over the Internet's invisible wires in order, I assume, to mediate the discussion and diminish my tone of disgust.

■

Three months before the wedding my mother visited me in New York to help shop for a tie and black dress shoes. My brothers had informed me of her intentions. It was a nice opening gambit on her part, the pretext of participating in the sartorial matters of my forthcoming wedding, and I would have thought little of it—she visited more than anyone else in the family, and unlike anyone else in our family had actually once, as a teenager, lived in New York. She'd worked at a department store the summer before marrying my father.

I stood under the main DEPARTURES AND ARRIVALS sign at Penn Station. We went to lunch at a large Mexican restaurant in midtown. The waiter crushed an avocado at our table in a large stone mortar that impressed tourists. My mother called it "one of those New York experiences." The waitress offered us Bloody Marys and we drank iced tea. It was at this meal, a last meal of sorts, that she told me she wasn't coming to my wedding.

It should have been a blessing. A generous wedding gift in disguise. Accept it and never think of it again—that's what my brothers told me. My mother was, in effect, asking to be permitted a pass. There was only so much she could manage, and functioning gracefully in close proximity to my father was beyond her abilities. She had refused to attend my brother Simon's wedding a decade before on the same grounds.

Either as a mature adult clearly expressing myself or a child unwilling to understand the limitations of another, I spoke with a calmness unknown to me, explaining my disappointment. "This really isn't an acceptable option. I thought by now you could handle this." It was a measured tone, cultivated in the years since my childhood outbursts and the resulting nodes that had formed on the throat of the youngest of four boys needing to be heard. It was a tone, admittedly, that could have been interpreted condescendingly. Our conversation followed the course of serious discussions with much more at stake than what was actually being discussed—with the gravitational pull of a black hole, they drew in the subjects that were orbiting the perimeter. "Fine, I'll come to the wedding," she said. I told her, "I heard you were drinking again." She looked away.

I will admit, I did what everyone who has been cheated on does. In the days following *The Phone Call*, with a new critical lens, I mentally revisited every phone call or email claiming she was delayed, working late, shopping for a suit for an upcoming conference. Every event attended without me was reconsidered with the worst intentions in mind. I spent a short lifetime searching through everything: the crumpled papers stained with coffee grounds in the trash, all her purses, the pockets of jackets hanging in the closet—ATM receipts, restaurant mints, a ticket stub, red lipstick.

I placed the past under a magnifying glass, each item burning away as I looked at it closely. My brain centered its attention on my extraordinary will to suffer. I discovered no new information, or what I found could not be identified, just as a blood cell under a microscope is a strange amorphous shape, an abstract expressionist network of branches, until the label tells us otherwise. Bacteria, a lilac leaf, a bee antenna. Or worse, with a theory in mind, I couldn't look objectively; each item fit into my new hypothesis. A new version of a person was being created. Each event happened a particular way. It occurred. I experienced it. Done. What was left to do? Break her things, piss in her lingerie drawer, and pawn the ring on eBay? Instead, I did nothing. I cried on the couch or paced the two rooms. She had decided to go on the cruise, and I wasn't going to wait around in our house until she left. I left California; there was no point in both of us staying in our apartment trying not to make eye contact with each other. My older brother Noah offered to fly me out to spend Christmas with him and I accepted the gift.

December 24, 2006
Nina,

I know you've been angry, upset, and disappointed with me. I'm sure I could list a litany of adjectives to represent the distance which has grown between us. Fine, you met someone else. I can only assume you fell in love with him. There's no evidence to contradict this and in fact you've actively refused to placate me; vacancy possesses your face, a ghost of someone else inhabiting the physical body I once identified as you.

For the sake of this email, I'll set aside your decision to leave for your family cruise without me. Even in this state, my mind can identify a number of reasons: a) it is important to save face b) they paid already c) time apart might help clarify this difficult situation d) all of the above. This is the part of my brain which wishes to create a dignified narrative in these undignified times. I can't help thinking I deserve a little more. I deserve a little more than your brief emails: "I arrived in Puerto Vallarta. The weather is fantastic. Time runs out quickly."

I'm just thinking, maybe it would be appropriate to spend a few more pesos and write me something of any substance, or more substance than the remarks you would note on a postcard to a co-worker. Time does run out quickly in foreign Internet cafes and marriages. I know I'm needy; you've expressed how unattractive a quality that is. I should face facts: you're uninterested in communicating with me. Are you writing to Him? I'm certain this is the case, because you continue to act like someone who doesn't regret their actions, someone without a speck of respect towards me. So please don't continue to tell me otherwise. It's unfair. I know where I stand. I know the responsibility I take in this relationship. And I am determined not to be pushed out to sea. The person I fell in love with wouldn't turn her back so easily on me.

Love,
B.

Dear Jess,

Thanks for calling and sorry I didn't pick up. I just can't bring myself to recount everything over and over with everyone. The conversations with Nina have been unthinkable. I mean, imagine. It's impossible to stop my mind from the impulse to ask her the worst possible questions in order to arrive at some perspective or clarity, to satisfy some rational aspect of uncovering any, for lack of a better phrase, need-to-know facts, whatever they might be. But this is the short of it: She told me they had been together three times over a six month period. And since I've already done the math: in June we were married, in August we moved here, and the affair began sometime before our first wedding anniversary. Who knows how long she was considering acting on this before it actually happened. She told me they were together a few times, whatever that means, that once they "made out" in his office; that once after a work event they went back to his place for a drink. "It just happened." She kept saying, again and again. "It just happened. It wasn't planned." I asked her if she used condoms. She looked at me like I was crazy. She told me "It felt exciting, like I was doing something dangerous." "Did you tell him you loved him? Did you talk during sex? Did you? Did you tell him you loved him?" "I don't know. We were just friends; it is something that just happened." "Do you understand anything? Do you understand that friends don't fuck each other? That when you do that it becomes something else? How do you not remember everything? Shouldn't you have been replaying this in your head over and over for months now? Shouldn't you know every last fucking detail? So you would fuck him and then just come home and watch TV with me? How did you get home from his house?" "He called a taxi, but it didn't come. So he drove me home." "He drove you home to our house? What the fuck did you talk about?" "I don't know, movies. I don't know. I loved him. He was my friend." "Did you think about what kind of future you would have with him, what fucking kind of car you would drive?" "I don't know. Yeah, but I knew it wasn't reality." "What was reality?" "Do you think this has been easy for me? You know, I lost a friend." "I'm sorry, that must be very difficult for you. I don't understand. It isn't like you were drunk, that you were both at a bar flirting and judgment flew out the window for a moment." "I don't know." "No, how? Please fucking enlighten me." "I don't know. I must have been in his office talking with him, and went to give him a hug." "Why are you crying now? Oh, do you miss him?" Nothing. "Why are you crying? You aren't going to tell me? Did you love him? Did you LOVE him?" "He was my friend. I cared for him. And now I know guys and girls can't be friends." "You weren't friends. If I hear that word one more time. Do you even want to be with me? Why would you want to be with me?" "Because I care about you." "That's what you said about Richard too. Why would you want to be with me?" "Because I still can't imagine a more perfect person." "You don't make me feel that way." "Yes, I care for him and while I wish I could just run off into the sunset or whatever bullshit, I know I have my own things to work through on my own." And so it went, and eventually I just went to sleep on the couch.

Brett

I'd hated Christmas since my parents' divorce; the holiday split between two households, each year the tense discussions of who was going to be where and for how long, all parties fastidiously keeping track in order to use it at some later point as a justification for anger or hurt feelings. I still wasn't speaking with my mother after I'd asked her to leave my wedding a year and half before. I had flown to Minneapolis and was sitting quietly on the couch when my mother called Noah on Christmas Day. I could hear him whispering in the next room. "I'm not sure. I think he will try to work it out with her. No, he isn't eating. He leaves the day after tomorrow."

We went to a casino on Christmas Day, tried to kill sadness with kitsch, knowing how depressing and false the pretense of celebrating would feel in my current state. At the blackjack table we were quickly up three hundred dollars. Fortunes change. Noah joked, "Just think of it as going to the bank to make a withdrawal." We quit while ahead and walked out past the indoor water park and drove to a Chinese restaurant, where I ordered a bowl of brown rice and ate a third of it. I'd already begun to lose weight, which I found a perverse joy in, hoping Nina might find me more attractive.

I cried on Noah's front porch, the Minneapolis winter falling indifferently. I charted the days in hours that needed to be occupied. I demanded the television wash over me, obsessively replacing and numbing my own drama with one that could be solved. TV justice was a simple formula: the show started with a dead body and ended in an hour with the apprehension of the killer. And dreary details were inevitably left out, things like meals and showers.

I began to keep a journal of thoughts and conversations in a conscious attempt to have a record. I knew how easily I would forget, how events have a way of changing, are conveniently pushed to a hidden cul-de-sac in the brain. I had done it before. I had done it with my mother. Memories of events with no backstory, simple facts I could no longer recall, forgotten, most likely, in the hope they would never intrude on the daily narrative I told myself: *The world is not terrible.* Details became distorted, the gaps widened, until I no longer believed that they mattered. I tied the threads of a history into a bow and gave them away. And here I was again, knowing someday, at some point, I would forget everything, and I would find myself trying to remember.

Flying from Minneapolis to visit friends in New York, I looked out the airplane window and recited facts, all the facts I could remember. The earth is round. It rotates on an axis of twenty-three degrees, towards the east, in the direction I was traveling. It spins at a calculable speed, and is almost a hundred billion miles from the sun. The numbers become too large to understand. It is the same with suffering—when contemplating a disaster, even when the number of victims increases from one to two, we begin to lose interest. I don't think I invented that fact. I may have. In elementary school we were told to imagine the earth the size of a peppercorn, the size of a golf ball, the distance between planets as some amount of football fields stacked nose to nose. We were told to change the scale. It is important to keep records, to document the behavior, or else we resort to staring at the sky for answers. I kept notes because I wanted to be able to return to that feeling, that moment, so that later, when the facts started slipping, there would be documentation I could examine like a detective working a cold case. And so I replayed the events of my suffering. On the airplane I wrote, "Please let this plane fall from the sky in flames."

I'm at a loss for how I arrived anywhere, how one foot was placed in front of the other to arrive at the security check-in with my messenger bag, how I focused my attention to hear the boarding call, found myself in line to board the aircraft. I began writing a letter to my mother. With nothing making sense, I retraced my steps to find out where I went wrong.

Dear Mom,

I know I will not send this, which I just mistyped as "say this." I begin this letter in anticipation of events that may or may not occur. The sky is gray—this is the season when gray skies permanently fix themselves through day and night, when crystalline lights are strung from trees, transforming what was bare into an object the mind holds with fascination. I remind myself to look away.

Our first interval of silence lasted four years, from 1992 to 1996. I'm not positive why you kicked me out. After the divorce settlement, my father gone, you returned to the family house and for a brief interval we were all together under the same roof again. It wouldn't take long before you were shouting at me to "Get the fuck out of this house." It's possible the next morning you would have forgotten. It's possible Simon phoned dad. "Maybe Brett shouldn't stay here in the house with her." I packed my things. Noah, Simon, and I moved in with my father the next day.

This is the season the wind shakes windows. This is the season I anticipate a letter from you, a reminder you continue to exist; a return address telling me you remain in the town I left over a decade ago. I know the trees you see, the train tracks and bridges you cross in your daily routine, whatever that may now be. I know this better than any return address.

The card you sent to me this year, care of Noah's address, read simply: "I don't care about the details and so forth and so on. I just care about my son. Love, Mom." The cards are never empty. I know once I open them that we share something. My fair skin tinted blue, my blond hair, my hands which tremor with no provocation, and your money. When I was thirteen, when I was fourteen, and so forth and so on, each year four or five drugstore cards. Elves surround a snow-covered evergreen. An elephant holds a flower in his trunk. A print of an old willow tree. A Japanese wood-cut wave forever about to crash. They moved with me, kept in a box in a closet or beneath a bed. We haven't spoken in almost two years, since the day of my wedding. I start this letter, which I will not send, because I want to account for you how I have lived.

I've lived in the suburbs of Philadelphia in three different structures; in Pittsburgh in four; in Brooklyn three; in London two; and in the Bay Area two. Not much occurred. The weather in each place was slightly different; the trees exhibited their own characteristics and were related. Hummingbirds in California reminded me of hummingbirds in Virginia where your mother Orpha lived until she was moved to the suburbs of Philadelphia to die in an air conditioned building conveniently situated off a turnpike exit. The body begins to shrink in old age. We transported her back to Virginia in a shoe-sized box in the trunk of your car. In Virginia, she is said to have done the Queen's hair, when the Queen was visiting and staying at the lodge in 1957. Every summer we visited Orpha in Williamsburg can be distilled into a list: tri-corner-hats, knickers, coloring books of the uniforms of the American Revolution, reproductions of the Constitution, a duck pond at a golf course where she would take us to feed Canadian geese. Standing on a bridge, I dropped pieces of week-old bread. I watched the fish fight, wedge themselves between rocks. I wanted the fish to beach themselves in the shallow waters, to watch them feverish with hunger and excitement. I wanted to see if I could trick them into acting against their own welfare. I wanted to watch them die. On one visit, we went on a candlelight ghost walk through the colonial town, each building distinctly remade to be haunted. Orpha held my hand. I carried her charred bones from the trunk of your car to a hole in the ground. Hard earth, damp earth, in the end it doesn't matter; she was placed two feet deep in Virginia soil. Under a green tent I read a poem to strangers. They all told me she was returned home. "You asked me recently why I claim to be afraid of you," Kafka began a letter to his father. It goes on, heartbreakingly, for some forty pages. The letter was given to his mother for delivery, which she failed to do, and returned it unread. "I did not know, as usual, how to answer, partly for the very reason that I am afraid of you, partly because an explanation of my fear would require more details than I could even begin to make coherent in speech. And if now I try to answer in writing it will still be nowhere near complete, because even in writing my fear and its consequences raise a barrier between us and because the magnitude of material far exceeds my memory and understanding."

I concentrate, sit in the dark with eyes closed, a warm feeling centering in the chest. All that passes through my mind are family photographs, stories with details colored in from echoes and echoes of stories. Fallsington, a seat of early Quaker settlement; preschool, a Quaker meetinghouse. I know each day I wept when you dropped me off outside the stone building. I know I sat all day in a corner with a wooden shoe as my learning aid. At the end of the day while I waited for you to arrive, the class played Telephone, a phrase moved from one ear to another, transforming it into another story.

Love,
Brett

The friends I was visiting went to work. I left their apartment and walked the streets of the city they lived in. Quiet house after quiet house. Bare branches set against a bare sky. A stray cat that followed me for a block. I smoked. I walked and listened to sad songs: "Take a forty-five minute shower and kiss the mirror and say, look at me, baby, we'll be fine, all we gotta do is be brave and be kind." I looked at my watch and waited for another day to conclude. I read the entire Internet. I searched for more music to download. Absent of the adjectives needed to express myself, I looked at the All Music Guide, which described the "moods" of the bands in my current rotation as: earnest, melancholy, gloomy, reflective, autumnal, bittersweet, brooding, cold, paranoid, angst-ridden, theatrical, and wintry. I turned the music up. When the playlist was done it would be time for dinner, then three television programs, then time to sleep. I'm going to make it through this year if it kills me.

Noah had asked if I could have made more of an effort. He said I could have demonstrated a commitment to my marriage by getting my driver's license. It was a ridiculous suggestion, or it should have been—it was exactly what Nina had brought up after *The Phone Call*. "I don't know how you could be a good father." She meant I couldn't take care of myself, that I would never leave the apartment, or drive our imaginary kids, Ezra and Lucia, to soccer practice. I hadn't needed a license in New York City, but if I'd shown some initiative in committing to our new life in the Bay Area where we owned a car, things might have progressed differently. Instead I was the perpetual passenger, turning the dial to find a song to listen to. She was exhausted with taking care of me, with my depression and fears. I understood, sympathized—I had felt equally exhausted with her depression and fears while living in New York.

Moving to the Bay Area was not my idea. Nina had been an undergraduate at Berkeley and she believed New York—the pace, the residual anxiety of 9/11, the distance from her family—was the cause of her uneasiness. There were days when I walked her to the door of her office or calmed her down when she called from work crying. She began taking medication, seeing a therapist. Things returned to a relative calmness, but she didn't want to remain in New York much longer. I never wanted to leave. It was part of the deal; I knew this before I proposed. The move to California was talked about with an inevitability that took for granted the sacrifice I would be making. Couples make these decisions. I'm not saying I didn't understand this. I understood this.

In Oakland, months before I had received *The Phone Call*, when she told me she wanted to go to couples counseling, I told her, "I don't have a problem with that." When she told me she stayed late at work because she hated coming home, I began taking antidepressants the next day. But it was already too late. The scenery had shifted for Nina.

I returned home to Oakland on New Year's Eve and took a cab home to our apartment.

December 31, 2006
Nina,

I'm not sure why I bothered looking. Maybe I knew what I would find. I was putting the laundry away in the dresser and I saw the ring box. I should have known what one finds in a ring box. I told myself I was opening the black box to make sure the cat-sitter hadn't stolen my grandmother's ring. I held the box in my palm. It snapped open. My grandmother's ring was safe and still there, and as you know, so were your engagement and wedding rings. Hope you are having fun in Mexico.

Thanks,
B

I placed a slim gift box beneath our miniature Christmas tree. I downloaded the learner's permit handbook and made an appointment to see a therapist at the Psychoanalytic Institute. She would be home from the cruise in a day, and I would be standing in the doorway. *Forgive me. I can overcome my fear of driving, all fears, for you.* I was partially aware at the time—how one is aware the sun will eventually extinguish itself, or each day lived brings death closer—that these last-minute efforts had missed their deadline by months, but that a failure to try was also its own form of failure. It was important to be noble, to be brave, to admit my wrongs. If our marriage was on course to end, I wanted to look back and say I did everything possible to prevent the outcome, that it was, indeed, not on my behalf, that I wasn't the copilot watching the scenery pass and tuning the dial, that it would be Nina's decision.

January 1, 2007
Dear Nina,

I answered the phone today: "Please hold for an important message," and me holding thinking you were calling to say Happy New Year. It was just a collection agency for a person who once lived here. I left behind everything, my friends, my career, to move to California and build from your happiness. I didn't want to be here, but it was important to you, and you were so unhappy in New York. The phone rang and your name came up on my caller ID. When I answer you are not there. You call back and all I can hear is a faint humming. I say: "I can't hear you but it is nice to hear your voice." Disconnected. I go outside to smoke a cigarette, the home phone rang and I ran in to answer it: "Happy New Year from Cal Girls' Basketball."

Thanks,
Brett

My friend Nick drove down from Occidental to check on me and we went to an outdoor mall. I attempted to articulate to him the feeling of returning to my empty apartment. "It's like when I came home for my first winter recess from college—everything was the same but slightly different. Like, we normally had a real Christmas tree, but my father had purchased an artificial one and it took me two days to tell the difference. Or have you ever had to pack up the house of a dead relative? Everything's there, exactly the same as it was the last time you visited, but the objects, only days severed from their owner, are already filled with nostalgia. I think Richard must have been in the house."

Nick's demeanor hinted that he wasn't going to let on if he did or didn't know anything. "You got married young. Things happen. You moved here and she flourished, started going to the gym. This is the best she's looked and felt in her life." Quietly I nodded. I told myself that if I ever found myself on the opposite side of this conversation at a future moment, walking with an anguished friend or complete stranger, to convey the exact opposite senti-ment. *This is awful. You'll get through this.* Not even, *Maybe it is for the best* or *What doesn't kill you. . . .* Nick's perspective wasn't driven by cruelty. He had already arrived at an emotional distance, discerned Nina's motivations that, years later, maybe I would come to grasp, but at that moment I could only think he was privy to something I wasn't.

We continued walking, barely speaking under the winter sun and palm trees amid post-holiday shoppers on the prowl for sales. Nick stopped at a taco truck. I didn't order anything. I understood what Nick was trying to explain. There was little I hadn't already analyzed with my brother, or friends, or hopelessly scrawled in an ongoing bullet-point list at airports sitting against a mauve wall with a raccoon or grizzly bear or some other cartoon animal on a mural behind me.

- She must have felt like she was reinventing herself. But to what end?
- How can she be content with who she's become?
- Has she actually changed, become someone new, or is she just fleeing who she is? Does it matter? Is there a difference?
- Does this new person have any regard for herself, for others, any ability to express herself?
- She's pushed everyone away she cares for, keeping secrets, acting on impulse. What does this say about her?
- How could we have misjudged each other so grossly?
- What does it say about someone who can so quickly and so radically revise themselves?
- Did she ever love me?
- Was he ever in our house?
- Has he touched my cats? He must have been in our house.

I asked Nick if he would dispose of the bottles of alcohol Nina had left on the kitchen counter. I didn't dwell on the lack of consideration, the willful provocation in leaving a cache of alcohol in the house with an alcoholic; it seemed inconsequential given everything else. And to be honest, what disturbed me wasn't the deed itself, but the number of bottles and what they implied. It was a quantity for an intimate holiday gathering, rather than just enough to obliterate one person's troubles. Two bottles of vodka, gin, whiskey. There were too many options. I could have understood a bottle of whiskey half-full, but not the two glasses in the freezer. I knew Richard had been in our apartment.

I asked Nick what I told myself I wouldn't.

"Did you know anything? Did you know this was happening? Tell me."

"I know she saw Richard before she left for Mexico."

I told Nick I needed to go home. We drove in silence. At home, key in the door, my body began to falter and Nick was required to prop me up, wedged against his body and a stucco wall as he opened the door. Inside he laid me down on the couch. He knew I hadn't eaten in days and immediately gave me a glass of water, pulled out the only thing in the refrigerator, Fakin' Bacon, and started to cook. It was over. After all this, she had seen him again. I didn't want to nourish my body in order to stand, to walk, to produce the energy my body required in order to live. Nick hand-fed me like an invalid and I acted like one, refusing to eat the small pieces he had broken up for me. I hadn't been to an AA meeting in years, maybe seven. I checked online to find the times and locations of my neighborhood meetings. I felt like I should know just in case.

FAKE MISSED CONNECTIONS · 31

January 3, 2007
Dear Richard,

Setting aside my absolute anger and disgust with you as a person, I believe that you, as an educator, must have possessed at some point in your life some understanding of ethics and common decency. It is to the memory of this understanding that I appeal when I ask you to discontinue your relationship and indeed all contact with my wife. Remember for the time being she is still my wife. Perhaps such an appeal is futile when made to someone who has exhibited such selfish, reckless, and gross disregard towards others, and moreover, to one so devoid of sympathy that he has chosen to perpetuate such destructive and hurtful behavior even after its devastating effects on others became well known to him. In the end, I just want you to stay away from her, no matter what principle or strength or fear you have to call upon in order to keep your distance. The damage has been done, and although you are certainly in part responsible for it, if there is any possibility of repair, it must certainly be done without you.

Brett

Richard's response was, for all intents and purposes, a business letter. My letter demanded his letter's composition, and it was composed with the precaution of a lawyer. I understand that there was nothing he could have said. He apologized. There was no response that would have satisfied me, short of: "I fucked up. As I write this my wrists have been cut and are slowly bleeding out."

January 4, 2007
11:35 AM

ME: What time is the marriage counselor?

ME: What does that mean?

ME: Did you listen to what Marty said when we were there last time? He said I could have helped us months ago. That if we weren't both committed to working on this together, there was no point. And in your last comment, were you meaning to hit such a sarcastic tone?

ME: Oh, good, then can I say fuck you?

ME: Pissed at what?

ME: At yourself? I hope.

ME: Not really any reason to be pissed at me.

ME: I don't think a marriage counselor is the answer to anything. He might be able to help if we were working towards something; but, let's face it, you are utterly selfish. You have made up your mind regarding how you feel. It is something YOU need to work on, not us.

ME: You keep using those words but have no insight into what they mean to you, and your choice to not make a choice is a choice and if it is not already very clear to you, here it is: Your choice has devastating results.

ME: You can't do anything to make any of this any easier on me, and now it is transparent you are trying to save face by going to counseling, to be able to say "I gave it the old college try. I tried to work things out, but things have progressed so badly we couldn't." And you know what, at this point, I would hate myself for making any of this easier on you, although on the other hand I also hate myself for suppressing my own impulse to do so, and I resent you for it. Having the choice made for you absolves you of some of the guilt.

ME: I think your confusion is about how you could hurt me or that you don't now want things to go even more badly for me, but these are all thoughts you should have had long ago. And you didn't. And you can't. And you won't.

ME: Oh by the way, I looked at your emails, and there is a new one from Richard waiting there in your junk folder.

ME: You don't seem to have any ability to shed any light on anything, so I thought maybe your emails would.

January 6, 2007
Dear Friends,

Thought I would drop you a line to let you know the marriage is over.

Love,
Brett

January 6, 2007
Marie,

Thank you for your email and your kindness and generosity. You've been an amazing mother-in-law. It sincerely means a lot to me, though it is not surprising since it is how your family has welcomed and treated me from the beginning. I've reached out to a lot of friends who are talking me through the day and I'm sure the days to come. I am flying to NY today for a week and staying with Sam and Evelyn. It is important to me that you are strong through this, especially for Nina. I know she feels devastated and it must be difficult for her to navigate her own feelings, as I know it has been for me. I appreciate everything, but really am not thinking that far in the future yet and really can't process more than a day or so at a time. It goes without saying that I will always be here and that I don't wish to lose you or your family and especially Nina from my life and will make every effort that is emotionally possible. This is just all very devastating for everyone involved, and I wish it had never turned out this way. It is not what I ever wanted. I love Nina dearly and will continue to keep a large place of hope in my heart for her and her happiness whether it is with me or without me.

Love,
Brett

January 16, 2007
Dear Nina,

This is my fundamental problem and how I see things differently than you do: At some point in time, in the not-far-off past, you loved me. We spent five years together happy and in love and made a mutual decision to spend more years together, perhaps have children and build a life with each other. Now, there may be some problems with that statement, emotions that I might be assuming which maybe are incorrect such as "happy" and "love," but I am assuming the best and that you felt that way and were not in a state of confusion, though it is possible you were. This is not to say there weren't problems or issues, but my assumption was that there was a strong foundation of love and a willingness to work through issues as they arose. I watched my parents' divorce and it wasn't something I desired to replicate, and thus didn't enter into this marriage lightly. I knew that life was not easy, that in fact it was tremendously difficult, and I had found a person who I would help through those times and who would help me through those times. I knew that marriage was a long affair and that things would shift and adjust like, how we thought about each other when we were 40, or how things might adjust when we had children. But I held onto the notion of "for better or for worse."

There is no way to reconcile anything. That's certainly what you keep stating and I keep feverishly ignoring. All I can leave California with are uncertainties. To remember and repeat each sentence uttered again and again in my head, to search what little you confessed for larger cracks, to lay the texts before me on an autopsy table to dissect and search for hidden signs. What does it matter that you told your mother "I have met someone else?" Was that easier to say than "I've cheated on Brett?" Does this betray you in some way? What does it mean that you keep telling me "I care about you, I care so much about you," but not "I love you?"

This is all relatively new or at least this rupture—just a month old—but you have been walking around with this feeling in your gut for a year, without providing me the opportunity to question it or work on it with you. Perhaps that time is too long to conquer, but I think I deserve a commitment to work it out, with the knowledge that it might not—but that we would fight for something we thought was valuable. And that is where my disappointment is strongest, because of course I would work on myself and my issues, and to suggest I wouldn't is to miss a large part of who I am, and the things I have done and overcome and dealt with. Life and love go through phases, and we let something drift to the brink, but that doesn't mean we shouldn't try to bring it back. That is what I am asking. To try. And you don't want to, you stand with your blank face, limp arms like someone who is dead, and that is what truly destroys me, since it erases the past and any imagined future. You will be erased.

Brett

A day before *The Phone Call*, the book that Nina and I had just finished editing arrived in the mail. A beautiful hardback of collected readings for wedding ceremonies with a silver dust jacket. It is true sometimes things are as predictable as a bad movie. The book was an anthology of "classic and contemporary prose, poems, excerpts from love letters and novels, and aphorisms" that we had spent the past year working on together. When I was in Minneapolis visiting Noah, the publisher emailed to ask if we would be available to schedule regional radio interviews. *Someday*, I thought, *this will be a funny story.*

2

I packed the three suitcases I owned with clothing and moved back to New York. I was temporarily staying with my friends Jess and Todd in Harlem and halfheartedly searching for my own apartment, stalled in a ditch of post-relationship apathy, depression, and the terror of starting over. I slogged through Craigslist ads: airy, great location, shiny hardwood floors, a window, a counter for a coffeemaker, fits a bed. I wasn't asking for much. I looked at apartments in Midtown, in Inwood, in Brooklyn. Brokers were quick to inform me I didn't earn enough to afford a studio in Manhattan; I should be looking in Queens or the Bronx, which translated as "I'd rather not waste my time on a small commission." Unfamiliar roommates were a distant option, though I came complete with two cats and their unattractive accessories—tumbleweeds of fur and stray litter kicked from a plastic box filled with shit—and my own pathetic baggage of sadness casting shadows across my face. In my early twenties, I had lived in apartments with roaches and small mice visible only by their small pellets on the gas stove. In one apartment, my landlord's cats crawled up in the space between the outer and inner wall and pissed—an oblong damp stain appearing on the ceiling of the apartment and a telltale stench that it was time to move on and out. I was getting too old for that. By chance, a friend emailed me a listing and in the rush to submit my application, I listed my yearly salary as my monthly income. I signed the lease the next day.

I furnished my new apartment in Brooklyn with half the knickknacks Nina and I once owned in Oakland. A shadowbox displaying my wisdom teeth, a painting of a caribou from a childhood friend, a pillow embroidered with the likeness of one of my cats, and an antique print of a Hindu god above my desk. When I left I hadn't wanted to take anything that was ours, the furniture we bought together at the Alameda swap meet, the vintage library desk, a large antique rug, a framed page of a fifteenth-century French breviary with our initials in ornate dropped caps that was a wedding gift from my brother Simon. I didn't want the dishes, the spoons, the forks, or anything else from the registry. I regret leaving my toolbox—a miscellany of screwdrivers, drills, nails, and a hammer—most likely all Christmas gifts from my father, and that realistically I never had occasion to use, but that were unequivocally mine. They were too heavy and impractical to ship, and I wasn't going to ask for anything. I took one pocket-sized tool—a stocking stuffer—a miniature screwdriver set shaped like a football. I left everything I could, every painting or bookcase still firmly there, hooked to a wall so an earthquake couldn't knock it down. Everything felt half full of half empty. I applied a fresh coat of paint to my apartment's bare walls.

Friends called to check in; we talked about what people in their late twenties talk about on the phone—whether we were going to a party at a mutual acquaintance's apartment and whom we would or wouldn't be happy to see there. My friend told me she had just painted the inside of her apartment door gold, in order to reinforce the notion that beyond the entryway the outside world wasn't sepia and slowly rusting. I was fortunate to have a job—my old job in fact, an administrative position at a poetry nonprofit that I'd held before moving to Oakland. I was fortunate my return to the city didn't involve hours sending form letters, waiting in a lobby for an interview, keeping my arms close to my body to avoid exposing possible sweat marks. There was a certain eerie stability in returning to the exact desk where I had already sat for seven years.

When I hung up, I was alone again with my cats—two felines in a small apartment keeping desperate company, fulfilling their duty to be there for me, a cliché and a subtle stay against complete solitude. I never planned it this way. Nothing made sense. The book of my life was suddenly inscrutable. I opened it to look for clues. When I flipped back to the beginning it was as if my entire story had been redacted by some middle-management clerk in an office park in Delaware—he had received orders from the higher-ups to erase the narrative actions and details that had propelled me forward. I needed to create order, to define a narrative, to reach out to someone.

Dear Mom,

As I write this, it is raining; I watch a puddle to confirm that the invisible is happening before my eyes. One pin prick after another. A passing garbage truck shakes the apartment walls. This letter will not reach your mailbox, will not leave my apartment. I swear this isn't a perfunctory assignment from my therapist to uncover a core list of grievances; an attempt to articulate and in so articulating purge all I wish I could or could not say. Nothing is that easy. Where does one begin? There is much which separates us, more than a shadow cast between two unidentified objects measuring the passage of time. There is much I'm unable or unwilling to explain, much that has accumulated and must be discarded in order to move forward.

Where should I begin? I concentrate; sit in the dark with eyes closed. This is how people try to remember things, to attempt to recall the earliest memory available, something like a slug moving down a wall, the blue backdrop, the color of the wall, my body and the edges it created, the air moving in currents against my head. I have no such memories—all that passes through are photographs, an outline requiring shading to become three-dimensional, stories which require me to color in the details, factual or not, based on some thread of history, a perspective from which to view anything. I think: A boy believes his mother loves him, until he doesn't. Then I think: Either the boy was unlovable, or the mother could not love. Somewhere in between there is an antechamber full of doubt where I wait; paintings of Monet's water lilies hang in a gold frame on the wall, I fill out insurance forms. Knowing there is no cure, I resort to paying a professional to talk about it.

The radiator is hissing. I try to recall everything. The dead end, with acres of woods behind our house. It is not a metaphor; it is where we lived, an actual location, a rectangle between two houses, baseball bases painted on the black asphalt. In the woods were a series of tree forts, ditches dug until we reached the tough red clay. Fireflies appeared when the streetlamps flickered on and we swung at the insects with yellow whiffle ball bats.

I remember the Torture Chamber, a "game" Paul and I begged Simon to play. In the middle of the summer months, he held us under heavy covers on his bed—sitting on our legs to prohibit movement, a wadded tissue in our mouth to muffle the squeals, and then, only then, he turned on the blow-dryer and aimed the hot air at our faces. Something in a younger brother wants so much the approval and attention of the older brother, by any means necessary. With Paul I was more an accomplice than victim. He was the mastermind and I was the face of the operation—whether it was a well-worn trick, like betting me I couldn't complete the task of cleaning our room in five minutes or sending me pleading for money for the ice cream truck. He stood lookout at the top of the stairs while I searched your closet for Christmas gifts: a drum set, Sega Genesis, a Walkman.

Mostly I remember that you were sequestered in the master bedroom drinking, watching programs on the black and white television with rabbit ears while your husband and four boys watched football downstairs. I recall curling up in the warmth of your green robe three times the size of a child. Later, you drove me in a blue Toyota to the hospital, my appendix about to rupture. I remember running out of my bedroom in the middle of a late night fight shouting "Stop! Stop!" You were at the bottom of the stairs, my father at the top. You threw a jar of peanut butter at his head. Noah cleaned it up the next morning, like removing chewing gum from hair.

I remember my childhood as a series of fights between you and my father, but the sizes and dimensions of childhood traumas loom disproportionately large in the imagination. According to my brothers, there were only three or four "major" fights. On several occasions you slept in the maroon family van parked in the dead end or left the house in the middle of the night to drive six hours to your mother's house in Virginia.

Eventually you moved to an apartment in a gray town closer to the city, twenty minutes away on the Pennsylvania turnpike. Each school morning you drove from affordable grimness to the house where you once lived, the house you cashed in an inheritance to purchase. Each morning, you arrived after my father had departed for work. You arrived to ensure I made it out the door to wait at the bus stop. Each morning, or so it seemed, your anger with my father found me. I was there standing with my backpack and books to receive every "fuck him" you uttered while reading the lawyer's papers he left out on the counter. Or worse, "He couldn't give a fuck about you; he only wants to fuck me out of money." Some days I'd walk to the bus stop, my hand in the air waving as you drove past on your way to work, then I'd double-back, hiding in the woods, waiting for the bus to arrive and collect my classmates. I waited a few minutes longer and snuck back to the empty house and went to my bedroom to sleep.

Do you remember any of this? You moved back home with a man I barely knew. He did landscaping at the Red Roof Inn. One night, he fell asleep drunk and naked on the pull-out couch in the living room. It was clear it wasn't my father's house anymore. Or do you remember how you gripped Simon's arm with desperation when he threatened to throw a six pack of Genesis Ale out the back door into the woods? It was dusk, a strange light still half-visible over the horizon, part shadow, part truth. A few weeks later, in July 1992, I wrote in my journal: "I slept over at my father's house. We played tennis. I am pretty good. My dad hurt his ankle really bad (he's on crutches now). The next day we went birthday shopping. I got three pairs of jeans, three hooded shirts, two cassette tapes. I still have my mom's birthday money too. That evening my mom got a case of beer. She was really drunk by 7:00. There was a huge argument. And she told me and my brothers to leave. I have to learn to keep my cool with the drunk and not to let her get to me. It's really hard. Simon, who hardly ever yells at her, was yelling last night (Noah too)."

It was the first time in years, with Simon and Noah home from college for the summer, that you would have all four sons under one roof. It was a month before I entered the eighth grade, two weeks before my thirteenth birthday, when in a drunken outburst you told me to leave. When I packed the last of my things, I stole your boyfriend's John Lennon records and his copy of *The Catcher in the Rye*. In my journal I noted: "We went by the old house to get a few things. My mother called that night. She told my dad that if I entered the house when she wasn't there, she would call the police."

Love,
Brett

After living in my new apartment for two months, I had begun to settle into starting over. A new combination of medications had, for the time being, brought a halt to tearful situations with friends recounting and questioning my failed marriage on the subway or in the booth of an empty diner at a late hour. In general my anxiety was mild enough to allow me to depart my apartment, out three consecutive doors onto the street to purchase coffee, and then back to my apartment. Grind more beans. Drink the pot black. Pace, and return to the computer screen.

I was slowly beginning to feel a part of my new neighborhood, had established routines: a favorite takeout restaurant, a coffee shop that played loud 90s punk music and gave me a frequent customer punch card, and a bodega where the man behind the counter reached for my brand of cigarettes as I opened the door. I began to recognize my block's regulars, mostly twitching meth addicts who bummed cigarettes from me in front of an aid building. There was a semi-homeless woman, who stepped out in front of me one evening as I stood at the crosswalk waiting for the light to change. She gingerly pulled her skirt up to expose her genitalia while staring directly at me, and let out the smallest tinkle of urine down her leg. Afterwards she asked for a light and kept her gaze on me as I lit her cigarette. "I saw you lookin'," she said.

There were the various men who stood against the metal gate to my apartment door selling porn DVDs and loosies. We would exchange nods and they would call out "How you livin', David Spade?" I assumed they had nicknamed me after the actor because I, too, was short and blond, but that was the extent of the similarity I allowed. (Sometimes when I had facial stubble they would call me Steven Spielberg.) These men always came to my assistance. When I was locked out, one of the gentlemen produced a screwdriver from his waistband to jimmy the lock. When a single pallet of seventy boxes from Oakland was delivered and left on the sidewalk in front of the liquor store in my building, one of the men offered to make sure nothing happened to them for ten bucks. I carried the boxes, mostly books, two at a time up the two flights and stacked them three feet high against a Harbor Fog–painted wall. One of these same men punched me in the face after I told him I didn't have any spare change, but the next morning upon exiting my apartment he was there with hand outstretched and an apology: "I think I knocked someone's glasses off last night." I'd lived in Brooklyn off and on for ten years, so I knew statistically I had it coming. I accepted his apology. I knew this neighborhood and there was nothing I would fear here. I felt welcomed home.

And by "home," I mean nothing more than a set of characteristics I had grown comfortable with. I preferred the verticalness of New York to the suburban sprawl of the Bay Area, a place without personal history for me and populated with people who made small talk too quickly and with too much ease. I preferred the day trip to Coney Island to eat a hot dog and watch the barges of trash gradually move across the ocean's horizon to a hike through ancient redwoods. The cars of California were everywhere. It was clear you couldn't make it there without a hatchback and reasonable gas mileage.

I knew I was a creature of habit, knew my city's quirks and had grown accustomed to them: how to jaywalk with a sense of impunity; that it took ten seconds to cross an avenue as the crosswalk timer counted down, but I could do it in four seconds if required; how long my eyes could linger on a stranger; or that as I waited for a friend in a café she would be either ten minutes early or ten minutes late depending on the trains. I first arrived in New York in 1998 to live with my college girlfriend. She was studying painting, and I arrived to become a poet. It was my city, and I was in love with it before I was in love with Nina. It was sentimental. It was a chip on my shoulder, like how I can speak ill of a family member and jump to their defense at the first disparaging remark from a non-family member. It was the city where I lost eighty dollars playing Three-card Monte, and the city where I attended my first poetry reading by poets whose books I had read. It was family, and its shortcomings were all mine now. My brief stint in another city, Pittsburgh, felt like a detour in a small town, until I accepted the burden of exorbitant loans—which only the wild-eyed stargazer would find wise—to transfer to a school in New York City.

I know these sentiments read like a starry-eyed love letter—distance makes the heart grow fonder, or stronger, or wronger. But having been so long absent from the city it became my estranged lover, and I was filled with anguish, like the lover who needs to see his beloved who is holed up somewhere in a hotel in a faraway city on a work trip, who is down the street, or at work. Back in New York, I thought of the year and a half I was not here and of a letter John Keats wrote to his lover Fanny Brawne:

> I cannot exist without you—I am forgetful of every thing but seeing you again—my Life seems to stop there—I see no further. You have absorb'd me. I have a sensation at the present moment as though I was dissolving—I should be exquisitely miserable without the hope of soon seeing you. I should be afraid to separate myself far from you.

I had sent a slightly less eloquent email to my friend Francesca in my first month in California when Nina and I were staying with friends in Occidental while we searched for an apartment in Oakland:

> Blah, blah, blah. Do you want to hear about my day trips and the weather? Should I tell you about the sheep and the amazing garden here on the property where I eat fresh carrots and peas and beans? Aren't you just frustrated with curiosity? This morning I woke up and asked Nina if we could go home now. We can't. And though it is super-relaxing up here in the country, it is beginning to get more and more difficult to believe that I will be living out on this coast in a stucco house. I don't know what I am supposed to do but deal with it and get

all mellow and dig the fresh air. Yesterday I heard someone say "hella" and they weren't kidding. This is how it goes.

Around the time I returned to New York from California, an excerpt of E. B. White's famous essay "Here is New York" was posted in the subway system as part of a public arts program. It was the section in which he distinguished between three types of New Yorkers: those who were actually born here; the commuters; and those, like me, who arrived from elsewhere with an idealized vision of the city. It is that final category of New Yorkers to whom he ascribes the city's "poetical deportment." We had arrived in the capital of commerce, the land of the wishful profiteers and poets, with romantic dreams of becoming someone or something, and if not, then to have the comfort of becoming anonymous.

April 1, 2007
N.,

I'm perplexed at your insistence that I refrain from anger in my emails to you; by your reasoning anger is not "constructive" and not helpful to coordinating whatever it is we have left to coordinate. This feels entirely disingenuous to me that you could pretend to be taking the high road, to suddenly be retreating to the language of therapy and self-help. Is this some strategy your therapist advised? Maybe she could have also suggested coming clean months ago, when for so long you were unable to address any of this in any productive or healthy fashion. Does my anger make you think less of me as a person? How much less could you possibly think? It's funny, since I think, in general, except for spitting at you, which was disgraceful and I'm embarrassed and sorry for, I have acted very compassionately and sympathetic to you, talking with honesty and candor about how I felt and what I thought without resorting to real name calling or destructive actions, which I think many others would have. I'm angry, and personally I think you should experience this anger and disappointment. This isn't the type of anger I will burn through in a week. In fact, I'm sure the self-help literature would suggest I express my anger rather than keep it subdued and shelved. Your constant insincere insistence of "I know you are angry" only attempts to minimize my expression of hurt, while portraying it as somehow invalid and irrational. I'm angry; do you expect me not to be? What do you expect from me? Do you imagine I could be wholly sympathetic to your position which intrinsically alienates me, or rather, how should I put it? Fucks Me Over? Do you truly think you are in any position to be talking about hurtful behavior? And though you say you wouldn't talk that way to me, well, I wouldn't cheat on you as a symptom of my frustration towards you or my relationship with you and then, get this, continue and continue to do it after it has been exposed, denied, downplayed. Your hands are dirty, and I know you must now have them full with working out how to forgive yourself.

As to pushing you away, how much further could I possibly push you away? Where to? Our relationship is clearly over. Destroyed. In your most recent email, you note casually our lack of intimacy started before any of this. Of course it started before this. But I have to say that your responsibility looms larger in my mind than mine. It was always your inability, your spurning my advances, your uncomfortable-ness with me and not vice-versa. You cooled on me. I recall numerous occasions asking if something was wrong, and it was always explained as your inability to share such a degree of intense closeness with anyone, so much so you told me you believed it would be easier to have sex with a stranger than with me. I remember asking you, even back when we lived in New York, if you loved me more like a brother.

But it wasn't working, and when something doesn't work, junk it. I will accept my failures. You're right, this was a relationship and I'm also responsible for my participation or nonparticipation which led to its failure, and though I would love to point fingers (and I'm pretty sure in what direction I would point them) I will accept my failures, which according to you include a neediness and anxiety, both of which I have experienced in varying degrees and imagine I will feel for the rest of my life, just as I believe you will deal with varying degrees of depression and anxiety at future points in your life. The only time you honestly addressed these concerns to me was the time you told me you stayed at work late because you didn't want to come home to someone so unhappy; I immediately went to the doctor and started taking anti-depressants. And the other time, when you said you would like to go to therapy together, I told you I "had no problem with that" which you took as a sarcastic or dismissive comment and never followed up. I know I could have also followed up on this, but I was shut down in my depression. I was alone in the apartment working while you were at work; I couldn't drive myself anywhere, and didn't know where to go if I'd had my license. I hadn't made many friends at graduate school, and missed New York, the city itself, the connection to my friends and a group of other writers. I could have shown some incentive. Rode the bus somewhere. But it was a vicious cycle: knowing I needed to find a group of people to interact with and yet being too depressed to motivate myself to make the effort.

You are right that depression is part of me, something I need to work on and be aware of. And it is important that both of us find a partner who can deal with the other's depression. You cast my depression in comparison to yours, to which you reacted proactively and with strength to work through it. You're right, you did, and it was impressive and I will never take that away from you. However, I would like to point out that you had a base of support to come home to, to call up on the phone and talk you through it when your strength failed you. This is something I didn't have or couldn't reach out for and it only created more resentment in you towards me. Your strength was amazingly found within you but was also fostered by those that loved you. Perhaps you overlooked my depression since it was not as outwardly tearful as yours, but a numbness which made it difficult for me to reach out, especially when I felt like there was no one to reach out to. Remember me telling you I wasn't even able to email my friends, to keep in touch with them about the most mundane everyday things? Surely that must have hinted at something much more than mere unhappiness. You seem to even resent it, that I wasn't proactive, that you had to nudge me towards help. I want to point out that is what partners do.

And you're right to suggest that it is only between you and me, and not the heartthrob you fell in love with and fucked only to come home to me and order takeout and watch *Law & Order*. Maybe I would be willing to place that in a cavern in my mind and hope that it disappeared over time, but it is still present in your willingness to seek out comfort in this person, even when you know it is destructive to someone you "care so much about." You wouldn't even make a provisional commitment to not see him, email him, or date him, and looked at me incredulously when I suggested you shouldn't continue to work there with him. If it was just about us, then shouldn't he have been out of the picture for at least the time we were trying to figure things out?

Clearly not,
B.

Most evenings, in Brooklyn, on arriving home from work, I smoked a thousand cigarettes and indiscriminately and illegally downloaded *Pitchfork*'s recommended albums by New England trust fund kids with asymmetrical haircuts who noodled away with effects pedals and keyboards, transforming bleeps and beats into patterns, or the newest hip-hop sensation from Ghana. It kept me feeling informed and, if called upon, able to participate in the conversation my demographic was having at the coffee shop. More importantly, I discovered the benefit of devising purposeless tasks to occupy and account for my leisure hours. I set time aside to reorder my Netflix queue, to curate a rotation of films with enough variety to anticipate the mixture of possible moods and minimize the potential that the rectangular red envelope remained unopened in a stack of junk mail and bills. I organized the list so that on any given occasion my selections consisted of a documentary, a romantic comedy, and a foreign or classic film: *The Bridge*, *Juno*, or *The Night of the Hunter*.

Some nights I would fall asleep on the hardwood floor, the back of my shoulders propped against the couch, a book folded open and resting on my chest. As I would come to the end of a sentence, the logic of its grammar would vanish and I would drift into the subject matter of dreams. Living alone with no supervision, I'd reverted to a childlike indifference to proper conduct, and with no parent or partner to wake me; I slept where I placed myself. In a small apartment, surrounded by all my belongings, nothing had been right for a long time and there was no one, except for myself, to remove me.

Once every two weeks I received an email from Nina. A UPS tracking number, a request for confirmation of receipt of legal documents, notice that The National were playing in Brooklyn, questions regarding the well-being of my cats, inquiries if I was receiving her emails, which I was no longer responding to, confirmation that she received legal documents.

Other nights on the floor, I watched the ceiling fan spin a continuous gray shadow while I contemplated the practical minutiae surrounding the single person's universal dilemma: dying alone and unnoted in their apartment. The archetypal slip in the shower. A gas leak. Heart failure. I calculated the probable amount of time that would pass before my body would be found. I liked to think of it as a version of Sudoku. Each factor placed in the scenario altered the course of events. *If I die tonight. If I die this weekend. If I die on a holiday weekend—I will grow cold. It would be a Wednesday night when, prompted by my work colleagues, my landlord knocks on the door; an eerie silence lingers, a locksmith is called. I'm not going anywhere. I should give a friend a set of spare keys.*

The fan kept spinning and my mind moved elsewhere, revisiting and taking inventory of every injustice perpetrated against me. When I'd exhausted childhood traumas, my teenage years, and my marriage, I started cataloging recent insults, friends who hadn't returned my emails from the day before. Even as I recognized the pointless destructiveness of such trains of thought, I couldn't stop. Instead, acknowledging my self-loathing sent me wandering further down dark corridors until I was standing on the welcome mat to rooms with more advanced torture devices, including the coup de grace: suicide.

I placed a Post-It note on my bathroom mirror that read "It will get better." I repeated over and over: "It is getting better." A book on cognitive approaches to healthy living suggested that I do something like this, that if we change the dead-end paths our thoughts follow, we are on a road to somewhere else. These books were filled with such insights. There were volumes to read, and so little to learn. Or maybe there was nothing to learn and the point was to have an objective third party state the obvious. I wanted to believe I was becoming a better, more self-aware person with each chapter, with each analogy I encountered in the vast body of self-help literature—the type of books that might posit men are from New Jersey and women are from New Mexico, books with titles like *Dang, Dude! You're Getting a Divorce* that your father might give you to navigate the emotional pain. Books that would contextualize my suffering with something like "The Parable of The Rusted Nail."

You are walking carefree through the autumn foliage on a weekend apple-picking trip. Close your eyes to picture this if it helps. You are walking on a crisp day; your thoughts are elsewhere, maybe on the game. Imagine the weight of the Golden Delicious apples you are carrying in a wicker basket. Really feel that weight in your arms. Close your eyes and begin to catalog all the apples you have ever known: Fuji, Gala, Granny Smith, Gravenstein, McIntosh. If you are a sensitive type perhaps imagine you were contemplating lines from a poem memorized in a high school English class: "But I was well / Upon my way to sleep before it fell, / And I could tell / What form my dreaming was about to take." Suffice it to say, you are preoccupied with your thoughts, as you often were in your relationship, only half-listening, with your eyes on the road or on the television. You are observing the clear blue sky, one foot in front of the other on the brown grass, not paying full attention to the path you are treading, and then it happens. You lift your left leg and place your foot down on a rusted nail in a discarded piece of wood, maybe from an old barn or picket fence. It will come as a painful shock. The nail pierces the worn sole of your tennis shoe, damp from the morning dew. Your partner says, "I need some time and space to think about our relationship." You are a man, so there are two options. You stoically ignore it, or you let slip the phrase "Fuck my world!" and try to take a few brave steps forward as pain travels slowly up your leg. You might hold back the tears, until, on further investigation of the wound, you notice the blood. At the sight of blood your eyes water, or maybe you feel faint. The point is that the pain will subside. You go to the hospital and get a shot. You walk tenderly for a month, perhaps a year, but after time your strut will return. In a few months, you might think: I should have known something like that would happen; it really was too cold out there for apple-picking.

I took *Othello* down from my bookshelf. Misguided, jealous, tragically flawed or not, I felt, *Finally, here is someone who gets me.* "O curse of marriage, / That we can call these delicate creatures ours, / And not their appetites! I had rather be a toad, / And live upon the vapor of a dungeon, / Than keep a corner in the thing I love / For others' uses." Even knowing the misfortune on the horizon, this meant more to me. I put out the light and went to sleep.

One night I settled on watching *The Bridge*, a documentary about "the mythic beauty of the Golden Gate Bridge, the most popular suicide destination in the world, and those drawn by its call." There was a woman in the documentary paralyzed with grief from her friend's 245-foot plunge. She was understandably unable to bring herself to drive across the bridge. The bridge was ruined for her. The bridge is ruined, each year, hundreds of times. Each time, in fog or sunlight, no matter what season and how grandiose the beauty of the structure, it holds up that memory. One young man interviewed had managed to survive his suicidal leap into the cold Pacific. There is a poem written by Ted Berrigan and Anne Waldman that in part recounts a similar story:

> I asked Tuli Kupferberg once, "Did you really jump off of The Manhattan Bridge?" "Yeah," he said, "I really did." "How come?" I said. "I thought that I had lost the ability to love," Tuli said. "So, I figured I might as well be dead. So, I went one night to the top of The Manhattan Bridge, after a few minutes, I jumped off." "That's amazing," I said. "Yeah," Tuli said, "but nothing happened. I landed in the water, & I wasn't dead. So I swam ashore, & went home, & took a bath, & went to bed. Nobody even noticed."

I abandoned the possibility of jumping from a bridge as a viable option. Self-inflicted death should be foolproof, or else one is forced to continue life with an additional failure. It isn't so much that I thought about suicide, but a substantial rest from an interior life. The profound advantage of being done. I thought, *It's possible that "one day at a time" leads to a life lived.* I smoked. I didn't want to ruin anything. The world didn't change. There it was again, always there, a lump in my throat, too awkward in shape to swallow, partially obstructing my breath. It was easier to shuffle from bed to kitchen for a glass of water and back to bed than to open the front door to what was on the street below.

There were times I thought I hadn't taken my own life not from fear, but from utter laziness. The work involved in figuring it out was exhausting. The easiest and most efficient method was to order pills from Canada, which may or may not be the item advertised. The blue sugar pills would sail through my veins in vain. How embarrassing to vomit up a bottle of aspirin or placebos as the body rejects the mind's wishes. I looked around my apartment for a beam that could bear the load. Therapists only take a suicidal client seriously if she or he has a plan. I wanted to be taken seriously. It was with more than morbid curiosity that I found myself following my thought experiments to their conclusions. It was a familiar pattern, off and on since childhood, in which the imagined events became confused with reality until I began to wonder if I'd already completed the act and was a walking ghost. Alone, with no immediate prospects to end the solitude, I thought: *Regarding suicide, nothing is extraordinary. To take action in one's own death isn't cowardly. It might be cowardly to remain.*

I remained cowardly. My brain traveled the familiar neural pathways that my past history of depression had worn, and my brain recalled the previous methods I utilized to deal with or forget my depression. I mean to say my gray matter is a solid hue of gray, devoid of hints of color, leaning neither towards a brighter shade of hopeful white nor the depraved black of nothingness. My gray is a perpetual cloudy day. The two most radical ways I had previously attempted to change this palette were 1) praying to the blue god Krishna or 2) drinking until I passed out, and both were options I had forgone long ago. Still, almost weekly, I checked online for the schedule of services at the Brooklyn Hare Krishna Temple and the times of the local AA meetings.

In my childhood household, alcohol served the purpose of faith—that is, it provided a coping mechanism for the inevitable death lurking in all of us. My parents' routine screaming matches traveled at light speed towards divorce, and then there was the viciousness, the pettiness, and the sadness of the divorce itself. Experts report that during such spells of emotional vulnerability, individuals are susceptible to new religions, cults, and utopian societies. After the death of a loved one, a tragedy, or an upheaval of their daily routine, they may find themselves waiting for a sign, like the lunar eclipse marking the messianic end or heaven's gates creaking open. The *Bhagavad Gita* explains that there are "four types of pious person that render devotional service unto Krishna; the distressed, the seeker of knowledge, desirers of wealth, and men of wisdom." If I'm being generous I was two or three of these—but I was unequivocally distressed. I had a distinct feeling that at any moment, my family, my whole world, might just cave in. The tectonic faults and vibrations were just below the surface and at any moment they could rupture. There was no identifiable "earthquake weather"; certain cloud formations on a calm day are as dangerous as certain cloud formations on any other day. The needle rested until it tremored unexpectedly, and I knew it was only a matter of time before the earth would open up to swallow me.

It all happened quickly. I was thirteen years old when I began praying to Krishna: a blue boy playing a flute to a herd of sheep on a green hill, a small boy with a peacock feather in his hair and beads around his neck, lotus in bloom almost everywhere around him. I burned incense and chanted the holy name, waiting for a mystical presence to make itself known to me, for a sphere of light to radiate from my fingertips. I began praying before I understood anything about the teachings of Krishna. I only knew it was incumbent to close my bedroom door, turn off the lights, and seek protection from the world. It happened quickly. I was young. There was little opportunity for a family intervention. I simply came home one night with a shaved head. The difference between the three-inch mohawk I had when I left for school and the ponytail tuft on the crown of my head when I returned must have seemed to my father a question of semantics.

I found ways to occupy my time. I made a suicide to-do list. It's important to delete computer files, history, cookies. My last site visited shouldn't be Cute Overload, Craigslist Missed Connections, or worse. When my computer arrived from Oakland, I plugged in my iPod. Twenty thousand songs were organized by date added, and the last one, by Beyoncé, had been downloaded by Nina. All Music Guide describes Beyoncé's music as "celebratory, good natured, and uncompromising," and the song "Irreplaceable" is no exception. I watched the video on YouTube, in which Beyoncé portrays a character who refuses to shed a tear for her ex-lover. She indifferently files her nails as the cheater walks out of their apartment with boxes of his belongings. The song is an anthem, empowering the singer to realize she "could have another you in a minute." My ex-wife listened to the song on my computer exactly twenty-four times. I placed the song on repeat and spent too much time contemplating the lyrics. I wanted to ask Beyoncé why, if her lover wasn't special, she bothered with the relationship in the first place.

I began to systematically delete all my photographs of Nina, including any photographs taken by her or suggestive of her presence. Our honeymoon to Dublin, Prague, and Paris went into the trash. I deleted the photos she took of me sitting at a café table with an espresso and a pink macaroon, me in a sombrero with a docile donkey in a port town of Mexico, me posed in front of mating sea lions from our picturesque drive down the Pacific Coast Highway that couples are required to take. All into the trash. I could still see her; almost feel her there on the opposite side of the lens framing me, asserting her existence. She was capturing my image under the false pretense of creating memories we could, at a click of the mouse, recall. The computer prompt asked "Are you sure you want to delete the 253 files?" How quickly they all disappeared, all the quirks and memories effacing themselves.

I should start at the real beginning. In the third century BC, some-where in Northern India near the border of present day Nepal, Krishna, the Supreme Being, an incarnation of Vishnu, was born. As a young boy he played in the woods, protected the villagers, dodged assassination attempts, lifted a mountain, killed demons, and eventually found himself on an epic battlefield. Refusing to fight, he was a charioteer to Arjuna, the greatest warrior on earth, with whom he discoursed on a variety of topics including media-tion and yoga, devotional service, and the nature of material exis-tence. It is this conversation that would become the *Bhagavad Gita*, the sacred text for the Krishna movement.

Five thousand years later, in 1965, the American beginning was marked when, on a religious mission to bring Krishna to America, His Divine Grace A.C. Bhaktivedanta Swami Prabh-upada arrived on the Lower East Side of New York City. A year later he established the International Society of Krishna Con-sciousness, which describes the tenets of Krishna Consciousness in its current media kit as follows:

> People are not their material bodies, but are eternal spirit souls. . . . To achieve Krishna Consciousness effectively, members chant and meditate upon the holy names of Lord Krishna. . . . Members also practice four "principles of reli-gion": compassion, truthfulness, cleanliness, and austerity. . . . They are strict vegetarians, not eating any meat, fish, or eggs. They also abstain from gambling and illicit sex, and do not smoke, drink, or take drugs.

Or maybe we should start at my beginning, 1978, the year of my birth. I wasn't baptized. The truth is, until my adult years, I'd only been inside a church twice. Once when I was seven for a cousin's wedding, and once more when I was eleven. It was the morning after a sleepover at a friend's house. His grandmother dropped us off in front of St. Joseph the Worker in Levittown, Pennsylvania, a town, according to the *Saturday Evening Post*, where "Everybody lives on the same side of the tracks. They have no slums to fret about, no families of conspicuous wealth to envy, no traditional upper crust to whet and thwart their social aspirations." In other words, a community in which everything was going to be okay. Jesus looked down, surrounded by Klee-like geometric stained glass in blue shades, from the main entranceway. I followed my friend down the red-carpeted aisle to the first row of pews. We paused at the empty seats, walked out the side door, and went to the mini-mart to steal cigarettes.

In America, Krishna caught on quickly, or at least the chanting part did. Two years after the arrival of Prabhupada, the poet Allen Ginsberg was singing *Hare Krishna Hare Krishna Krishna Krishna Hare Hare Hare Rama Hare Rama Rama Rama Hare Hare* and playing his harmonium at Vietnam protests. Peace. Love. Freedom. Happiness. The religion received a shout-out of sorts in *Hair: The American Tribal Love-Rock Musical*. And in 1970, George Harrison was topping the charts singing about the Sweet Lord. It was a decade later in the movie *Airplane!*, that Krishna Consciousness was solidified as material for parody:

The Krishnas are approached by the Religious Zealot.

ZEALOT #2: Hello, we'd like you to have this flower from the Church of Consciousness. Would you like to make a donation?

KRISHNA: (shakes his head) No, we gave at the office.

I realized that if I did decide to go through with killing myself, all traces should be wiped clean. Instead of just clearing my browser history, I would remove my hard drive altogether, hammer a nail through it and submerge it in a bowl of rubbing alcohol. Municipal strangers with walkie-talkies would track dirt on my wood floors. I spent an unhealthy amount of time scrubbing those floors. There was little else to do. One of my brothers would be contacted by the authorities. Contagions and rot might hang in the air. The floor would need to be scrubbed with lemon disinfectant, to remove my blood, vomit, and shit. I'd need to leave cleanser out beside the kitchen sink and extra bowls of food for the cats.

To leave the business of sorting and disposing of the debris of a life to someone else might be too cruel. My belongings would be a window one couldn't help put peep into, to search for answers to how and why. What book was on the bedside table? There were volumes of poetry, the *I Ching*, and Cioran's *On the Heights of Despair*, in which this passage would be found underlined: "Is there anything on earth which cannot be doubted except death, the only certainty in this world? To doubt and yet to live—this is a paradox, though not a tragic one, since doubt is less intense, less consuming, than despair."

I concluded one shouldn't die amongst one's things. I thought of taking a cab to one of the airport hotels miles from the city's center. No one would ask questions. If they did, I was a sales rep, I was heading home for the funeral of a distant uncle, on a layover from Houston, from Pittsburgh. I thought: *Let housekeeping find me with my passport on the dresser.* I made lists, noting that each gift I'd been given would be returned to the giver, collections dispersed: a ceramic swallow, a wooden sparrow, a painting of two finches, the photograph of birds on telephone wires, Francis the upholstered swan. Each bird would be given a new home to haunt. It felt no different than packing to move to another city, another borough, just down the street. Each box would be labeled with a person's name. *Fragile. This side up.* The sadness I imagined was someone else's, never my own. Memories would exist in their daily routines, and then months pass and soon a talisman of mine would gather dust in their apartment or be sold at a stoop sale in five years with their Linda Ronstadt records, travel guides, and chipped ceramics.

At thirteen I began the process of renunciation by becoming "straight-edge." *Don't drink, don't smoke, don't fuck.* It was a rigid motto to prop me up. I had fellow straight-edge friends, most of whom I had grown up with or knew from school because we dressed the same, skated the same empty municipal parks, listened to the same music, and were filled with a similar suburban ennui. We acted out; found ourselves in crowded basements and garages, at fire halls with cheap speakers and guitar fuzz. We banged up against others dancing with anger, listened to hardcore music and shouted *Don't drink, don't smoke, don't fuck.* Minor Threat. Chain of Strength. Burn. We marked the backs of our hands with thick black x's that wouldn't wash off for weeks.

In 1992, at a small hardcore club in Center City, Philadelphia, the lead singer of the band Youth of Today was headlining with his new band, Shelter. Teenagers with shaved heads wearing concert tees, chain wallets, baggy jeans, and messenger bags were throwing themselves against one another, against anything, on the checkered dance floor. I sang along: *Security. How secure are we? Making our plans in a castle of sand as our dreams get dragged to sea.* This was the first band of a new movement: Krishnacore.

There are those who, if approached at the right time and place, will convert to anything; perhaps, sadly, I was one of them. And, further, it is reported, these individuals will often experience a "relief effect," a decrease in levels of stress and anxiety. That seems reasonable enough. I find it is important to note that I wasn't alone. There were a dozen or so of us in my high school and we walked the hallways with shaved heads, wearing white undershirts dyed saffron. Our classmates called us the Krishna Mob. In the large cafeteria we bowed our heads over our ice cream sandwiches and chanted a Sanskrit offering to Krishna. I wore the saffron robes to attend my girlfriend's school dance, and then refused to dance with her. I would only dance at the temple or down a crowded street selling books and roses. It was important others see me in this way, that the inner transformation was marked with an outer transformation.

At home, I offered Krishna a freshly washed apple. In the corner of my bedroom, I constructed a makeshift altar: a milk crate covered in a multicolored Mexican blanket, a wooden figurine of Jagannatha (the round-eyed god seen on SMILE stickers sold by Krishnas), a jar of sacred sand from Vrindavan (the forest of Krishna's childhood), a small bronze vase with fresh flowers, and an image of Krishna clipped from the temple newsletter. There were times I kept my right hand clean and my left dirty and did not wear the pendant of Narasimhavatar into the lavatory. I hung the pendant on the doorknob outside the bathroom because such devotional items should not enter unclean spaces. After much adjustment and difficulty I learned to wipe with my left hand. The right hand should remain clean. Eat with the right hand. I looked in a mirror to apply tilak, a chalky sandalwood paste, to the middle of the forehead. Some say the space between the two eyebrows is a sacred spot where the third eye—the sixth chakra, Shiva's eye—appears. Some say the tilak has a cooling effect to aid concentration during meditation. Some say the mark is meant as a sacred distinction, identifying you publicly from nonbelievers.

There were times I refused my body its wishes. Times I gave in to my wishes. Times I turned the wooden figurine towards the wall, as if an all-knowing deity didn't have eyes in the back of his head. Times I could not pinpoint my wishes so I chanted a round: *Hare Krishna Hare Krishna Krishna Krishna Hare Hare Hare Rama Hare Rama Rama Rama Hare Hare.*

My father asked me very little about the religion, but I think he was happy to know my teenage acting out didn't yet involve drugs and alcohol. I was home on time and calling to check in at regular intervals; that, it seemed, was enough. I closed my bedroom door when I burned incense, and though we didn't eat our meals together he purchased microwavable vegetarian meals for me. I placed a small plate of the reheated rice and green peas in front of a wooden icon of Jagannatha, prayed, added the offering back to the larger plate, and ate.

My father did draw the line at my spending the night at the temple, but on Sundays I was permitted to attend the free weekend feast and lecture. It was an hour and a half trip. I took a southern commuter train from suburbia and transferred at the Center City transit hub. Families from around the tri-state area attended the free feast. The gravel parking lot filled up with lawyers, businessmen in khakis, people who worked retail jobs, people who most likely had savings in their bank accounts, hippies with tie-dyed shirts, some people with shaved heads, some people without, some people with kids, numerous Indian families with women in saris, and a few homeless men. All were welcome, all variety of shoes and sandals were left in the main hall. It felt more like a potluck for a progressive school than a religious gathering.

I prayed to God cross-legged on a beige carpet in my father's condominium with jasmine incense burning, waiting for thunder to release from my heart. Night after night with the lights out I chanted before sleep, but morning arrived like any other day, a disruption to my dreams of being elsewhere, of being transported to another life. I had inherited a household absent of religious practices and iconography. There was no cross above the doorway. No holidays for which we were corralled into the station wagon for midnight mass. I looked to the mystical heavens for answers in an attempt to make sense of life, to find an alternative solution in which I was not the only person I could depend on.

I drew lines of comparison. I'd read a Joseph Campbell book or two and created my own personal visualization of all belief systems as a giant rope. Along the rope large knots were tied at equal distance, each one representing a distinctive tradition. I linked chanting the mantra with the garland of roses, linked 108 prayer beads to the fifty beads of the Catholic rosary; linked the act of offering food to Krishna to the Christian "grace," linked a life of celibacy to monks in monasteries in Belgium and nuns in convents in Ireland; and linked the dietary restrictions and vegetarianism to my Jewish neighbors who kept kosher. The four regulative principles of Krishna Consciousness seemed less and less weird: No gambling. No illicit sex (or rather, sex was meant solely for procreation). No intoxicants. No meat, fish, or eggs. I was embarking on a life of purity. A round of chanting takes ten minutes. It is important to keep count, to surrender to the process. Devotees chant sixteen rounds daily. Sixteen rounds takes almost three hours. Three hours of service to the lord took less time than watching a James Cameron movie.

I wanted to believe there was only the moment before I was conscious of Krishna and the moment after. As is often the case, nothing lasted for long. One possible solution to the suffering of *maya*, or illusion, was replaced by another. It all happened quickly. The initial feeling wore off. I could chant the Maha Mantra ad nauseum and the world felt the same. The words I began chanting in 1992 lost meaning. When one door failed to open, I went looking for another exit. I started drinking in 1993.

I watched the fan spin. It had a job to do and did it. I lay in bed and visualized my body as a corpse painted a hue to match my living paleness. I imagined rain falling on the damp earth and the cemetery grass shining with a healthy greenness, nourished by the organic chemicals of the lives below its surface. I had selected the poem to be read at my grave: "Afterwards," by Thomas Hardy.

When the Present has latched its postern behind my
　　tremulous stay,
And the May month flaps its glad green leaves like wings,
Delicate-filmed as new-spun silk, will the neighbours say,
"He was a man who used to notice such things"?

If it be in the dusk when, like an eyelid's soundless blink,
The dewfall-hawk comes crossing the shades to alight
Upon the wind-warped upland thorn, a gazer may think,
"To him this must have been a familiar sight."

If I pass during some nocturnal blackness, mothy and warm,
When the hedgehog travels furtively over the lawn,
One may say, "He strove that such innocent creatures should
　　come to no harm,
But he could do little for them; and now he is gone."

If, when hearing that I have been stilled at last, they stand at
　　the door,
Watching the full-starred heavens that winter sees,
Will this thought rise on those who will meet my face
　　no more,
"He was one who had an eye for such mysteries"?

• • •

And will any say when my bell of quittance is heard in
    the gloom,
And a crossing breeze cuts a pause in its outrollings,
Till they rise again, as they were a new bell's boom,
"He hears it not now, but used to notice such things"?

Nothing was happening. I spent my days uninterested in the days that were happening—repetition, which is some version of living, was the dominant mode. I imagined the GPS data from my cell phone visualized as a map—the same route to and from work, the digital lines traced over and over with no variation. And then one night, in bed waiting for sleep to arrive, something did happen. A human-shaped shadow appeared before my bookcases. My cats sensed little or did not perceive a threat. The building I lived in was nondescript. It lacked the character ascribed to haunted sites (i.e. a rambling Victorian in disrepair set apart from the street, shuttered windows and antique furniture covered in white sheets). And yet, something did appear.

On television ghost-hunting shows, a dog will refuse to enter an attic and bark wildly until historic walls are dampened with holy water. Until sage is burned. My cats rested comma-like in the curve of my arm, eyes closed. On television the host announces, "If there is a spirit in the room make yourself known." And then a knock is heard from a location off-camera, the house creaks, a jar filled with sacred sand from India slips from the bookshelf and shatters. A bird—most likely the foreboding raven—caws outside the window. Someone off-camera whispers: "Did you feel that sudden chill?"

I followed the advice I'd gathered from such shows. I spoke to the empty room: "If there is a spirit in the room make yourself known." The next day I bought sage and burned it. Nevertheless, the figure returned that evening. In bed I thought: *It can do me no harm I can't do to myself.* I looked at it from the corner of my eye. Both intimate and unidentifiable, it paused in position. It paused in thought and reached no conclusion. Did it waver from its station or did the slow rise and fall of my breathing create the illusion of movement? In a house alone one must be very still. There was no sound. The cats were breathing. I regulated my own breathing carefully, slowly becoming aware of my pulse. I looked at it as if it was not happening to me, like I was looking out my window and into the apartment across the street. *Who's there? Nay, answer me: stand, and unfold yourself.* Not much unfolded.

I looked at it straight on. It was nothing, a misinterpretation of moonlight obscured on an overcast night, a double agent of my own invention, an apparition of dust and light playing on the wall and moving through me, allegiances both natural and unnatural. It was just my brain defragmenting: collecting and sorting the debris accumulated throughout the ordinary course of the day. It was just my brain defragmenting and encountering a glitch in the system. The imagination is colored, predisposed to shades of gray, a symptom of a vulnerable emotional state. If there was indeed a spirit in the room and it was what I was witnessing, I didn't anticipate convincing a jury on cross-examination.

I said nothing to anyone. At work, I began researching my apartment building via various online newspaper databases looking for a report of horrific events having transpired at my address. In *The New York Times*, I found the following article from March 12th, 1898: "Murder Mystery Solved Hilda Petersen Mother and Slayer of the Child That Was Found Dead at Rockville Centre. MAKES A FULL CONFESSION. A Swedish Servant Employed in This City Carried the Little Girl Away and Poured Carbolic Acid Down Her Throat." My address was mentioned in the article, but the crime didn't happen there. The father of the illegitimate child, a watchmaker, lived in my apartment with his five children and wife a century before me.

One night unpacking and organizing some boxes, I found a letter from my father, along with my reply.

July 1994
Dear Brett,

I can see that we are going to have some difficulty communicating over yesterday's drinking episode. I'm going to give the adult slant and you're going to try to give me the teenage spin. They are simply not compatible. Every kid in the world likes to think they are special, unique individuals, (and they are to some degree), but the situations they incur continue to be the same generation after generation. The talks I have with you are the same that my father had with me, and will be the same between you and your kids. I didn't want to hear it when I was your age, and I'm sure you don't want to hear it now. The bottom line is, I do have your welfare at heart. I love you and I want you to grow up to be as happy and successful as possible. You are bright, witty, and talented, but you are fifteen and nothing can change that but years. Without those years under your belt your judgment is skewed. You are still functioning on a teenage ego-trip, which only allows you to see how to get the things you want. And like most teenagers you'll manipulate and lie to get them. Also you will convince yourself that some of the most outrageous things are okay. Things like throwing parties in your father's house and driving around drunk. Hey, I'm not really as stupid as you think. I know these things. Fortunately to this point, as far as I know, most of your drives and desires have been handled within the law or at least with a bit of luck and without too much risk, I hope. But then I am not privy to much of your life. Parents are forced to do a lot of guesswork. Anyway I have given you a lot of trust. I have allowed you much leeway in your comings and goings. As a teenager, no doubt you believe everybody lets their fifteen-year-old go to DC on a whim, and head up to NYC on any given day. You know that just isn't the case. I have probably allowed too much to go by. And at times for selfish reasons like wanting to go away overnight. So I trusted you. I guess that really is not your fault, but mine. I should have known better. I chose not to see. I guess it's time that the door swings back. I do not condone kids drinking or using drugs. That the use is rampant is no excuse. It is bad policy for kids to do these things for both of the obvious reasons. They can be harmful both physically and psychologically and it's against the law. Believe me it is only a dumb kid argument to say the substances are not harmful. You know they are. You've seen the abuse. To say that you will not get caught is equally ridiculous. There is no crystal ball. And nobody is that smart, they just don't run out of luck. I see only bad things coming from drinking, smoking, and lying. None of those three will help you get by better in life. As I said, my hope for you is a healthy, happy, and successful life and I see that you are doing things that put those goals in jeopardy. As your father I have to do something to get you back on track. Hopefully you will understand that my judgment is not screwed up. Possibly you can see that I truly have your welfare in mind. In the past I have left many of the decisions up to you. I think I mistook your intelligence for maturity. I've done that before. I want to correct the error. Getting good grades is wonderful, but it doesn't buy you unlimited chances to screw up. To that end I am going to do my best to convince you that teenage drinking, smoking dope, and being untrustworthy are not in your best interest. I know what peer pressure is like. The brightest buckle under and actually believe that being staggering drunk, cursing out their father, and retching are cool. I hear the stories all the time. Still I want better for you. I don't want to get calls from the police department or, worse, the hospital. I've watched your brothers go through this, and maybe I've finally learned something. I've got to be, and I hate to say it, less trusting. Let's face it;

you've all lied to me. I guess I should expect it. For last night's performance I want you to give some serious thought to where you are going, and what is happening in your life. I believe the best way is to keep you in for a while. My decision is that you should stay in for five days. I won't take away your phone privileges this time, but next time you'll lose the phone and ten days of time. When your restriction is over, some new ground rules need to go into effect. I don't think it will be wise for you to spend the night at anybody's house. Because at this point I'll be thinking you are drinking. I'm not going to clip your curfew, but I will want you home every night at midnight. Over time, if you can build up my trust, this can be relaxed. If you can't get a ride, as usual, you can call me. I'm sure this will seem harsh to you, every punishment does, but I doubt it is much different than the rules that most fifteen-year-olds live by. Brett, trust and love are the foundation for relationships. I will be glad when we don't have to be adversaries. Until then I'll do what I have to do. I love you, and I hope you can regain my trust.

Love,
Dad

The night before I had arrived home with Elizabeth, a classmate I'd been dating for a week. We walked up the flight of steps into the condominium and my father was sitting in the living room. I attempted a high-five—a nonchalant gesture to demonstrate that all was well, I was not drunk, and nothing was out of the ordinary with my bringing an unfamiliar girl home near midnight. I missed the high-five and went to my bedroom to make out with Elizabeth, to kill time until her curfew.

Dad,

Please excuse my handwriting (my hand is broken from last night?). I waited around, then left because I didn't know if I was grounded or not. I understand your position in condemning my actions. In no way were they acceptable. But as a teenager I do do some things like that. Simon and Noah were into bigger and badder things than me and hey they're alright. I understand if those actions are repeated I will suffer and you would have to take some action as a parent. Even if you lose an argument with your opponent doesn't mean you still can't call them names.

I still love you,
Brett

My wrist was indeed broken—and not from a clumsy high-five with my father, but from punching my friend in his chest at a party the night before. It was a dare. We were in the basement of someone's house. It made a sort of sense at the time. We were drinking forties. I was posturing, and it escalated to its logical teenage conclusion: "I bet if you punch me as hard as your little ass could, I wouldn't even feel it." He was three times my size, the biggest in the room, one of my friends who was faithfully two steps behind me when I was drunk at a party, out of control, and spitting on a stranger. I didn't go to the doctor for a week—and then, once at the doctor, they needed to re-break the bone. My father photographed this event in the doctor's office—not from a parental impulse to document the pain I had caused myself by drinking, to have a record of my misdeeds, but because he had a disposable camera in his sport coat and it seemed like a funny thing to do.

I've recited the narrative of my addiction, the desperate and strange situations, so many times, it feels as if I'm reciting the first presidents using a mimetic device: What a Jolly Man Makes a Jolly Vixen. I can repeat the itinerary of my addiction; provide a cursory glimpse of childhood in a tone absent of any emotion or shock, having recited it numerous times in the rooms of professionals, on the first visit to a therapist or at Alcoholics Anonymous. "I did this. I did that." I begin in medias res like an epic poem:

There were times I was intoxicated and walked miles home with a black mind, and hours later could not recall walking home. I poured swigs of each liquor my father had in his cabinet—sambuca, vodka, kahlua—into a plastic sports bottle. I threw the bottle in my backpack and left for the weekend. Other times my jaw locked to the left or the right, filled with the anxiety of methamphetamines, leaving a pain that would remain for weeks after the night a white pill was swallowed in a room filled with strobe lights, filled with bodies, filled with music, filled with darkness. And mostly this is a matter of fact. It never lasted long enough. I would eat painkillers at lunch because drinking was too difficult, because the smell of weed would linger in the fabric of my clothing, and teachers could not easily identify the high of prescription pills. I smoked blunts driving around in a friend's car before school. Someone reported me and the nurse's office called for me in Algebra class. My heart rate was insane. I told the nurse I had three cups of coffee and she let me go back to class. I dropped acid at lunch, so when the last period bell rang and I walked out into a spring afternoon, I could sit for hours in a field of neon-tinted grass at Tyler Creek Park looking for a four-leaf clover. I drank forties and thought I could rap. We all did. I drank mushroom tea and played Sonic the Hedgehog, racing across the screen grabbing coins. I didn't smoke crack, though once I held an empty pipe to my lips as a joke. I was fishing for a reaction from my friends, who were with me in a living room where we were buying coke at three in the morning. If I hadn't noted their horror and feared their mentioning my actions the next week at school, it is possible I would have paid to refill the pipe. But we can play this game with anything. We drove home on River Road with the headlights turned off, curved along the Delaware River, miles from where George Washington crossed on Christmas Eve to surprise the British, miles from the spot where my family had watched the reenactment the previous Christmas morning.

There are no adequate similes or metaphors for addiction. There is no setting the broken bones back in place. And if there was, they wouldn't heal properly. The bones, forever injured, would develop a click in anticipation of dramatic changes in weather. With addiction, you simply know it when you feel it, when you admit it to yourself, and then, day by day, admit it to others in your life. Everything else is just an approximation, a literary device to advance an understanding, a voice of a loved one complaining. Or rather there is the addiction everyone else observes, and then there is the addiction the individual must come to terms with. It is an afternoon television special: *I don't have a problem. I can control it. I can stop if I want.*

When I was drunk there was a twenty-five percent chance I would cry and tell my friends they didn't understand the heights of my suffering. There was a twenty-five percent chance I would pick a fight, smash a window, or piss in the closet on a pile of dirty laundry. Or there was a fifty percent chance I would be fine and dance in the corner or play spades. There was no logic. I always had two bottles in my hand and a plan to raid the medicine cabinet of whatever house we were in. I didn't drink to cut the edge, to loosen up, to be right in the world—I drank to oblivion, to not remember anything or anyone.

It would be easy to say that my alcoholism was a weakness. That is the conventional narrative. But there are moments in which I want to admit that it was a power. A hero's singular ability to temporarily make the world invisible, to forget. I didn't want to remember. Perhaps here is where I should confess I wasn't loved enough, where I report that my genetic material was predisposed toward alcoholism, and worry over what I might have done to cause the difficulties and unhappiness in my parents' lives that weighed on me like a symbol, for the person I was doomed to become. There is my confession. I knew alcohol provided me with the power to avoid answering those questions, to eliminate them for an entire evening. There were no answers, and I wanted to be rescued from and defended against a world absent of them.

In 1996, at 7 AM in the basement of the University of Pittsburgh's Cathedral of Learning, I attended my first AA meeting. I had moved from the suburbs of Philadelphia to live with my brother Simon for the summer before starting my freshman year of college. He had started attending meetings three months earlier. He dropped me off on his way to work. I was barely awake. The other fifteen alcoholics were dressed for office jobs. At eighteen, in Pittsburgh, my recovery was a novelty. My bottom hadn't reached the horrific depths of the man who said he started snorting heroin because if he drank at work his boss would smell the alcohol on his breath. He had a wife, children, and a job—real responsibilities to fuck up. I'd barely had a job and didn't even have my driver's license. And yet I identified with such plots, the desperate way the mind warps to find and justify any method to obliterate feeling. Each addict's story provided a touchstone to my own life experience and there was something frighteningly sobering in the disastrous levels their addictions had reached. And I was relieved to know I wasn't alone, that there were others sitting beside me who were worse off.

Something can be called an addiction when it interferes with your life. That is what they say. My responsibilities as a teenager were limited. My father made sure I woke up on time for school, ignored each batch of fake throw-up I concocted from chewed-up cereal and a can of chicken soup, and stood at my bedroom door while I dressed. A third of the time that fake vomit worked— there were years I was absent from forty-something days of school. But in my household for the most part I did what was expected of me, and was lucky to avoid getting arrested, getting caught. When an actual *21 Jump Street*–style undercover police officer arrested three of my close friends in high school, I was waiting at the bus stop to buy mescaline dots from one of them. When his locker was searched and turned up a list of names with corresponding amounts of money next to them I was called down to the principal's office. The principal was a friend of my father's. If I had been caught, things could have been different.

The decision to admit the first of the twelve steps was easy. It had become transparent that I was powerless over alcohol at that particular moment in my life. The first several months went smoothly—I was physically removed from the triggers of old friends and places, of access to alcohol. I showed up at meetings once a day. I drank the Maxwell House coffee and ate the stale cookies and listened. I stood up and got a one month sober chip and people clapped.

I made no friends in AA or at college. My age made me an anomaly at meetings; I was too young to know the suffering of the world and "real" addiction and was treated more or less as such. As a freshman who didn't drink, I didn't leave my dorm room that often. On Saturday nights as the hallway filled with drunken cackles and the annoying voices of my peers, I sat alone in my room, shadows shifting down the hall visible through the crack at the bottom of the door. I made myself feel sorry for my peers in order to feel more mature, to feel superior to the people and activities I was no longer part of. I told myself they were exploring something for the first time that I'd discovered years ago. I was wiser. I was who I was because I refused what they were. And I had the battle wounds, and the morning meeting I attended while they were sleeping it off.

I listened to AM talk radio and fell asleep. Even in sleep I couldn't avoid the facts. For the first months of my sobriety, my brain formed dreams filled with drinking that were so vivid and haunting, featuring versions of real scenarios, that for weeks I was unsure if I'd relapsed. Even now, if asked how long I've been sober, I pause and question the fact. In the dreams I found myself wanting to avoid anyone I'd ever known—I would wake from a night of drinking and find myself at a department store with my father and an acquaintance from high school, the person whose bedroom wall I had punched or whose sister I had called a slut, or just the stranger whose name I couldn't remember even though they sat behind me in chemistry. In the dreams I felt compelled to say *I'm sorry. I'm different from last night. I'm sober now. I'm sorry.* And worse than the dreams was the waking guilt, the inability to swallow that guilt in drunkenness. For that first semester I dreaded going home for Christmas break, knowing the identity I had identified with was nowhere to be found.

I found another letter from my father while unpacking—this one from two or three years later, when I was in my second year of college, written in response to a phone conversation in which, possibly for the first time, I attempted to discuss my recovery and my ongoing depression. It's a strange thing about recovery—one is galvanized to finally address the years of behavior that, out of necessity, one was silent about. It is a little like holding a grudge over a friend's small slight or inattention and then months later exploding over a minor incident with disproportionate anger. Which is just to say, perhaps it was just my first step toward an adulthood being off on my own, my newfound sobriety, my first experience with therapy, or maybe my father had just telephoned on an evening I felt like talking. Whatever the case may be, I told him I wasn't doing well. And, perhaps as was characteristic of my family, my father responded with a letter.

Dear Brettski,

I sat back the other night and thought about what you told me about your depression etc. It is something you have kind of masked from me. Remember I've really only seen you a couple of times in the last nine months and our visits have been pretty brief, our conversations relatively superficial.

If it makes you feel any better (from the old misery loves company line of thinking), I went through many of the same feelings when I was in school. I certainly don't say that to minimize how you feel or what you are going through, but I do believe some of it is the maturing of an intelligent, sensitive young man.

It has always been difficult for me to make "close" friends. I don't suffer fools gladly. That meant for long stretches in my life I was alone, if not lonely. Particularly in college. I did have a few friends in the dorms, but as I've related in my stories to you, most were pretty weird guys. They were fringe characters, but interesting in their own way. I guess I was attracted to them, because they were not what I considered stupid folks, just eccentric. The "stupid" guys in my dorm are all now CEO's of large corporations. But I couldn't connect with them. Go figure.

There were times I pulled back and kind of shut myself up. I did a lot of reading, a lot of basketball by myself, and a lot of walking around Williamsburg. It was pretty depressing. When I got out of the dorm and I was living alone, I did some serious drinking. I was good and depressed a number of times and definitely contemplated offing myself. But then from time to time, I'd get my shit together and search out folks. That's how I got involved with theater. There were a bunch of goofy people there too, but at least many were interesting. If nothing else they were somebody to drink with, and of course there were always some pathetic characters that made my life look so much more worth living. But mainly I think my bad times were all due to my being too introspective. I'm afraid it's the bane of us pseudo-intellec-tuals. When I was selfishly thinking only about me, and my puny place in the world, when I only dealt with how things made me feel . . . it was pretty depressing.

As luck would have it, I fell into that job at Williamsburg's Eastern State Hospital. My approach to life started to change right away when I got involved in teaching. My emphasis shifted somewhat, but certainly not entirely, to the rest of the world, and specifically the kids I worked with. It didn't stop me from being cocky. It didn't mean I never thought about myself, but it did shift my focus away from me . . . me . . . me.

Obviously you and I are not the same. We only share mil-lions of genes and some childhood experiences. Certainly many of our experiences are different, but some are more similar than you know. Similar enough for me to offer at least these sugges-tions. Try to look outward. Take what you have and share it with others. Don't force it; share it. Try to engage with other people in a caring considerate way. Try to do things for them. Basically I know you are already this way with your acquaintances. Make sure you do it with family and most certainly with girlfriends. Again I'm not 100 percent conscious of trying to do it. I don't want to sound preachy, but it's worked well so far.

I know turning your emotional outlook around is not easy. I don't mean to suggest that one little minor change and everything will be well, but I did feel that I wanted to share a little about my life in case it helps.

I know the Lauer boys (and their Mom) all love and care about each other. Hopefully we can all help each other out.

Love,
Dad

My problem with AA surfaced early. I had already done my time sitting in a circle listening to lectures that required I surrender to Krishna, godhead, to Him, to the program, to a higher being. My experience with groups suggested group logic prevails no matter how many times it is stated otherwise, as it is on the AA website, that "AA is not allied with any sect, denomination, politics, organization, or institution."

Through my sponsor I came to understand that there were options, intellectual wiggle room, other than the "He" and "Him" who appears in the language of the later steps—alternative ideas or substitutions that lead the addict to understand that he or she is not the center of the universe, to relinquish that control or narcissism, to place oneself humbly before something else. At one meeting, I shared my uncertainty in my beliefs regarding a conventional "higher power." I explained how I attempted to feel a comfort in the process of breathing ("breath" being from the Latin for "spirit"), and the knowledge that the cycle of the body continues unbeknownst to me. I am sleeping, and there it is keeping time. The man who spoke after me simply said: "God and Jesus are the higher power, youngster." Someone across the room said "Amen."

I wanted recovery, but I wanted to feel right in the world without the aid of a charismatic group or dogma. I had a chip in my hand marking a transition from the old life to the new, but I did not carry it in my pocket and rub it any time I had an urge to drink.

The truth is, I'd already exhausted my righteousness with straight-edge and Krishna Consciousness. I'd like to believe we are allotted a certain amount of such arrogance, hopefully spent entirely in our youth or expressed in the heat of the moment when a push-button topic divides a Thanksgiving Day table. The next day we wish we had reacted more humbly and generously to our aunt's neighbor regarding her view on capital punishment.

We can't go at it alone, and yet I needed to go at it alone, absent another belief system. "Humble yourself or be humiliated. Excuses are words put together to extinguish your guilt. Today will be here again tomorrow. It works if you work at it." The words of these new mantras were part of a system of indoctrination that I couldn't fully accept. I understood that if it wasn't for those rooms I wouldn't have been able to get sober, but I knew I needed to develop my own framework in which to understand myself in the world.

I've been sober for over a decade. I haven't been to a meeting in eight years. I've read that the human body replenishes all its cells on a seven-year cycle. Cells and atoms wear down and disappear or are replaced; skin flakes into the dust that surrounds us, resting on the windowsill. If this is the case, I'm no longer the same person after thirteen years of sobriety. I am almost doubly different. The transgressions and follies of youth are important to any life story: a cherry tree is chopped, St. Augustine steals a pear from an orchard, a boy runs off with a cult. These things happen in childhood, and you grow up and forget them, or you grow up and they haunt you, or, more than likely, you grow up and spend each morning dismissing the facts and waiting for your ghosts to appear.

I sat at my white desk. There was nothing to do but sit and wait. I put my legs up. I read *Baudelaire* by Jean-Paul Sartre. Above me on the wall was a framed print of Vishnu. I began the book in hopes of a close reading of Baudelaire's work and instead, twenty pages in, Sartre was still developing his psychoanalytic portrait of the poet:

> But the child who has become aware of himself as a separate being with a sense of despair, rage, and jealousy will base his whole life on the fruitless contemplation of a singularity which is formal. "You threw me out," he will say to his parents. "You threw me out of the perfect whole of which I was part and condemned me to a separate existence. Well, now I'm going to turn this existence against you. If you ever wanted to get me back again, it would be impossible because I have become conscious of myself as separate from and against everyone else." And he will say to his school-fellows and the street urchins who persecute him: "I'm someone else, someone different from all of you who are responsible for my sufferings. You can persecute my body, but you can't touch my 'otherness.'"

I bookmarked the page. I could say that Krishna Consciousness provided a framework, a coping strategy for the chaos of my childhood, for the age of Kali Yuga, the age of sin and vice lasting almost half a million years. Some of it stuck more so than AA, most likely because it got there first, because it was more complicated and mystical. The tradition of Krishna and its attractiveness to Westerners is no different than fascination with other Eastern religions—the appeal and fetishization of the esoteric, the exotic, and an "otherness." It sets itself apart—shaved heads, saffron robes, beatific faces dancing, playing cymbals, and chanting in an ancient language down Broadway at rush hour. It has all the signs of new-age crazy taking a wrong turn. However, I never quite experienced it that way. Of course there were rumors of cult-like brainwashing, or Krishnas involved in gun-running in the 70s, but the most I experienced was a feeling that the possibility of that zealous dogma was just around the corner, the dogma of any religion, of Evangelical Christians, of Hasidic Jews, that asks one to give up one's so-called "self" for a larger single-minded cause. But I didn't. I passed through. I was young and it was simple: there was a blue god, there was music, the devotees were happy and fulfilled, and not in a glazed-over way, and there was delicious food, but ultimately, I felt no different in or about the world.

I put down the book and looked at the image above my desk where Vishnu hovered above a lake, holding a lotus flower, a light haloing him. A crocodile retreated from an elephant it had attacked. The elephant's leg was bleeding. In his trunk he also holds a lotus. The elephant was Gajendra, the king of elephants. He was rescued from the crocodile because he was a devotee. In this moment of attack he prayed not to be saved from the crocodile, but from this life of ignorance. He struggled, some say for a hundred years, and only after his family left him at the edge of the pond, thinking death was imminent, did he pray. Many years later on September 11, or driving in a blizzard, or on an airplane in the moment before lift-off, or before falling asleep, without thinking I chanted the Maha Mantra, like a lullaby. *Hare Krishna Hare Krishna Krishna Krishna Hare Hare Hare Rama Hare Rama Rama Rama Hare Hare.* I was hoping the transcendental vibrations would still the psychological ones.

Soon I came to anticipate the ghost's presence in my apartment: watchmaker father, the murdered child, her mother Hilda, or otherwise. I smoked cigarettes at my computer and waited for nightfall, gathered myself for bed, forgot to eat. I grabbed another book—what else was there to do—and read a poem in Rimbaud's *A Season in Hell:*

> On the roads on winter nights, homeless, half-naked, hungry, I heard a voice that gripped my frozen heart: "Weak or strong: there you stand, and that is strength. You don't know why or where you're going; enter anyplace, answer everyone. No one's going to kill you, any more than if you were a corpse." The morning, I looked so lost, so dead in my eyes, most likely everyone I met never saw me at all.

For three consecutive nights the ghost clung to the exact same spot. I had done my research. I had contemplated purchasing devices that measured changes in the air, humidity, positive and negative ions, barometric pressure; that could pinpoint warm, cold, or bright spots, or disturbances in the electronic field. If one wanted surefire proof, night vision goggles were an available option, as were chimes to measure the movement of a spirit, if placed at an appropriate distance from natural drafts. Mostly, during the day, I read articles about the murder in *The New York Times* and *The Evening Telegram* online archives.

> My name is Hilda Peterson and I live at No. 58 East Fifty-Third Street, I have been employed there for three weeks and have been in the country for four years. I became acquainted with Charles Johnson the first year I was here. I met him in Brooklyn. Afterward we became intimate, and a girl baby was born. She was named Annie. He was the child's father. Subsequent to the birth of the child I did housework. I put the

baby to board with a family in DeKalb Avenue, Brooklyn. I had Johnson arrested and he was ordered to pay $2 a week to the Charities Commissioners to support the child.

Her daughter had been found:

in a chicken run . . . dressed only in a knitted undershirt and black stockings, fastened with elastics. The child was well developed, and well nourished, beautifully formed, and handsome, having large gray eyes and long, waving blonde hair. The chicken run is a square box made of slats, five feet long by two and a half square, and is used to allow young chickens air and exercise. . . . It was evident that the child had been killed by a heavy dose of carbolic acid. . . .

Hilda was depicted as calm, sane, and with "no indication of distress or remorse," as she confessed:

It was still snowing a little. There were some houses near the station, so I took Annie up a couple of blocks into some place and gave her the carbolic acid. I don't remember whether she swallowed it or not but she lived only a few minutes. When she was dead I pulled her clothes and threw them along the ground. I took her shoes and brought them home and put them in my trunk.

I was living and sleeping in Charles Johnson's apartment, the absent father of the murdered daughter, or at least the plot where his house once stood at the turn of the century. My ghost detective logic led me to believe Hilda was in the house with me, haunting Charles, the descendants of Charles, the domestic life in the New World that was denied her. Or rather that was the possibility I allowed, since the size and shape of my ghost discounted Annie. That is, if one believes how one dies is how one haunts. It might work this way: Those who died in dungeons drag their chains, those in straitjackets forgotten in a mental institution continue their screaming, or the man who met his death on the guillotine carries his head cradled gently against his waist. I could find no record of Hilda's death. The last article in my searches reported on her arraignment; and on the same newspaper page, in the column directly adjacent her story, a new story was beginning, that of a different family and another child found lifeless in a trunk.

They say that when one is weak illness attacks. I will not, at this present moment, go on record as believing in such things as apparitions traveling through keyholes, doorknobs turning and turning, disembodied voices whispering—all proof of vagrants held captive to wander the prison-house of the material world as reminders of the misdeeds they were subjected to. I remember a Krishna devotee speaking of waking up and being clamped by demons. He was barely able to mouth the mantra: *Hare Krishna Hare Krishna Krishna Krishna Hare Hare Hare Rama Hare Rama Rama Rama Hare Hare*, and then the demon fled. I kept the mantra on my lips in case the ghost approached.

My mind transformed a shadow into a visitation. There was a strange comfort in the shadow's existence. It did not harm me, it knew that I would die, that we all will die, and there was comfort in this inevitability. It conveyed the obvious—there are worse lives, circumstances. There is, after all, no rush—despite the anxiousness to deplane a recently landed aircraft, we exit in the order we are placed. Row by row, our turn arrives. The edge of the cliff we will fall off is always right there in the last place we look, like misplaced keys. What does not harm you only makes you calmer. I thought: *The seasons continue to change and you will be with me, my friend.*

She was there and then she was gone. I want to believe I was there for her and she was there for me, that even the undead were searching for some other to confirm their existence. It is what we do when we're alone in the world.

3

My friends either told me it was too soon to start dating or that the grass was growing tall beneath my feet. It had only been six months since my separation. The last time I was single, the world anxiously watched the news for reports of missile systems misfiring as the year ticked into the new millennium. Postage was 33 cents. *NSYNC was touring and it wasn't a reunion. The world had changed, and even if it hadn't, I wouldn't have been any more adept at courtship. I dated my first real girlfriend on and off from middle school until I was a sophomore in college. The beginning of our courtship involved moments standing awkwardly beside each other at a friend's bar mitzvah and talking on the phone until two in the morning about The Smiths, our parents, movies. I sent her hundreds of love letters, which she later burned. I'm sure it was deserved. And when that ended, it was only a few brief months before I was in a relationship with Nina.

I never would have approached Nina, and in fact it was Nina who approached me at a friend's party and asked me to dance. I was at the party to be set up with a different friend-of-a-friend, Stephanie, and at the end of the evening when we shared a cab home I couldn't bring myself to ask Stephanie for her number. What can I say? I'm shy. I'm insecure. I couldn't even maintain eye contact with a woman walking by me on the street. I feared rejection and the possibility that my male gaze (I'd taken one survey class on feminism in college) was offensive and an objectifying intrusion. I wouldn't want to make anyone uncomfortable with my advances, silent eyeballs or otherwise. I didn't let my eyes linger on a sheer shirt and black bra. I watched the eyes of other men; watched them turn around halfway up the block to look at an ass in short shorts, watched them trail everywhere after everyone. I was satisfied smelling perfume as a woman passed. And so Stephanie drove into the night without me and I remember the scent of the woods and fig leaves.

But it was spring, that heady time in the city when we tell ourselves we should be outside walking on a promenade, or sitting under a blooming tree, identifying our own lives with the shifts in meteorological patterns. My divorce was being finalized and I found myself at Jess and Todd's apartment, and the computer was on Jess's lap and she was signing me up for a dating site. It started simply enough. I didn't resist, besides a requisite roll of my eyes and shoulder shrug, as we flipped through *The Collected Poems of Wallace Stevens* and John Ashbery's *Hotel Lautréamont*, playing a parlor game with my dating profile, finding chance phrases and lines that both amused us and provided a possible answer to the question being asked. A distant third consideration was whether the phrase, plucked at random, sufficiently represented my sensibility, or the sensibility we were crafting for me. There was no harm in signing up—the act itself didn't necessitate my active participation in the dating life. In the end my profile read in part:

- The best or worst lie I've ever told: The apples fall without astronomy.
- The role religion plays in my life: He felt curious about the winter hills.
- Why you should get to know me: Prefers the brightness of bells, imperceptible errors, and a speech of the self that must sustain itself on speech.
- If I was given a million dollars: A little island full of geese and stars.
- More about what I am looking for: Canaries in the morning, orchestras. My heart pinned in a trance to the notice board.

We included the bare minimum of facts:

- The last thing that made me laugh out loud: Doing this.
- If I could be anywhere right now: New York City.

- Five items I can't live without: Books, my cats, coffee, my friends, the artificial world.
- My personal style: Sexy casual.
- Body art: None.
- Favorite item of clothing: Glasses.
- In my bedroom one will find: A deer decal, a sleeping cat, books.
- The last great book I read: Wallace Stevens's *Collected Poems.*

Following the fill-in-the-blanks there was a series of true or false questions. "People ask you for dating/sex advice." "I love to host dinner parties/board game nights/orgies, etc (where 'etc' is your activity of choice)." "My heart controls my brain (among other organs)." "When I'm in a relationship, I believe there's always room for improvement." "I like to grasp the details first, then big picture later." "I'm a head-in-the-clouds kind of person." False. False. False. True. True. False. And just like that, my so-called "romantic profile" was revealed to be the "Gentle Artist":

You are nature's balm: the soothing presence who calms us when we are stressed, who reminds us of the delightful spontaneity of childhood, and who shows us how to appreciate nature and all living things. But as easily as you bring happiness to others, you can bring sadness to yourself when you fail to see your strengths, focusing only on your limitations.

Love for you is an all-or-nothing experience. Because you tend to shut out the rest of the world so you can experience love more fully, you can be vulnerable to the whims of your beloved. Devotion and flexibility are two of the most important qualities you, as a Gentle Artist, bring to a relationship. You can meet the Gentle Artist everywhere art, fashion, nature, children, and animals are present or discussed.

There wasn't much else to do or learn about myself—my curriculum vitae completed, now I needed to apply for the job. We hovered around the computer on Jess's lap and disagreed about who was or wasn't attractive. We made pronouncements like: "Who wants to be with a hedge fund broker?" or "I hate yoga," or "She looks like she could be your sister." The night ended and I rode the N train home and signed back in, this time with the necessary privacy to determine my own dating qualifications.

It wasn't an easy task—the dating site was a rabbit hole, each profile picture labeled "Click Me." Click Me: "Sugar on Spikes." Click Me: "New in Town." It was a frenzy of clicking, self-doubt, arrogance, lust. *I wouldn't have sex with her. Or would I? She is too good for me. She wouldn't have sex with me. Her favorite movie is* Father of the Bride? I refreshed the dating site. I stared out my window at the skyline waiting. I sat pressing F5, the site reloading a fresh grid of faces. Click Me: "What's wrong with a little self-destruction?"

I might be of the last generation born without full immersion in and preoccupation with technology. I played the early computer game Oregon Trail, followed green dots to safety. I wrote all my college papers on a Brother word processor with a two-inch preview screen that fit three lines of text. The total disclosure of my personal life wasn't my natural state. It felt foreign, strange, and awkward. I was more adept at watching the stream of comments and posts than with sticking my foot in to test the waters. I'm not saying I walked uphill both ways in the snow to the church dance to hold my steady's hand through a white glove, only that I did believe we were meant to meet our friends and lovers the old-fashioned way. Via college, the workplace, at a bookbinding class, a third-party introduction, or at a café on Sunday, sitting patiently reading a book all afternoon anticipating someone would notice.

Instead, I was inside devising searches by height, age, and location to generate a photo of someone new. It was spring outside on the avenues, a parade was happening somewhere in the city and I thought: *Let the couples who find themselves outdoors observe that it is spring. Let them be intoxicated with noting that it is spring, pointing out flowers about to bud, and wandering with their golden retrievers to cafés serving microbrews.* When logged in, my photo appeared on the homepage for others who were logged in. *I'm watching you watch me flickering on the screen in what looks like an orchard or pumpkin patch. A left arm is around your waist. The body of a stranger is cropped out. Your ex-boyfriend's phantom wristwatch is still glimmering in the corner.*

I posted another photo. I learned it was important to post several photos, current, and in good lighting, preferably wearing a shirt. I wanted women to think I was serious and beautiful. I posted a photo in which I was wearing, please forgive me, a fedora and looking past the photographer. There I was, positioned according to the rule of thirds, with the Empire State Building lit up over my shoulder out the window in the background. In the final photo, I was in Jess and Todd's kitchen wearing a Halloween mask of a horse's head.

■

The first email I received was a single sentence:

Please describe an "imperceptible error."

Mary

■

I wrote back:

Dear Mary,

That's a good question, but to answer adequately I might need to sketch diagrams and would definitely require a dry erase board. But I will give it a go; it is, after all, in my profile. I would say imperceptible errors are the errors which define a person, and in defining are imperceptible as parts. They are what make the person who she or he is and adds to their charm. I just looked up "error" in the Oxford English Dictionary. Its original meaning was "to wander," as in Alfred Lord Tennyson's "The damsel's headlong error thro' the wood." I like the idea of wanderings which cannot be "apprehended with the mind or senses" or be captured. How is that?

Brett

Dear Brett,

I'd like to see some Venn diagrams and maybe a Gantt chart. Are you saying "quirks"? To me, quirks don't equal errors. I was thinking imperceptible errors would be like, very tiny mistakes that add up over time and then climate change happens or your stove explodes. Bad examples, maybe. I can see how wander would come to mean error. It's interesting it would go from literal to figurative like that.

Do you like poop?

Sincerely,
Mary

I emailed a different girl, and she emailed me, then I emailed her, then she emailed me, and then I emailed her. Soon almost a week had passed without a reply. *She's busy. She's dating someone else. She noticed I'm divorced. Note to self: That horse head photo is a distinct sign of creepiness and not whimsy. Buyer beware. We would never work out. She lives in Hoboken.* But a virtual brush-off was still a brush-off. So I checked Craigslist Missed Connections, a virtual bulletin board of personal classifieds written by individuals who met or momentarily noticed someone else across a crowded train or in line at a movie, but due to whatever particular chain of events—train doors opening before the nerve to speak arrived, a phone number lost to the washing machine—they were unable to contact that person directly. One could write a post about the moment in hopes of reconnecting, if indeed the other party happened to find the post and was interested. I felt safe checking Missed Connections. My voyeurism was protected. There was no real expectation of being located and understood, no photos of prospective dates, no pressure to psych myself up to write a witty introductory email.

It was a fairy tale, a distraction that allowed one to believe a letter in a bottle was washing up on the distant mythical shores of Atlantis, where every single woman was beautiful: in tights and cowboy boots, red flats and a black miniskirt, a tattoo of a star on her wrist, a broken heart on her arm, skinny gray jeans and white sneakers on the train. But I was never anywhere—at 2 AM I was asleep, not dancing at Home Sweet Home. I didn't shop at Whole Foods on Tuesday with a green tote or ride a mountain bike across the bridge. I rode the subway to work. I had baby blue high-top sneakers, rectangular tortoise frame glasses. I didn't want to be overlooked. Someone must have seen me. "We sat across from each other. You were reading *The Year of Magical Thinking.* I was reading *Regarding the Pain of Others.* You got off; I wanted to say something." It would be one thing to be noticed—to inspire

intrigue or wonder, eyes not passing over me but pausing to con-
template a little further who I was, feeling the blush rise around
my neck. It was a gigantic other thing to have that person follow
up, an hour later, three days in the future, unable to shake thoughts
of what a voice sounded like, so that in the middle of the night or
a lull during work, the interaction is typed, a descriptive missive
floating out into the Internet's cosmos. I told my friend Charlie
that when a person does this in an attempt to find you, you are at
the peak of your desirability. It should not be squandered.

I was vigilant. It was important to remember each person I
exchanged chitchat with was a possible Missed Connection. A
woman approached me at the coffee shop. "I think you dropped
this." I was caught off-guard. I looked at her left hand for a wedding band. Todd told me that Missed Connections don't happen,
you make them happen. "I like your scarf. I just finished reading
that book." Pathologically pathetic, I held the door open for
anyone. I tucked in my shirt. I wanted to be presentable. I had
difficulty smiling at strangers. One day I walked past Parker Posey
and made eye contact. We were on our cell phones. *Let it start to
rain so we can duck under the same awning to wait for the storm to
clear, let the rain fall as I walk on without an umbrella stepping on
every electrical manhole waiting for the stray voltage to notice me and
knock me dead.*

I got back to my apartment and checked Missed Connections
out of loneliness and boredom, which are the same. There is a
beauty in anonymous strangers reaching out into the ether to find
someone they believe they have shared a moment with—a cab
from the airport, a phone number smudged off a sweaty hand. I
wanted to find faith in others looking for each other—and not
just the "you bought me and my friends a drink at an anonymous
bar" types, but romance, or an uncanny quality in how, in a city of
millions of characters, there is bound to be a story starting somewhere. But once I had read them for a week, for two weeks, for
a month, the stories began to sound the same. If a dating profile
was the curated language one was required to enter in order to

participate, a list of likes and dislikes and witty phrases crafting an identity we hope another will share or find value in, then the Missed Connection was just another outlet for longing, and the longing had carved out its own genre. In the end, the algorithm for online dating is just a pretext. It's not perfect and it doesn't matter. I had pretended to subvert the process when creating my dating profile, but that was just a trick to get myself to feel comfortable with participating. So there I was. My phone wasn't ringing. *Nothing is happening. I must make something happen.*

I composed a fake Missed Connection from the headlines and marketing slogans of the dating site, using words that others had selected to present themselves to the world, to prove they were lovable.

SUBJECT: Rain or Shine / m4w / Brooklyn

It may or may not be unfortunate that people search for certain sex, anonymous travels, individuals for laughter, or text messaging all night. It takes time to write these emails with a personal account reduced to various forms of opportunities and objects I can't account for. Click here: just what you never knew you were going to get, a girl prowling about town, sugar on spikes, what's wrong with a little self-destruction, placing the ass in Cassidy since 1979. Set standards, and bingo, break 'em. It takes time to uncover each other, start off and finish the walk in the park, later dismiss the passage or the symphony heard on the barge circling sirens from the island. It may be artificial, it is artificial, but I won't shoot myself footless, brave waters in a kayak and some shy garment. Others are determined to attend fashion week or a free bluegrass concert on an abandoned pier. I swear I want this whole world, just not most of that. Let's just talk about this sunset, or the rosy fingers of dawn, better still dirty-talk if you say so, both of us, at once, starting now. It may end up being a touch to never scrub away. This may or may not be mutually beneficial, but here I am, two miles away, your three-night stand, rain or shine, on foot.

And, small World Wide Web that it was, Cassidy responded:

Dear Mr. Mystery Missed Connection,

I'm not sure if your post had anything to do with me, but my friend passed it along because my MySpace tagline is "putting the ass in Cassidy since 1979." Although fashion week and bluegrass concerts aren't ringing a bell, that's potentially my ass you're talking about. Have we met?

Cassidy

Dear Cassidy,

I don't know you. I wrote the Missed Connection based on pro-files from a dating site. It was meant to be a project to see if I could take all the interesting language and tag-lines and craft it into a text that represented that strange experience. Perhaps I didn't think it all the way through. I didn't expect you'd stumble upon it, and hope it didn't freak you out too much. I'll remove the posting if it did.

Jake

Hey Jake,

It's no problem—I was mostly bewildered, since 90% of the entry was unfamiliar (. . . but since I was at McCarren Pool twice this week, I figured I would check it out). It's pure luck that I have a friend that peruses Missed Connections! Don't worry about taking it down. It's not really deprecatory, just odd. I do feel sheepish for being busted for being on a dating site, though.

Cassidy

Cassidy,

Oh, don't feel sheepish. You got "caught" by someone who is also on the site. That doesn't really count. Also, to come clean, and make this entire thing even more creepy, my name isn't Jake.

Yours,
Brett

It took me three weeks to realize my aimless and compulsive clicking throughout the dating site had consequences. Each click was recorded. Every person I clicked on could see that I had been viewing her profile, had clicked through her slideshow of four photos. There were few photos on the site I hadn't spent time contemplating. Let's face it; there wasn't much else to initially go on, and the fact that someone was looking at my profile was a form of interaction. An affirmation. Even if we were all trigger-happy, clicking away until dawn, still I was relieved to know others found the miniature image of my face worth the minimal effort of pressing their pointer finger down on the mouse. Maybe I shouldn't have been so reckless with my clicking, but "sending a wink" seemed immature, silly—having a middle school friend ask a girl if she thought I was cute, while I held down mute on the three-way call. *I should just take the chance and email the person.* I wanted to start each email: "Forgive my trespass of your personal space and please don't feel obligated to reply to this note in which I demonstrate that I have read 'your' and not 'you're' profile, and have spelled everything correctly, despite my ugly habit of homonym mistakes." It did, I admit, feel good to be "hot-listed," even by women with fuzzy matchbook-sized photos. Each click straightened my slumping shoulders. I set a goal of 1,000 views. I'd "hot-listed" fifty-seven people. That seemed like too many. It was just a list to return to, like bookmarked websites or an online shopping cart—I could decide tomorrow whether or not it was imperative I own gray desert boots, maybe I should wait to see if my sudden interest in Russian icons wanes. It was also a way to let the other person know I was interested, that I was there and available. I signed in and wrote a note to Daphne, with whom I had already traded a few emails.

August 17, 2007
Dear You,

I guess it was forward and inappropriate for me to ask you over last night, to place you in a position where you felt there could be any danger to your well-being, and I am sorry I did that. And your co-worker of course was right, you shouldn't show up alone at a strange boy's house in the middle of the night to watch Japanese anime, a million terrible things could happen, and often do, and I guess I felt somehow like it wasn't quite a first meeting, that with the illusion of the connectedness of the Internet I somehow knew you more than a complete stranger. But I guess that is true and not true. You don't really know me yet, and I don't know you, and it would be better to do that in a safe location. It 3:30 AM and I am in a safe location and thinking about sleeping and meeting you tomorrow or today actually as I write this and you read it. There are helicopters hovering over the projects. The night is over, for me at least. Maybe you are still awake. Maybe you will get this before morning, though I hope not. Tomorrow we will walk around in public at the zoo and talk and nothing will come of it or else I won't be able to tell. And I have said enough already. I'm feeling pretty ridiculous at this point. I think most people are laughing at me. Especially you. That's fine. For now. I guess. Though not for much longer. And yeah we can get to know each other and look at all the caged birds, and animals, pretending they are happy. I think I will not expect anything. I will expect to say hello and talk and see what you have to say, and tell you things. And then, goodbye. I know these things take time, and I won't place that pressure on myself, or you, or is that what these emails are meant to do? I'm feeling a little sad today. I'm not sure why. I wish I wasn't divorced and that my refrigerator was full.

Brett

August 17, 2007
Dear Bretton,

I don't want you to feel sad. I honestly don't care that you are divorced or have nothing in your fridge. I'm single and have expired everything in mine. I mean I was dating someone for about 7 months not long ago and all those feelings and the closeness that I thought I had with him was obviously nothing. I'm by myself now and it makes me feel dumb. I mean that's nothing to what you have been through so it makes me dumb to even say anything. I like your heavy emails.

Daphne

August 18, 2007
Dear Daphne,

I know you think my attention and affection are not merited yet in the situation, on account of it being so soon, that you feel disconnected from it and that makes you sad, and that makes me question myself and my own actions. Am I just sweet and that is how I interact in the world, or am I more like how I think you are perceiving me: desperate for love? And maybe it is both. And that makes me sad, to know that about myself or even imagine that about myself. And if it is true, what do I do with it? Slow down little pony. I tend to gallop. And I will try to rein myself in a little, though it will be difficult. As last night proved. I guess in that regard I am a boy lying next to a pretty girl and my body takes over and seems to fit too nicely with yours. I don't want you to regret anything or think about it the next day with dread. I want you to be excited about me, about seeing me, sleeping next to me. And it made me sad on the subway to see you strange and sad talking about your ex-boyfriend.

All of that,
Bretton

August 20, 2007
Dear Bretton,

I don't think you are desperate for love. . . . I mean maybe we all are a bit, including me but not in the evil way you are thinking. I think you are like me, you fall easily. The amount of affection does make me feel a little empty . . . and it has nothing to do with you. It's just odd to me. . . . But since you have gone through what you have—that makes me question how you can be so affectionate with me. I think you are just an extra sweet and emotional guy. Nothing in the world wrong with that. I like hanging out, I just hate the empty stupid feelings I get when I, for lack of better term, "mess around" with someone. It's not you, it's me. I don't know why I get like that. The extra affection that I don't know the source of makes me confused. I don't know how to reciprocate that. And I don't blame your friends for telling you it's too early to date, but how can they give you advice for something they have not lived through? And you should not be sad and stuck in your house. It's not healthy. It's also not healthy to jump from relationship to relationship . . . I'm having fun and you are too so that's what matters. And I was a little bummed that you said we might not hang out because you wanted space, because I want to hang out. I wanted a picnic and I sort of want to see you today. That's nothing new. Wish you were online, bleh.

Daphne

I had the month of August off from work and so I was available to spend a good deal of time with Daphne. My days were free. I rode the subway with her to work in the morning, met her at the end of the day and rode back to her apartment and straight to her room. We lay in bed and ordered food and movies. There was a canister of Easy Cheese permanently on her bureau, it could have been half-empty or half-full; I never saw it in action. We went to the zoo. We held hands. She had beautiful eyes. She bought me my own boyfriend pillow when I began ending up with hers in the morning. She was the first person to send me images that made me blush—I squinted at my tiny LG flip phone screen to take it all in. She began to call me her "pretend" boyfriend, an acknowledgment, I think, that we were playing house. I think she liked having me there as much as I liked being somewhere. I'd only dated a few people after the divorce and she was recently out of a relationship, and we were trying to make sense of what it was like to be caring and cared for. The "pretend" helped us both impersonate love, until, of course, it no longer did.

September 3, 2007
3:21 PM

DAPHNE: I don't like you emailing people on Nerve.

ME: I know you don't.

DAPHNE: Well, quit emailing. I like having a pretend boyfriend, it works for me. I can't share.

ME: Well then, it isn't pretend, is it?

DAPHNE: I prefer it pretend. You have too many issues for it to be real. If one of us finds someone more awesome, fine, but you shouldn't be emailing around each day because you can. That's lame.

ME: Where do you think finding someone else is going to happen?

DAPHNE: If you are emailing around that is just like telling the world "Here I am" and it makes it easier for you to poof! and disappear, but if you are dealing with real life you will be too busy hanging out with me to ever meet anyone.

ME: And real life is a pretend relationship?

DAPHNE: Yes. You're too shy to meet anyone in real life unless they are whoring it up and in that case they will be trashy.

ME: So I should be spending all my time with you. That sounds like you have me in your clutches.

DAPHNE: Pretty much. I like it that way. I'm very selfish.

ME: You want something which is totally understandable but something I'm not willing to give you.

DAPHNE: Ok.

ME: Right?

DAPHNE: Yes. I said Ok.

ME: I mean we could try to see each other more casually.

DAPHNE: No. I'm not capable of that. I have a bad problem jumping into things like no one's business. I'm very dysfunctional. I'm a serial hang-arounder, but I can actually stand you and you aren't an addict or an asshole. I promise you I don't like most people. I have a feeling though that you fall easily and it must feel nice for you right now because you are so starving for affection.

ME: Some of that might be true. I mean, I guess it is. Some of that.

DAPHNE: Well at least you got some nice affection that will hold you over a bit.

ME: I don't think about it that way.

DAPHNE: Well it's the way I said. You are being all true to yourself! You go boy! Dr. Phil would be very proud.

ME: Thanks Daphne.

DAPHNE: I really can't be your friend. I've let you know how I feel.

ME: I understand.

DAPHNE: If I was awesome I would be your friend, because that's what you do if you like someone, but I'm all or nothing unfortunately.

ME: Maybe you will be able to at some point, just not today or next week.

DAPHNE: No I won't. I'm very good at eliminating people, for lack of a better word. I don't want to be your friend. I don't want to see you dating around. I won't be happy for you. And I don't want to wait around while you find other stepping stones to maybe one day want to hang out with me more, that's gross. Whatever, look how fast and out of nowhere you did this to me; wanting affection and being cute isn't a good combo to avoid that kind of stuff. It's romantic and unabashed and vulnerable blah blah blah. Thanks. You are kind of dumb because I'm the coolest girl you will ever meet.

ME: Ok.

DAPHNE: You are going to have a hell of a time dating people. Because anyone ok with you fucking around is going to be dumb and have AIDS. Don't be offended, but I am deleting you off email, Facebook, etc. You should write a girl back and meet someone to stay distracted, it will help.

ME: I can't deal with rehashing how much of an asshole and wrong and fucked up and cruel I am.

DAPHNE: You aren't, really.

ME: So I'm just going to get AIDS?

DAPHNE: Well with the situations you want, yes you are. You are fishing around a crummy pool of people.

ME: I told you I don't know that I will be dating, and if and when I do I will set up parameters to keep things from getting serious.

DAPHNE: That's impossible. You tried to set up parameters with me. People don't work that way. Hello. Blah. I feel like I'm going to cry.

ME: What can I do?

DAPHNE: This makes me think you are a pretty crummy person and that I have been duped. I'm beginning to hate your fucking guts.

ME: You can think that if it makes it easier to think I'm a fuck-face. But that isn't true. And I'm sorry that there were some things that were crummy and didn't work out. But I wasn't dishonest or disingenuous with you at all.

DAPHNE: Ok. Fuck off. Thanks for fucking me. Glad I could get another guy off.

ME: Are you done?

DAPHNE: You really added more fucked up shit to my lovely record.

ME: Don't hold me accountable for your record.

DAPHNE: You are part of it now. The end result is always the same. Go fuck some girls to get it out of your system. I thought you weren't like that. Asshole. But guess what, you are! Hooray for me!

ME: That isn't true.

DAPHNE: If it makes you feel better to tell yourself that then go ahead.

ME: It is taking all my power to not tell you to go fuck yourself.

DAPHNE: I'm not making anything up, it's true. Did it take all your power to fuck me and know you didn't want anything more?

ME: You had every opportunity to end it.

DAPHNE: You just want to keep doors open with various people, yet sleep with me. That makes sense.

ME: You can go ahead and chalk me up as some boy who is out there fucking around. I don't think that is true, and didn't ever treat you that way.

DAPHNE: Facts are facts.

ME: You are the first person I have been with after my divorce. I'm sorry.

DAPHNE: So what. Lucky me, oh lucky me.

ME: Please stop. I'm at work. Can we talk about this later?

DAPHNE: THIS ALWAYS HAPPENS. You should have left me alone and known not to fuck a girl who has told you this is what happens to her. Don't do it again, asshole, to someone else when you know you can't do anything but jump around from person to person. It's not fair to others.

ME: Lesson learned.

DAPHNE: You are playing with people and that's so fucked up. You should take down your fucking profile.

ME: You are treating me like someone I'm not.

DAPHNE: Facts are facts.

ME: Don't blame me for them.

DAPHNE: Do you know how long it has been since I've slept with someone sober?

ME: That is fucked up, and not my fault.

DAPHNE: Or with someone who actually liked me? You walked into a train-wreck. Just leave girls alone.

ME: Fine. I will. I've clearly no grasp.

DAPHNE: The worst part is you just think it's cool by saying: "Hey I'm so nice. I don't do this to people." Just say: "Yes, Daphne, I knew I couldn't do anything more, but I was real nice to you and spent a lot of time with you and made you think there was actually something there and I fucked you because it had to be done. There had to be a first after my divorce. I knew it would end up with nothing, but I need to start somewhere."

ME: Fuck you.

DAPHNE: Stop fucking around with girls.

ME: Ok. Fine. Done. I have work to do.

I told myself it was an untenable position. *I should stay home, stare at the brownstones across the street, search the computer screen for new books and ties, make a cup of tea, watch a movie, go to bed, wake up and clean up the cat fur with a Swiffer.* In the heat they never stopped shedding, even the ceiling fan somehow managed to gather their fur on its blades. The cats begged to be brushed, and then the fur didn't stop coming off. It gave me something to do. A task to complete. Maybe, as friends suggested, I wasn't "ready" to be dating. Is anyone ever prepared for anything? Maybe the Buddhists, with a mind detached from desire and ignorance sitting quietly watching the material world pass.

I saw only two options: either I would live with loneliness or continue to attempt to make connections and fail, in any number of new ways. I couldn't allow myself to be interested in every new person I dated. It had only just started and already it was exhausting, a math equation across a chalkboard devised to prove its own difficulty. It would be a series of failures until it wasn't. I was broken and slowly fitting the pieces into some self that could walk through the door. And I walked through the door. And yes, I fell too easy; a sweet word shattered me into a thousand shards. And what was I supposed to do with this? How to settle into anything, without awkwardness, with the earth at a slight tilt and me leaning against the wall avoiding the eyes of others? And what does anyone really need but an email in the morning from a stranger that says "Tell me about yourself."

The more time I spent combing through profiles the less weird it felt, and I became a little braver in contacting people. I showed up for the dates, was there on time or five minutes early, smiled, carried on a conversation, asked questions, laughed as I paused to sip my coffee. I was forever sipping coffee at a café on a first date since I couldn't bring myself to meet at a bar—I was less worried about relapsing than giving off what I feared was a distinctly creepy vibe of not drinking while my date was, me standing too close and too sober as if at any minute I was going to spike her drink with Rohypnol. It might have been a sense of arrogance, a misguided male characteristic in a city populated with more women than men, or my insecurity masquerading as confidence, my timid standoffishness misread as self-importance, but I came to view myself as an average catch in the world of Internet romance. What I mean to say, to clarify, is that it was enough to not be a complete fucking monster—the people I met had come to expect another awful encounter in a series of awful encounters. I exhibited a strict personal policy of not yelling at my dates on our first meeting. I didn't ask if "they always dressed so slutty." I didn't get up for another drink and never return. I hadn't been unemployed for years. My hand didn't drift to their neck with a hateful grip when we were kissing. These were all real experiences relayed to me on dates. I learned this was something to talk about on first dates—all our past dates from the site were an experience we bonded over.

And though I understood there was a world of dating in which two people fooled around and it meant nothing, with me, it turned to something else quickly. They saw the absence of harm, they saw potential, and they thought I might be the one to settle down with for a period of time. I wasn't complaining. So what if I spent the entire weekend with them in bed, at the farmers' market, ordering Thai food? I wanted to be that person, thought I was that person, needed to believe I was the boyfriend type. I couldn't stand to see myself as anything else.

September 4, 2007
9:30 AM

ME: On my way to work from girl's apartment.

CHARLIE: Yeah man, how did you swing that?

ME: No idea, magic or something. But what's the worst thing that could have happened, because it did.

CHARLIE: Couldn't get it up?

ME: Bingo!

CHARLIE: Did it happen eventually or one try and that was that?

ME: One try. I'm cursed.

CHARLIE: Then what—did you go home?

ME: No spent the night.

CHARLIE: Shouldn't be that big of a deal. Was she cool?

ME: I think she was disappointed.

CHARLIE: Any idea when you will see her again?

ME: This weekend.

CHARLIE: So no sweat. Make up for it with round two.

ME: What if I can't? It is bumming me out.

CHARLIE: Handle that ass. Don't doubt yourself. If you're that worried lay off on jerking off for a minute.

ME: Whatever, see you at the hookah spot.

Nothing will be original again. That might be the motto of the twenty-first century. Not "Know Thyself" engraved in gold letters above the entrance to a Delphic temple, but rather on the archway into an empty public pool in Brooklyn where summer concerts are held, written in a font meant to capture the nostalgia of handwriting: "Nothing will be original again." On the first date I disclosed everything: my ex-wife had an affair, I was a recovering alcoholic, I was estranged from my mother. I sabotaged myself, while simultaneously providing an exit strategy. The next day, I sent a two-page email. I didn't understand the rules. Wait two days to text back, three days to email, a week before IM-ing: "It was nice hanging out." The sad fact was I dated anyone for three weeks, committed all my attention and affection, out of romantic desperation meant to reinforce my own self-worth. I placed a doodle of a bird and a heart on her pillow as I left for work. I called the next day, maybe twice. I didn't want to be alone. I needed to set clearer boundaries for myself. What is the appropriate timeline to feel something like love again? *I'm supposed to feel consumed. It happens like a thunderbolt or a fork in a socket.*

I couldn't help but envision how each person had rested their hand on a chest not so unlike mine, watched their favorite movie on this couch at night, months before, with someone else. There are too many people in the world, and sitting in front of a screen exchanging messages and staring at photos creates desire and boundless possibilities. Once face-to-face in reality, it's not so much that expectations are tarnished, but that there was a fear of missing out on the host of other options. But more importantly for me, it was as if my own individuality, if there is such a thing, felt insignificant, felt routine, felt like a bit part played night after night onstage. I don't have any way to say it without feeling like Bridget Jones; I wanted it to be distinct with me. And yet what if history was doomed to repeat itself, like the sad man living in the desert struck by lightning four or five times in a life? The lightning's electric charges lingering within said man's circulatory system like a parasite, defying the laws of science and recruiting future bolts of lightning from the sky to strike the body again, and then again, and then for good measure once again, not delivering love, but burns, disfigurement. I wanted to believe my luck at finding someone was neutral—my odds the same as my peers—the customary 50/50 chance of success. Heads or tails. It is the law of probability. Each time we begin again with renewed optimism or faith in our luck. The alternative is too depressing to maintain.

Throughout it all I wouldn't let myself forget that on the rare occasions in my marriage when I did have sex with Nina, she was also having sex with someone else. Thinking of him as she was with me, coming home after she was with him, or going off to see him after she was with me, each time returning to play out a domestic routine I believed to be scripted only for us. Sam asked me if I still thought about her. He told me he did as well, that he missed her too, and I knew it was important that he tell me that. After a half a year without her, he was the first one to say that to me. It was easier each day for me to write her off. I'd become accustomed to such a position with people. It was my life's work. I didn't tell him that I had recently found her Social Security card in a stack of random papers. I brought it to work to shred before thinking better of it and mailing it to her mother in a package of other miscellaneous documents.

September 5, 2007
Dear Sophie,

I apologize for emailing you, particularly at your work address, and hope it is not too much of an inconvenience. Really, I just wanted to write to let you know that I do appreciate your calling me and providing me with information I undoubtedly deserved to know. I have since left the Bay Area and moved back to Brooklyn. I hope all is as well with you as it could be.

All best,
Brett

Sophie Reynolds's reply was generous, kind, and sympathetic. She was relieved to know how I felt, that I didn't hold *The Phone Call* against her. We were sharing a trauma, attempting to make sense of our pasts and finding support in our friends. We were alone in the world together, distinctly undergoing a similar range of emotions—the predicament of infidelity by no means unique to us, except that regardless of our separate lives we had somehow become characters in the same drama.

■

After posting that first fake Missed Connection, I convinced Jess to write some more with me. It became slightly obsessive. I was posting one or two a day. Craigslist had begun "ghosting" my posts—meaning they were published, but not included publicly in the queue. To get around this, I had to post from different computers with new IP addresses, using different email addresses that I had to create weekly. If I was at a friend's for dinner, I retired to their office to post from their computer. It wasn't quite cloak-and-dagger, but I allowed myself to entertain the idea that it was.

I found it didn't really matter what I posted. Responses would flood in almost immediately:

I look every day, wondering if someone feels like I got away :) Oh well . . . we can't all be the "cute hipster girl reading *Pride and Prejudice and Zombies* on the G train." But sometimes I'd like to think when I catch a guy stealing glances that the universe is setting up a moment that will ensure that I will stick in his mind for at least an hour ;) I read missed connections too, for entertainment, and for the slim chance someone spotted me on the train and thought I was the most beautiful thing in the world. They are like little love stories. I reconnected with someone on here that I spoke to once, because I too looked to kill time at work. I thought I would go for it—the one written about me. The guy ended up being tragically boring. What a cliché. Romance is dead. LOL. I still read them.

Jess and I emailed back and forth during work hours, sometimes writing just a phrase, sometimes a full sentence or two, the other person adding on from there, and then I posted them to Craigslist.

SUBJECT: L Train this Morning / m4w / Brooklyn

You were on the L train wearing skinny jeans and an expression of doubt. I share that doubt, and wanted to share my thoughts on podcasting, 19th century Russian novels, and French pressed coffee. Your body language implied you are interested in these things, as well as polka music (in a strangely unironic way), East Asian horticulture, and car racing. I could tell that you were listening to some minimal techno, or electro, or Silver Jews, or Jigga. And so was I. I think that if we meet, I will explode into knowing the exact way to sing in the shower and cook pasta for your tiny mouth. If you felt the same way, let me know, smoke signals, etc.

I waited. Smoked a cigarette. I refreshed my inbox. A reply:

I'll bet you enjoy the *Times* on Sunday, spending your week-ends lounging on a blanket at McCarren Park playing Scrabble after a large brunch. If you'd like to, we can watch independent films, cook dinner listening to 60s Motown records and you can marvel at my random use of antiquated diction and perfect spelling.

And another:

What color were the jeans and what time was it? I'd hate to be the wrong person to converse with about polka music over pasta . . .

I searched *The New York Times* for articles about online dating and found "Looking for Love: Online or on Paper," in which the author noted that in 1841 a German aristocrat, Baron von Hallberg de Bröch, placed a full-page ad in the *Journal of Munich* boasting of a sumptuous castle and received seven hundred letters in response. Among the qualifications the seventy-year-old baron required in his prospective partner: "She must be from sixteen to twenty years of age; she must have beautiful hair, handsome teeth, and a charming little foot." Where were my seven hundred emails?

I refreshed my inbox:

> I was sitting on the L train this morning though I'm positive
> your missed connection was not with me. I can't help but want
> something big to happen soon. Like really soon. Like in twenty
> minutes soon. When the class is over soon. I hate Wednesdays
> and expectations always harm more then they help. Maybe one
> day I'll inspire a random show of affection in the form of a
> shower bravado and pasta cooking . . .

And

> Quite possibly could have been me. I make coffee for a living. I
> prefer clover pressed. Am I yours?

I refilled my coffee. I looked up "clover pressed." I learned that
the final step, "when a cake of spent grounds rises majestically
to the top, is so titillating to coffee fanatics that one of them
posted a clip of it on YouTube." I watched the video on YouTube.
I refreshed my inbox:

> I'm not your lady, but I hope some kind of poetic justice is
> served in that you and your lady will be sharing a cup of French
> pressed coffee in no time. Possibly even each of you having a
> cup of your own. Good luck.

I felt awful. I emailed Jess and told her I was awful. She wrote back: "Maybe you are filling the world with hope rather than toying with it." I fancied myself the perfect flâneur, as described by Baudelaire, though instead of strolling the physical avenues and arcades of the modern city of Paris, I was idling my time away taking in the personal ads of the Internet. The flâneur, according to Baudelaire, has the unique ability to set up home everywhere in the world; "being at the center of the world and remaining hidden in the world," he experiences "some of the smallest pleasures of those independent minds, passionate, impartial, that language can only clumsily define. The observer is a prince who rejoices in all his incognito."

But that was just a theory to tell myself. In fact, it was more like I was trolling the universe. Though I never did write back or engage beyond the initial posting, I wasn't an observer. I was inserting myself into the activity of the passing multitude. I believed, for the most part, the majority of people reading the posts were somehow consciously or unconsciously in on the joke, that in the end the Missed Connection post itself was the point, was the event they were responding to. The joy was in knowing that others were out there, passing strangers, just like me, secretly hoping, quietly looking.

Someone responded:

That might be one of the best Missed Connections ever, you made my day.

After dating online for several months, I was caught off-guard out on a second date when the girl mentioned a specific life detail I hadn't yet confessed: "Didn't you meet your ex-wife at a pencil factory?" I changed the subject, made a lame joke about erasing a rough draft. I was positive it wasn't something I had shared. In fact, I had forgotten that detail entirely. At home, I searched my emails for confirmation. Nothing. I googled myself. The first result to appear, after .15 seconds, was my wedding announcement in *The New York Observer*. *Fuck the Internet.*

NINA AND BRETT
MET: September 2001
ENGAGED: December 13, 2003
PROJECTED WEDDING DATE: May 21, 2005

The two bards first met back at a party in Williamsburg held in an abandoned pencil factory. The long-haired Brett was wearing big Gucci sunglasses with clear lenses. "I knew who Brett was, but I had never formally met him," said Nina, 25, a tall brunette. "I was watching him all night. He was leaning against a wall, smoking, and just looked mysterious and cool." When Marvin Gaye's "Let's Get It On" started playing, she walked up to Brett and asked him to dance. "He turned around, looked at me and said no," Nina remembered. "I thought, O.K., so he's a jerk."

"I was shocked!" protested Brett, 26 (and no relation to Matt Lauer). "I was on my way out and saying goodbye to people, and this person who I had noticed earlier in the night to be quite beautiful approached me. I remember going home and asking my roommate if I should go back to the party."

Luckily, the circle of young poets in New York City is quite small and several weeks later Brett got word of a publication party for a magazine Nina publishes in her spare time. "I was sort of waiting for the right time to talk to her again," he said. "My temperament is not the kind that I could have contacted her and said, 'Hey, remember that time you asked me to dance?'" He missed the party, but sent her an e-mail requesting a copy, which she delivered at a subsequent reading held by his office. The scribes then made plans for a hipster pilgrimage to an art exhibit at P.S. 1 in Queens. Sitting in a small room with a Janet Cardiff installation involving choral music playing through speakers, Nina realized that she had stumbled into something big. "It was so beautiful, and I think we ended up just sort of staring at each other," she said. "It had this very personal and intimate feel to it," Brett recalled.

Yet their first kiss didn't come until almost two months later. "Nina took the lead on that one," Brett sighed, who rallied by buying her a recording of the aforementioned choral music for Valentine's Day. Nina explained that she "knew right away that he was it."

The couple picked out an antique 18-carat filigreed gold band with a small flat diamond set in the center, from Doyle and Doyle on Orchard Street. "I wanted a ring that looked like my mom's," said Nina. When the crucial moment arrived, Brett gallantly tried to drop to his knee, but Nina stopped him. "I freaked out," she said. "I didn't want to be looking down at him. So I made him stand up. He asked me to marry him, and then we sat down and stared at each other like morons."

There were rules to my new world order. It is safe to assume that each active participant on a dating site has at least three queries out at a time. People say things like dating is a numbers game, a game of chance, but also implied is that the more people one dates or meets (think speed dating), the better their odds are in encountering someone who is bearable. It's also about timing: Mercury is in retrograde, I'm not quite over my last lover, I had a bad day at work and wasn't in the mood for sushi.

A month had passed when Lindsay emailed me again. We had exchanged a few emails on the dating site and then silence—she disappeared. It happens. Lindsay's email didn't explain much, she was traveling, she was sorry so much time had passed since her last email—it would be reasonable to assume she had been dating someone else or trying to date someone else, just as I was. Lindsay's timing wasn't exactly great; I was reading the email at the end of my workday, right before heading out of the office to meet a date in the Lower East Side for tea. Or actually, maybe it was perfect timing.

September 7, 2007
Lindsay!

Oh you don't need to worry about blowing me off, leaving me out in the cold, high and dry; you just owe me for all the tissues I wadded up with tears and the pints and pints of ice cream I consumed in sadness. It is nice to hear from you, though of course, I have met my Internet life partner, actually all lucky thirteen of them.

If you can believe it, I haven't and am emailing you on a Friday night. I should have waited until morning. Anyway, now, I have a strange-ish question: Were you by any chance at Teany tonight?

Here I am,
Brett

And, small as the real world can be, it was in fact Lindsay sitting five feet from me, hours after she sent her email, and an hour into my awkward first date with someone else.

September 8, 2007
Dear Lindsay,

It goes without saying that it was incredibly weird. And I was sitting there thinking why is this pretty girl smiling at me, that never happens, am I going to have to look at Craigslist Missed Connections or something, and then a split second later, I though OH, maybe . . . I admit though I'm happy we got the awkwardness of our first date over with. It was a demo. And I'm not quite sure that I was out on a date last night, but I will roll with that since it was a person who contacted me from my profile, but she lives in Boston, and was in town and wanted to meet, and so I thought, eh, whatever. When I described her "accent" to a friend, he informed me that "weally" isn't a Boston accent, but a speech impediment. So, I can promise there was no hand-holding. I can also promise my favorite color is blue, that I like birds, and just got a manicure. And where will you be for the weekend?

Soon,
Brett

PS: I had my intern at work crunch some numbers today as to the probability (in percentages) of an encounter at a tea shop in the Lower East Side.

See attached file.

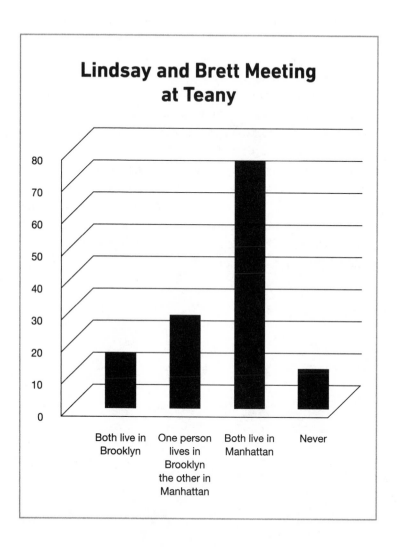

Lindsay and Brett Meeting at Teany

80
70
60
50
40
30
20
10
0

Both live in Brooklyn | One person lives in Brooklyn the other in Manhattan | Both live in Manhattan | Never

We traded a few more emails, and then for whatever reason, laziness or life intervened, and a week passed without my responding. Late one night an angry and indignant email arrived from Lindsay. Among other things, it questioned my basic decency and offered the advice that I refrain from acting like an asshole, if not for her sake, then for the sake of all my potential future dates. It would save everyone a good deal of time, waiting, suffering, and expectation. She wasn't exactly right, but also, maybe she wasn't wrong, and it was certainly the opportunity for me to bow out gracelessly. I will say, though, her email was funny, well-written, and full of passion, and I'd become recently accustomed to apologizing for performing incorrectly, knowingly or unknowingly. And so, I didn't move on to someone else and instead sent an apology and made plans to meet in person.

October 11, 2007
Lindsay,

I'm sorry to receive your email and did have every intention of emailing you back and while I could list reasons (from an insane and draining work week to my own recent dating experiences and taking a few days before leaping back in) they are still not adequate, as I'm not dead, and there have been no deaths in my immediate family and so I should have emailed you. And I do sincerely apologize for that. I couldn't agree more that dating is exhausting and perhaps a little disheartening and I certainly had no intentions of exasperating you.

Having said all that, I can't help but think that your email is a little misdirected. We didn't date or even really meet; we exchanged a bunch of emails that I really looked forward to receiving and there was certainly the expectation of meeting. So maybe "unstoppable moron" might be a little much? You took over a month to respond to me and I don't think you should be so quick to hold others to a standard which you yourself are unable or unwilling to live up to. I was disappointed when you didn't email me, but I certainly would not judge you so harshly because of it.

And still don't,
Brett

My friend Charlie and I constantly found ourselves at the hookah spot. The walls were painted with a form of hieroglyphics. It was as if the person hired had recreated the symbols from the memory of a half-hour school lesson on ancient Egypt rather than modeling them on actual images, or as if strict copyright laws required each hieroglyph to be altered 30 percent to avoid a lawsuit. The lights were dimmed and that helped. We sat on fringed cushions and ordered cherry mint tobacco and mint teas. We were both single and we both didn't drink, so late in the evening, after a movie, instead of ending up at a bar, we found ourselves there. On Wednesday nights a DJ played Top 40 hip-hop and R&B, on Thursdays it was filled with drag queens performing lap dances for middle-aged men, and on Friday nights it was filled with teenage ravers. All the waitresses were young women from former Soviet countries. The place wasn't going to last but it was three blocks from Charlie's apartment.

I sat with the long hookah hose in my hand puffing scented tobacco. We handed it back and forth. We looked at our phones and talked about girls and my online dating. I told him how someone had emailed me who recognized me from an Oakland coffee shop, that I exchanged emails with her about the differences between Brooklyn and the Bay Area. She lived ten blocks down the street from me. We IMed each other for a month or so, she sent me a mixed CD of moody songs, and we never met. I told him about how Daphne still wouldn't let me completely end our relationship, though I wasn't exactly standing my ground either. One morning before work, we were on the roof of her apartment building smoking, and ended up having sex on plastic patio furniture. We stopped when the condom broke. I called a pharmacy near my work to find out if they sold the morning-after pill. We rode the subway for twenty minutes in silence. At the pharmacy, as I pulled out my wallet to pay, a strip of three condoms fell onto the counter. Daphne had slipped them into my pants when

I was in the shower as a joke. I told Charlie how, on the way to meet him, I received three text messages. One from Bella, asking if I wanted to go to a concert; one from Christine asking why I wouldn't text her back; and one from Lindsay asking for a picture of my penis.

We looked at our phones and browsed online profiles. I had signed up for the dating site at the standard free membership level, but recently upgraded to Gold Status for $34.94 a month. A date told me she thought I must be "loaded" because I had paid the premium fees, while at the same time wondering how pathetic a person must be to splurge for the Gold Status. But now I had such benefits as: "Show up at the very TOP in searches; Be the FIRST to contact new members; Get FULL access to members' recorded video intros; FULL access to blogs and group features; and most importantly, Access to EXTRA LARGE photos." We looked at the extra-large photos and we noticed there were trending similarities for the women I clicked on. These women liked a night out, but also, a night in watching movies; travel; someone who felt comfortable in a suit, but also looked good in a T-shirt and Converse. A surprising number of women listed *Secretary* as their favorite movie. Or rather, the women whose profile pictures resulted in a click of my mouse tended, overwhelmingly, to list *Secretary* as their favorite movie. We were trying to find the next person I would wink at or hot-list.

We watched videos online related to the book *The Game*, mostly as a joke, but I couldn't help waiting for some secret to be revealed. We passed the hookah hose back and forth. The videos were a series of informational demonstrations on how to "neg" a girl—to use a mild insult meant to shift the power from her to you and capitalize on her insecurity. There was the technique of feigning interest in a prospective mark's friend, presenting a nonthreatening personality while also creating a spirit of competition between two women; or using an opener like: "My friend and I were taking a poll, do you floss after you brush your teeth or before?" Something, anything different to distinguish yourself from others, even creating a larger-than-life personality by "peacocking." Wear a top hat. Wear a gold dookie chain with a tiger pendant. I devised my own opener: "I was just talking with my friend and we can't remember: Did Kevin and Winnie ever finally date on *The Wonder Years?*"

I told Charlie that the antidepressants my doctor had prescribed made it difficult for me to reach climax, and that my doctor had tried a variety of cocktails to offset the side-effect (half a Wellbutrin and a whole Lexapro, skip taking my pill on the weekends I had planned a date). I finally just gave up and tried to turn it into a positive—I could last forever! One woman told me that I "fucked like a girl." I asked her if she meant it was difficult for some women to reach climax during sex. I felt proud to have a window into the female experience. She clarified by saying, "You never just jack-hammer me like a man."

Somehow even after her less-than-gentle reproach proclaiming I was a moron, I had been dating Lindsay for a month, by which I mean she was making the trek to my apartment in the evenings to binge-watch *Veronica Mars* and spend the night. Questions about the status and nature of the relationship became part of the conversation. I could say I still hadn't adequately absorbed proper dating etiquette, but that would be disingenuous, and yet, knowing better, I ended the relationship via email.

Lindsay responded and let me know, in summary, that I could go fuck myself. I deleted my part of the correspondence and forwarded Lindsay's email to a few close friends. I had come to think of it as my civic duty to keep them up-to-date on the breaking news of my post-marriage Internet dating life, to provide amusing rubbernecking at the wreck I managed to make. The majority of my friends were married, had been married long before the popularity of Internet dating. I had been in long-term relationships since all my friends had known me, and thus they had no context for this version of me meeting potentially amorous strangers. Dating and talking about dating had come to consume my life. I had moved through the various stages of grieving to arrive somewhere on the border between depression and acceptance. These dating stories, at the very least, were good brunch conversation, but also—my friends had hope for me. They believed my failures would eventually pass, that there was a pinhole of grayish light and fog becoming visible at the end of the tunnel, revealing a girlfriend I would feel comfortable enough to bring to brunch and introduce in person.

But after sending Lindsay's email to my friends, I might have regretted it. I began to see her email not necessarily as a case study for my overall dating conduct, or the definitive evidence to corroborate my failings, but as a pretty damning indictment. In part, this was a result of having shared her words with friends. They were no longer private—they were a narrative I felt I was required to defend, to articulate why and how this person could harbor such hostility toward me. Her email wasn't just expressing a desire for me to die in the most gruesome and horrible ways, but contained pointed words. She noted that, at the very least, she expected to receive some poetic words while dating a poet, and she should have known it was a bad omen that I never provided her with any. She wasn't misguided to expect appropriate gestures, even of the false variety. When I was sixteen and required to write a few sentences about poetry, I proclaimed: "Poetry is communication, and what on this planet is more important than that? Communication saves marriages, stops wars, and keeps the heart beating." I certainly thought poetry's value was in its attempt to communicate something that had the potential to alter the course of events, that it was the pure expression of truth and emotion. But almost twenty years had passed, and that feeling had degraded, or mutated, or modulated into a feeling of estrangement, disconnection, and helplessness at attempting to communicate anything, through poetry or otherwise.

All we are given during the initial dating period are such small signs, omens of future behavior: how our prospective partner tips the waiter, if they walk you to your subway station or hail a cab, if they smile back at a toddler on the street, or if there is aluminum foil on the ceiling of their apartment in order to prevent alien communication from penetrating their inner sanctum. It is always the small things. All I could provide for Lindsay, or anyone I dated, was the illusion that she could understand me. I supplied the plot points for each woman to construct her own narrative, rather than expressing my own.

Certain things were taken for granted: our stances on abortion; the importance of art and culture; we would of course vote Democrat; but the surface hid everything beneath, and the illusion on her part was that I would share those depths with her. Lindsay, for one, had believed whatever data was presented before the poet's eyes would be transformed into an emblem of feeling and an exclamation ending with an exclamation point! Instead, I had sat across from her in silence as she talked to me. The clock ticked slowly in the intervals it had perfected and we looked up at its face when there was a pause in the conversation.

Her email stung, and stung more once I had shared it with my friends who might have held better opinions of me. She didn't spare any four-letter expletives or cruel words in explaining that when we watched the documentary *The Bridge* and I didn't even hold her hand, that I was in essence an unfeeling monster. What

Lindsay was remarking on wasn't just my aloofness regarding commitment, but rather almost a model of withholding that couldn't be explained away as reservation or shyness. It suggested a cold indifference and cruelty. And furthermore, she was more prone to expect an openness and expressivity because I was a "poet." If indeed one spends his time thinking and attempting to articulate some strangeness in the world, it could be assumed that said person might extend such thought and care toward the person he is sleeping with, might wear his emotions on his sleeve like a blue flower, and share his overwhelming feelings about the world, love, the bare trees framed out the window, the songbirds in those trees singing as we drank coffee in bed on Sunday morning.

Instead, my impulse was to provide a smokescreen of facts as a version of sincerity. It was easier to say that my wife had an affair, and I was devastated, and leave it at that, than to begin the unpacking in a game of armchair therapy. It was easier to say I didn't speak with my mother than to discuss the ins and outs of childhood. Instead, I blew smoke out the window and summarized an article I just read, said things like: "Children of divorced parents divorce at a much higher rate, continuing the divorce cycle, the transmission of some cultural genetics, and so half of us are walking around with the mantra that we will not repeat the mistakes of our parents." I sat across from Lindsay, in silence, or she talked. Sure, I could have presented her with my daily inner monologue tentatively spoken aloud, watching her face for a reaction—some twitch, or raised eyebrow, or nod of recognition indicating we had stumbled onto some shared values. It would have been easier to lay a limp hand on hers as we watched a documentary showing footage of another body throwing itself off of the Golden Gate Bridge than to begin a conversation in which I expressed my sympathy with and desire to toss my own body off a bridge. Press repeat: *I am divorced, I am a recovering alcoholic, and by the fact of confessing such personal details, I have shared with you.* And perhaps we would have gotten to know each other over time through our working theories of the world. She'd learn to understand and appreciate mine and vice versa. But it was a bad sign I wasn't going to take the leap of faith beyond that.

I remained in touch with the many of the women I had dated. I'm not sure why, except that it required virtually no effort. I'm certain it was the same for them. We had friended each other on Facebook and there they were in my feed, or there they were a green dot in my Gchat contact list. I wanted to believe I displayed the comportment of an adult who had conducted himself properly, that sometimes things don't work out, and every instance of that is not a reflection of my poor behavior. There we were, still friends, though they had probably muted my posts. And yet, on the other end of the spectrum, sometimes that lack of a decisive and clean break led me to Bushwick or the East Village to spend the night with an ex long after we were in the habit of spending the night together. But in most cases, the connection I shared with my exes was a pretense of manners. I didn't really know the details of their lives, names of their family members, their particular tics and habits, and in fact we had made an active decision not to extend the effort to get know each other better. When we did chat, we were stuck with the limited shared subject matter—our time together—which meant rehashing that time, and how our respective dating lives had progressed.

March 18, 2008
9:38 PM

BELLA: Hello.

ME: You are always online these days.

BELLA: You know, I'm just here to see how your life is going to keep me awake in the wash of boredom and bad office lighting.

ME: That makes me sad. Should I send you emails to keep you updated?

BELLA: Actually, I really just want to know about the cats. Can you send me hourly reports on their movements?

ME: I gave my kittens to the Salvation Army to help with missionary work.

BELLA: What noble creatures.

ME: They are in Darfur right now.

BELLA: How selfless of them. But seriously, how is your life these days?

ME: You know, it is just kind of average.

BELLA: Details?

ME: What do you want to know? I cry myself to sleep. Stuff like that.

BELLA: Like, cry yourself to sleep after you have sex with lots of different women?

ME: T O N S. No, nerd.

BELLA: But some women, right?

ME: That is what us boys do.

BELLA: It seems like it. Like everyone wants to see lots of other people.

ME: Do you mean people want to see other people AND you?

BELLA: I guess. I just pin a lot of hope on these dates because they seem special and then I feel used when nothing comes of them.

ME: But you felt that I used you, or that you wasted your time with me?

BELLA: Yeah, like I invested more time in what was happening and then it was over.

ME: But dating is set up that way.

BELLA: Maybe that's the problem. I have too many.

ME: Too many what? How many dates do you go on?

BELLA: One a night.

ME: Really? You tramp, I thought I was special.

BELLA: You were special.

ME: Um, so were you.

BELLA: Then why did you keep your profile active?

ME: I just never ever signed out.

BELLA: Why do you think it didn't work out with us?

ME: Why do you think other girls didn't work out? I didn't want to commit.

BELLA: That makes me sad.

ME: Sad why?

BELLA: Sad that you go out on all these dates knowing before-hand that even if it's an amazing girl and an amazing date, in the end, it will end.

ME: Isn't that what people do?

BELLA: All people don't screw over other people.

ME: I haven't. Look who is talking.

BELLA: All people don't assume a relationship's end from the beginning. That is not what I call a real relationship.

ME: What else is there?

BELLA: There are people who stop looking at other potential girls for a whole week when they start seeing someone they might end up liking. Why do you check emails from strangers when you're with someone who isn't one? Why would anyone do that?

ME: Because it is there. Because someone has emailed them. Because they might have had other emails in the works.

BELLA: It's not just there. It's there because you set up a profile and asked it to be there.

ME: It is there. It is like checking email or something. It doesn't even really mean anything.

BELLA: Do you think that all men think this way? Or that it's fair to ask a guy to shut down his profile if I'm seeing him for a few months?

ME: I don't think there is anything wrong with asking that and doing that, but if it is there then they will look.

BELLA: I don't understand men, I guess.

ME: I am useless with providing insight into the male psyche.

BELLA: This is seriously keeping me up at night and not in a good way. My not understanding. It makes me want to give up dating for good.

ME: Then give up.

BELLA: Or maybe I could go back a decade and meet a guy at a bar or through friends.

ME: But let's also think this through a second, what would the equivalent be in a more traditional setting? You go on one or two dates with someone. Do you ask them to stop flirting with other people?

BELLA: What's your point?

ME: I'm brainstorming. At what point does someone ask for exclusivity?

BELLA: I guess when you've been dating for a while and it seems like the relationship could get more serious while still being fun.

ME: That is what is weird about online dating, it speeds everything up and one gets the feeling that they know a person really well.

BELLA: If you were seeing someone and started to feel like you knew that person well, would you close down your profile?

ME: I guess. I don't keep looking, not when I am seeing someone.

BELLA: But you didn't feel like you were seeing me.

ME: I didn't really, and that was because the whole thing was new and it was more from curiosity and more to make me feel like I was cute or interesting after having that taken from me from my marriage.

BELLA: Do you think I'm being needy or mean?

ME: I don't think you are. And I can take it.

BELLA: So what if when people start dating, they take it slow?

ME: If you saw a person once a week getting to know them it might be different. It is also a little about taking a risk or a leap of faith in a person, but that makes you vulnerable.

BELLA: Is it silly that I want someone to take a risk with me? To think it was worth it to be vulnerable for me?

ME: I don't think that is silly at all.

BELLA: I feel like we get each other. We get along well. Why can't we just hang out?

ME: Ask me to do something, we can hang out, we can go see a movie, but you can't hold my hand. I have been lucky in meeting people who are interesting and smart. I mean everyone I have spent time with I would still want to be in touch with. I like them all.

BELLA: But even if you're with a great person, you end it.

ME: Yes. Something just ended today!

BELLA: Why did it end?

ME: Why do you think?

BELLA: Ok, fine.

ME: Fine what?

BELLA: Fine, I get it, you don't want to commit to anyone, no matter how perfect, no matter how much that sucks—there is no person on earth you would commit to right now.

ME: I don't feel like I am ready, but don't want to be alone with my cats watching *Law & Order* either. Or maybe I do.

BELLA: I just ended something too.

ME: How long did you see them for?

BELLA: A few weeks.

ME: Why am I a little jealous?

BELLA: Because you have a little soul left. It actually sucks, the breakup I mean.

ME: I'm sorry that didn't work out. What was his problem?

BELLA: He didn't have a problem.

ME: I mean what did he say?

BELLA: He said that he needed more from me, sexually.

ME: Did you write him and tell him that was shitty?

BELLA: No.

ME: But you slept with him?

BELLA: No. Does that make what he said ok?

ME: I think that is understandable, sometimes people need intimacy, so can you just chalk it up to that, or is that such a guy thing?

BELLA: It is a guy thing.

ME: Yeah, you are such a girl.

BELLA: I feel bad because I actually liked him. I feel cheap, emotionally cheap.

ME: Don't feel cheap. You let your guard down and were vulnerable and the person wasn't right.

BELLA: It just feels raw.

ME: How recent is this?

BELLA: This week.

11:37 PM

BELLA: Why did you hook up with me if you knew you weren't going to keep seeing me?

ME: I didn't know that then. That is something I am figuring out.

BELLA: It just seems like you knew your state of mind well enough to know that people could get hurt. You said you wanted more intimacy and then you said you weren't ready for it.

ME: I'm not sure I know what you are getting at. I didn't know those things when I was seeing you. I knew I liked you, but I was worried that you were one of the first people I dated, and didn't have a handle on what I thought about dating. I said that about more intimacy, because I did want that, and was hurt when you blew me off, but I knew why, and thought you were acting reasonable.

BELLA: I guess.

ME: I don't know. The other thing might be that I get close enough to people in a certain space of time and then realize whoa, I like this person but don't love this person, and so then break it off. I don't know. I have no grand theories. I try the best I can.

BELLA: Did you have sex with the other girls you dated?

ME: Why would you need to know that?

BELLA: Just wondering.

ME: Yes.

BELLA: Maybe that is why they fell for you.

ME: In each case, I tried to say that wasn't important and that we shouldn't have sex, which is apparently a foolproof way to have sex. But also, I think you are giving my sexual prowess too much credit.

BELLA: Oh, so you have your tricks to get girls to have sex with you? Sex can actually be a big deal.

ME: I was kidding. And I know it is, and was one of the reasons I was trying to delay it.

BELLA: It is really good we didn't do anything.

Maybe every woman dating a poet deserves to have him tell her flowery things. Even given my complicated indifference to dating, it was strange I didn't write an ode to anyone's eyes, breasts, or particular gait. Lord knows I had nothing else to do and I've written poems from less, from assignments from professors restricted to the lexicon found in the business section of *The New York Times*. I could have said something. And it wouldn't be much of a lie to say that is how, in fact, I came to write poetry in the first place—from a wooing derived from lust.

I was in elementary school when I wrote my first poem for a classmate, but before I wrote poetry I pretended to write poetry. I don't mean this as an aesthetic or qualitative judgment, but rather as fact; I declared something written by another as my own. Really, it only happened once, in fourth grade. I handed Carolyn a note about how it would be pleasant if I could caress her body, because unlike a lot of girls, she had an especially nice one, but even still I should have had second thoughts before I just simply handed my heart over to her.

I was an eleven-year-old boy in pegged stonewashed jeans, and I was certain these direct and heartfelt verses would woo my crush—just as a twenty-four-year-old pop sensation with frosted hair, a dangling cross earring, and eternal sunglasses must have thought when he wrote them. They were, of course, the lyrics to George Michael's "Faith."

In my defense . . . actually, I'm not sure where to start. I could say I was young, overeager, and hadn't received a classroom lecture on the ethics of plagiarism. I could say it had been a difficult year—the year my parents' divorce became finalized. I don't want to rationalize my actions or be embarrassed to say George Michael's poetry spoke to me, but it did, and I am.

More importantly for this story, I was stuck with a staggering inability to speak with Carolyn in public. It was more than just generating the nerve to walk across the wood-chipped playground, from the jungle gym where I was positioned with a group of boys to where Carolyn stood each day near the seesaw with two or three other girls. I was sick with something, obsessed with a new-found bewilderment I was unable to articulate. I'm sure I didn't understand the relationship of boyfriend and girlfriend beyond the names assigned. Abstractly, I knew bodies touched, as in holding hands. So I listened to George Michael's album over and over in my living room. I put my headphones on. I turned up the volume. I felt the lyrics and emotions of the song were part of my own psyche, and I apparently came to the conclusion that there was no more perfect way to express my inner feelings than to transcribe the lyrics and address the note "for your eyes only."

I am sorry I didn't even quote lyrics to Lindsay, or Daphne, or Bella, to say "I was listening to this song, and thought of you," or at the very least write an acrostic poem constructed from the first letter of their names. It would have been painless for me to do, to conjure the muses for a bit of occasional verse—something I certainly had done for birthday cards for friends, even as a post on Facebook walls. All I can say is I wasn't ready. *Sadly, let me explain, let me try to tell you everything. All I can say is I wasn't ready to commit to a level of faith with you. Yes, everything I said was honest and true.* I could have used those for the last lines of Lindsay's acrostic. But I was already working on this document. I was compiling and rereading the emails from my marriage. I knew this story wanted to tell itself, and I knew deep in my heart Lindsay wouldn't be there for the end of it.

I can't remember when my father started dating again. I'm not sure what advice the self-help books have for single fathers, but they can't possibly dwell enough on the unnaturalness of a child waking up to his father making eggs for a woman in a robe who is not his mother. I think I was eleven.

What remains more potent, more available to the complex mechanisms and pathways in my brain, is the moment marking the end of my parents' marriage. They had been separated for years when my father told me it was official; he and my mother were getting divorced. We were driving home from a department store, and I was in the backseat—I'm not sure why, this was before families adopted such safety precautions—and I began to cry hysterically. The word itself was like a curse being cast. Enter the dark clouds, thunder, sinister howling from a black cauldron. Even if I knew that a divorce was a possibility, it was the first time one of my parents, not an older brother, was explaining it to me. It wasn't just the acknowledgement of a family unit splitting; it was that the people I had instinctively trusted as beyond reproach in their authority and wisdom, because they were my parents, because I simply didn't know any better or wouldn't let myself know better, even when I had witnessed their undeniable sadness and anger with each other, were failures. And as a child crying, hyperventilating and banging his chest with his fists in the backseat, "divorce" seemed to mean that, if the people who were given to me as models were failures, all failure was now possible. My uncontrollable outburst was reason enough for him to slip a note under my bedroom door after we had a fight. If email had existed, surely he would have emailed me from a laptop downstairs. I don't recall the particulars of the fight; all I have is his letter.

August 8, 1990
Brett,

Sometimes in conversation we bang heads . . . we don't really listen . . . even though we do understand. It is hard because we are both trying to look out for our own interests and they may not always match up with each other. Certainly what you said about Janet is correct . . . but times and situations have changed. You know that of course. In past years I could easily take you to the mall, soccer game, wrestling practice, art fair, you name it, because I had a partner to come home to. What crosses my mind now, and maybe it is somewhat unfair to you, but it's a fact nonetheless . . . in six years you'll be gone . . . college, work, who knows. If I don't establish some other relations or relationships, Brettski, I'm going to be alone. I don't like that thought. So here's what happens . . . I'm trying to develop a relationship with Janet. (I like her a lot . . . she's a nice person and already cares a lot about you guys.) At this point I can't predict what'll happen between the two of us, but I certainly don't want to lose you because of her. That is why I try to include you in many of the things we do. I like to share my experiences with people. You for one . . . and certainly Paul and Noah and Simon. I'm not trying to cut my time with you, I'm just trying to fit you in. Believe me she recognizes the awkwardness of the situation. She's a very sensitive lady. She is constantly on me to spend time with you guys and rightfully so. Many of the days she doesn't come over occur because she knows I want to spend time with you. Of course often you're out with your friends, but I do see you in passing, and can at least keep up with what is going on in your life. I like to know what you're doing, who you're hanging out with etc. I'm not nosey. I care about you. It would be nice if we could avoid the guilt trips, yelling, and cursing, but I guess that is going to be a part of our lives. As long as we know we love each other . . . I think we can always overlook and even laugh at the silly moments when we lash out at each other. There is certainly a lot of frustration in all of our lives right now. . . . I'm sure we'll work through it. Let's pull together. Talk if we can . . . write if we have to.

I love you very much,

Dad

Technically, I still wasn't divorced. It was some purgatory in-between stage like Dante's Belacqua waiting: "O brother, what's the use of climbing? / God's angel, he who guards the gate, would not / let me pass through to meet my punishment." The documents arrived on a Tuesday. Nina had addressed the envelope herself. What I had expected was different: a man in a tan suit would approach me and bum a cigarette. As he fumbled to light his cigarette he'd ask me to hold an envelope for a moment. Upon returning my lighter, the document still in my hand, he'd casually remark: "Mr. Lauer, you've been served." Then off he would walk down the road into the sunset. I don't believe this was an unreasonable expectation. I deserved a dramatic ending; I'd witnessed it countless times on television. Instead, in the top left-hand corner of an envelope, familiar cursive handwriting. Quite possibly, the last physical traces of Nina I would encounter. Of course I expected to be caught off-guard. I was caught off-guard. It was always the days when my mind was preoccupied, when I was in the middle of a conversation on the phone, balancing it between head and shoulder, that correspondence from her arrived. Never the day I paused, exhaled a breath, and turned the mailbox key.

The documents were just a template on white paper, the paragraphs of text a fading gray ink as if they had been previously Xeroxed a thousand times. Like the W-9's I sent out from my office. Some hand had touched them, though, as there was a blue checkmark in the box beside "Dissolution of the marriage based on," and then in a sub-box below, another blue checkmark beside: "irreconcilable differences." That's a phrase for you, a very simple umbrella phrase encompassing nearly everything. "She beat me." "He stole money from my parents." Really, anything. The familiarity of the phrase did provide a strange comfort. *Yes, I've heard that phrase before.* Every divorce is a series of stock phrases, actions, and emotions, but I wanted to leave a fucking paper trail of her deceit. I wanted it on public record. Irreconcilable differences.

It both articulates perfectly a series of events and feelings, and omits a particular brand of accountability from the official record. I spent two hours looking through files and transcribing income and expenses in duplicate. It was as if a coworker left a stack of work for me before going on a three-week cruise. I knew it wasn't rational, but I felt I shouldn't have to lift a finger for this divorce. It was her doing. I wanted it to be enough to say "Yes, it is over," but we had entered this contract legally, so we had to end it legally. Somewhere amongst all the boxes another was checked: "There are no minor children." That was what friends said. "At least you didn't have any kids." If for no other reason than that it expedited the process. I signed in duplicate. I paused before pressing the blue pen to each page, paused not from a feeling of uneasiness or mourning but from an obligation to note the moment without actually noting the moment. Maybe the pen wasn't blue. It doesn't matter; the documents were signed and sent to a government office building in Oakland. A period of time was legally required to pass. I waited. I waited some more.

4

It is true. I looked for Nina. I looked for her on the streets we had walked regularly, in the shops of our weekends, the restaurants we once frequented. In the distance any woman with long brown hair and bangs might be her, until after a time she was nowhere, or those places took on different meanings, or stores closed and were replaced with different stores.

At work, part of my day involved killing time—either as a result of boredom from repetitive office tasks such as stuffing envelopes, such as answering the phone, such as writing another email, or, on the other end of the spectrum, a respite required from the work stacked in neat piles on my desk, or rather simply, my boss was at a lunch meeting and the option to whittle time away presented itself. I read *The New York Times*, *Pitchfork*, friends' blogs, and friends-of-friends' blogs. And then I would find myself at my desk, watching the workday clock as the last hour of the day stuttered to conclusion, and place Nina's name in the search engine. It was what was expected of me. I want to say there was nothing special about it, that it wasn't loaded, that if I had work correspondence with someone living in Texas, I found myself doing the same for him as well. But the curiosity that drove this wonder was linked less with placing a face to a name and more about checking in on a wound. I wanted to know if her life had become "better" than mine, different than what she once envisioned for herself without me. But it also was no different than a changing of the seasons, an unpacking of my sweaters and scarves, placing them back under my bed, and preparing for what would come next. Mainly I searched for her name because I could, because it was there to be searched.

According to the Internet, Nina seemed to have embarked on a quiet and boring life of little digital relevance. Nothing came up. If she was on Facebook, she'd blocked me from accessing her account. I didn't blame her—I had blocked her from my page months ago. The majority of search results just spat back a list of the magazines and books we edited together, their availability now at a deep discount. The only images were the covers of the books themselves. No new information.

I went back to working, adding content to the workplace website, and after an hour of squinting at code, I posted what would be one of my last Missed Connections.

SUBJECT: Lorem Ipsum / m4w / 31 / New York

I'm placing this here for you. I will change it later.

Memories are forgotten with interference, when new objects of attention are placed in their pathways. Instead of looking for Nina—instead of looking at the morbid car crash on the side of the road—I looked the other way, across the grassy median and off into the distance. I signed in to the dating site. I hadn't seen "Croque Madame" before, hadn't sent any winks, and hadn't clicked the button adding her to my hot list. My user name was "The Emperor of Ice Cream," after the Stevens poem, and our two names sounded like a nice meal, a good date.

May 15, 2008
Dear Croque Madame,

That is a pretty funny username. But better yet, it led me to this: "Croque-monsieur's earliest published use has been traced back to volume 2 of Proust's *À la recherche du temps perdu* (191 . . . . . 😎 ," which for some reason I think is amusing. Maybe that amusement is a result of a long and relatively unexciting work day. And your work day?

Yours,
Brett

In came one response to the Missed Connection:

Hey baby I'm here.

And then another:

Hey,

I'm working on a project about Missed Connections on
Craigslist in NY and I was wondering if you would be willing
to answer a few questions about your experience. I know that
Craigslist is kind of sketchy to begin with and it's hard to
trust anyone here, so we could talk via email and of course
you could remain anonymous if you feel more comfortable
this way. I am getting in touch with several people who post
here so I could get a broad view on some of the issues I'm
interested in. In general, this project will deal with the way
people interact with each other, meet new people, and cope
with loneliness; all in relation to living in New York.

I wanted to be done with it all. It wasn't just that the full-time job of posting Missed Connections had worn me down, that the creative impulse was waning, and that the thrill was gone, so to speak—all of which were true—but that the initial question of what would happen if I wrote and posted a fake Missed Connection had been answered. The responses had become invitations to someone else's bright idea for a project or dissertation, someone else's investigation into the art of loneliness. We come full circle to reporting on why any one of us is doing anything. And here I was, writing my own dummy text. *Lorem Ipsum*, the beginning of a block of Latin text used as placeholder text for graphic designers to return to later with the actual content of the design, the two words that begin it derived from a phrase meaning "pain itself." It had come to mean nothing, and yet was filled with the potential to be something, anything but itself. Here I was mourning my marriage, itself its own simulation of the outcome of a tradi-tional connection and the failure of the supposed connection, so much so that a term was soon minted: starter marriage. Here I was having another coffee, half myself and half a version of who I thought would be desirable to the person sitting across from me. Here I was writing letters to my estranged mother, which I wouldn't send. I should have just been posting the letters to another section of the Craigslist bulletin board, Rants and Raves. Here I was placing the words one in front of the other, filling in my life's template until the real text was written and could be dropped into the design.

May 15, 2008
Dear Brett,

My work day has been uneventful. I work in the marketing department at a museum, and we're in a bit of a slow period in between
exhibitions at the moment. What do you do? I'm sitting here day-
dreaming about my weekend plans. Brunch will definitely figure
in. What are you up to this weekend?

Cheers,
Ingrid

May 15, 2008
Dear Ingrid,

Ok, and so emoticons are cool, and maybe I even use them every once and again etc. but, I don't know how that ended up in my last email. I work at the Poetry Institute as the Managing Director, and have been here for almost ten years now. I have the day off tomorrow to wait for a DSL service repair, conveniently any time between 8 AM and 7 PM. And then a friend is reading on Saturday, and maybe a little writing . . . but no big dreams.

B.

May 15, 2008
Dear Brett,

I enjoyed that little bespectacled emoticon! Even though it was obviously a mistake and made no sense. Poetry Institute? It's nice that you were able to actually find a job doing what you love! So rare. You have the WHOLE day off tomorrow? Granted, waiting around for a repair guy is the pits, but I'd love to laze around the house and watch daytime TV. Especially since it's going to be so rainy tomorrow.

Anyway, I have to run off to a work event. Ta for now!

Ingrid

P.S. This may be a little premature, but if you wanted to have a very low-pressure Sunday night drink, I could be up for that.

May 16, 2008
Dear Ingrid,

I would love to meet up for drinks on Sunday, but I don't drink, which isn't weird for me at all, but thought I should tell you. Maybe we could get coffee, tea, scones, play Boggle, something super high-pressure. Here is my email brettfletcherlauer@gmail.com if that is easier for you.

Hope your work event was fancy with cubes of cheese,

B.

Sometimes I looked at the Facebook pages of classmates from high school: puffy red faces, weight gained, and photos of newborns. Sometimes I googled myself and sometimes I googled my exes. I wanted to believe that elsewhere in the world, blocks from me, or somewhere in Middle America, in a moment of shared boredom, one of my exes sat at her desk engaging in the same pastime. I'd left them all a digital memoir, had been tagged by friends in embarrassing photos, posted my own photos in a horse's mask, in a rabbit's mask, posted an essay I'd written about online dating and Missed Connections. In one such workday search session, I was happy to discover the article announcing my engagement to Nina was finally on page four of search results for my name. Time moves on. According to the wisdom of the algorithm, which I can't pretend to understand though I've read the Wikipedia entry on it at least twice, I had been busy with more important things. It was during one of these googling sessions that I discovered Lindsay's blog.

I read the entire archive in one sitting and learned she was writing for a variety of comedy and pop culture websites, mostly recaps of *Glee* and *Parks and Recreation*. I also learned that she had started performing stand-up comedy. In the "About Me" section of her blog there was a list of upcoming dates where she could be found onstage. She'd been busy—when we were dating the requisite background search produced only records of the college clubs she'd participated in as an undergraduate. Among the various links on her blog, there was a link to a video of one of her shows.

It was the end of the day. I took out my headphones and plugged them into the computer speakers. I clicked the link. It looked like any stand-up club I'd seen on television: a person standing on a dark stage with a microphone, a brick wall in the background. Mostly her jokes were observational humor on dating and love; ridiculous things her mother said to her about her troubles finding Mr. Right. Midway through her bit on dating failures, she began a new bit on her Internet dating adventures. My palms started to sweat. I swiveled in my chair to take note of whether my coworkers were watching, if they had sidled up behind me and were now looking over my shoulder—as if the headphone cord had jerked loose and the audio found itself being broadcast for all to hear—to participate in wherever this setup was going.

She talked about being on the third date with a guy, and how the third date is traditionally the moment when people come clean, reveal something they were holding back, like when her date, says, "I have something I need to tell you," she is ready for anything: he has a kid, he killed a man in Reno to watch him die, his wife thinks she's cute. And it was funny; the way a person discussing with confidence what we might not reveal in the checkout line can be funny, and always more funny if you are sitting in the room with friends, preferably friends who have had a few drinks. The reveal—what the person disclosed on the third date, the date of intimate confession—was that he had witnessed a ghost in his apartment.

I paused the video, took off my headphones, went outside, and smoked a cigarette. I mentally replayed all our dates. We watched *The Bridge*, watched *Veronica Mars*, watched porn on my computer. I thought about how at the end of the relationship she kept texting me, once a month, always on the weekend, most often after midnight, and I would respond. *As long as she doesn't use my name. As long as she doesn't use my full name.* I smoked another cigarette.

I knew nothing was private anymore; everything was content, a story to retell as a blog post, a screenshot, a podcast, a stand-up routine, a memoir. This isn't exactly new. When you open yourself up to another person, or in my case just crack the door, a slim beam of sunlight shines through, and with or without the Internet you are subject to the possibility of humiliation, ridicule, or, at best, indifference. This brief video was allowing me to eavesdrop on the joke that was told about me at brunch the next morning. I was acutely aware of this from my own participation on the other end as storyteller, my inability to locate any higher moral ground to stand on. I had taken pains to present myself in a certain way to the world, and of course I had no power in how it was interpreted, particularly now, to an audience, to the hundreds of people who had watched the video. There was nowhere I saw this going that wouldn't humiliate me. I finished my third cigarette and walked slowly back to my office chair, head down, prepared for the shame I had coming. I put on my headphones.

It was funny; funnier in her telling, because she was animated, she was over-the-top, and so demanded the audience smirk and laugh with her. The big punch line wasn't so much a punch line, more a dramatic eye roll at how idiotic her date was, because, let's face it, people who see ghosts are the same people who see UFOs, who disbelieve the moon landing, or belong to the Flat Earth Society. And then it was also funny (again, in her retelling) because if the person telling her—me—actually did witness a spectral haunting, it means that said ghost was still lingering in the small apartment, hovering over the lovers, available at any moment for future appearances, such as, and not limited to, moments of lovemaking. So it was either ridiculous or spooky, maybe both. I wiped my palms on my jeans. Braced myself. I knew that this was just the lead-up, that a one-two punch was coming in which I would be thrown in front of the comedy train for maximum laughs. When the second hit didn't materialize and she moved on to other dates, other failures, I was relieved, possibly even grateful; I wanted to email "Thank you" but thought better of it—all emails lead to something else, further correspondence, more material— by then I knew not to commit anything to writing. What was written and sent, what was written and posted, became someone else's source material.

Dear Mom,

I fear in your private moments of contemplation at a copy machine at work, driving home, washing the dishes, that you have altered the version of events that have led me to my small desk, writing this letter I will not send. Memory does that, provides its own process of natural selection to ensure the survival of a species. I'm no different; each time I recall a memory I move on to something else. I light a cigarette, check my email. I try to forget.

"How dare he tell me not to drink," is what you told my brothers. I didn't tell you what you could or could not do. As god is my witness, I walked up after the wedding ceremony as you were ordering a glass of wine. I walked up without malicious intent. Noah was there. Let him testify, since later the story became: "He accosted me, he sabotaged me, he set me up." I asked you twice what you were doing; you kept your eyes on the wine list. "If you are going to drink, I'd prefer you leave." Such a tempered word, really, "prefer." To regard one more than another. I repeated myself. I repeat the events over and over. I've edited this down to a paragraph in order to not dwell too long on what can only be described as your willful obliviousness to the damage your alcoholism wreaked over the entirety of my childhood, spilling over into our present relationship. Since little will come from such accusations, I'll settle for calling what occurred simply a demonstration of bad manners. I can't help myself: that you would take my comments so lightly and disregard them at my wedding is staggering to me, and simultaneously a staggering testimony to the force of your addiction.

You told my brothers you didn't even want to go to the wedding, conjuring a false anger at the absence of a rehearsal dinner where you would have been provided the opportunity to meet my future in-laws and feel more comfortable. I understand this is traditional, but there was no rehearsal dinner because I was attempting to mediate your interactions with my father. Quite frankly, the anxiety of having two events at which something could go awry was a risk I wasn't willing to take. I had assumed there would be awkwardness for the group photographs, father on one side, and you on the other. I allowed for the possibility that you would utter some vicious words to my father or my step-mom as you found yourself accidentally waiting in line for the bathroom behind them. A snub. A "fuck you." This is what I had prepared myself to live with. But definitely not drinking. Some contracts I had thought were as good as spoken. The fact that you were there was an assumption you would not drink, was a condition I didn't actually foresee needing to be addressed. Some contracts are made with a general feeling of faith in right and wrong. Mom, I did not speak to you for those five years when I was a teenager because you were an alcoholic. I had experienced firsthand the effects of your alcoholism. This wasn't a secret.

Love,
Brett

May 17, 2008
1:44 PM

INGRID: So, did you enjoy snooping around my Facebook profile?

ME: Yes. I know too much now. I feel dirty.

INGRID: Ha! What? I hope you're joking.

ME: You aren't going to get much from mine.

INGRID: This totally gives you a leg up, conversationally.

ME: Do you need to know something? Like my favorite snack?

INGRID: No, I'm fine, but you can tell me if you'd like!

ME: Nah, I will keep it secret.

INGRID: Suspense!

ME: I'm a little surprised you didn't ask me about being divorced. That is always the first question.

INGRID: Oh, whatever. You can just tell me about that whenever you feel comfortable. It's not like you're asking me for my dating history right off the bat.

ME: Actually, if you could provide that . . .

INGRID: Ha! I'll tell you whatever you want to know, I'm an open book. I also have some amazing online dating disaster stories, if you're interested.

ME: I don't feel uncomfortable about my divorce or most subjects at all. I haven't had any dating disasters . . . yet.

INGRID: I have some doozies. It has made for some good stories.

ME: Oh, by the way, I lied about my age, height, and body type.

INGRID: How old are you REALLY?

ME: 45, and I've lost A LOT of hair since those photos. No longer a horse's mane.

INGRID: I actually have slightly darker hair now (really). Hope that's not a deal breaker.

ME: Ugh, really?

INGRID: Yes, really, you jerk!

ME: I was teasing.

INGRID: I know.

ME: Your day is over?

INGRID: I'm still working and then I'm meeting a friend for a drink in Williamsburg (ugh) at 7:30. So now I have to kill time. What are you up to tonight?

ME: I'm not sure. Maybe staying in. I have a packed day tomorrow. Brunch with a friend, then a reading that seems like it may go on forever, and then a going-away party.

INGRID: Brunch! Where?

ME: I'm not sure. I'm tagging along with a friend to be a buffer for another friend.

INGRID: Ah. Well, brunch is my favorite thing pretty much ever.

ME: Why exactly?

INGRID: I can't believe you're asking that. But, obviously:
1. Bacon
2. Sweet and savory combinations
3. WAFFLES
4. Maple syrup and butter

5. Many drinks (coffee AND juice!? crazy!)
6. It's relaxing
7. Often outdoors

ME: But that can be breakfast as well.

INGRID: True. What do you have against brunch? This is very upsetting.

ME: So much.

1. The neologism
2. Deciding between lunch and breakfast
3. Crowds
4. The national deficit

How many did you have? I don't have seven in me. The coffee isn't working anymore.

INGRID: This is quite the revelation. What if I took you somewhere that wasn't crowded and we went early enough that it could be considered breakfast? And it was TASTY?

ME: You are some kind of magical problem-solver.

INGRID: I just can't live in a world where people don't love brunch. It's too sad.

ME: No, I love brunch. How long have you worked at the museum?

INGRID: A little over six months, so not long.

ME: And you like it?

INGRID: I love it! It's such a fun place to work. Everyone's lovely, it's great to be working for an institution I believe in and care about, blah blah.

ME: Did you go to school for art?

INGRID: No, no, no. I majored in journalism and dramatic literature.

ME: Dramatic literature as in studying texts, or acting out the texts?

INGRID: Studying. Not acting. God, no. That would be my worst nightmare.

ME: I was hoping that was the answer.

INGRID: Don't worry, I'm not some kind of theater nut.

ME: You so are. We should go see *Hairspray*. Or have you already, like, five times?

INGRID: No, no, I have not.

ME: It is okay if that is where you're salary goes too.

INGRID: Oh, brother.

ME: Is that because of my typo?

INGRID: Ha! No, I was feigning annoyance at you giving me grief.

ME: I know. I was being sassy.

INGRID: Sass doesn't always come across well on chat when you haven't yet met the person.

ME: I know sass doesn't, but what is weird is that I like that it doesn't come across.

INGRID: Why's that?

ME: I'm not sure. I think it is the confusion of language and tone, and that it highlights or provides proof that it is difficult to communicate. Like, here I am trying to be myself and it fails, and that feels like a big DUH to me. And it is reassuring.

INGRID: I'm totally picking up on your sass, I'm just giving you a hard time (sassing back).

ME: I just got played. Is that what you are saying?

INGRID: Yes. Well, you didn't get played, but YOU weren't picking up on MY sass. You can pretty much always assume I'm sassing.

ME: Wait, could you point to the sass in the above text?

INGRID: I don't know, I guess I wasn't sassing that much.

ME: You have an awesome name btw.

INGRID: Oh, thank you! You have a lovely name yourself (<-- not sass).

ME: Thanks. Fletcher is my mother's last name. That is why I use it.

INGRID: The three-name thing is hard to pull off, but you do it with aplomb.

ME: I made a choice to use it a while ago. What is your middle name?

INGRID: Holly (meh).

ME: Holly Scott works nice though.

INGRID: Yeah, but Ingrid > Holly. I'm much more of an Ingrid. You haven't met me yet, you'll see.

ME: Ok, am I going to meet you? I forget.

INGRID: No, actually, I'd prefer to just have a relationship over chat, if that's okay.

ME: Deal. I think that might work better for me too.

INGRID: So what time is good for you on Sunday?

ME: Whenever. I have nothing planned.

INGRID: I'm just going to say this once, because I don't want you to get on a high horse, but you are quite a dish.

ME: Aw, I just blushed.

INGRID: Ha!

ME: I blush easy though. Skin tone and all.

INGRID: Oh god, I'm half girl, half-beet. So pale, the slightest blush is noticeable.

ME: I'm a ghost.

INGRID: Oh my god, what if you were ACTUALLY a ghost? If only.

My first post-marriage kiss was initiated over instant message—I'd been on four dates with Bella and there had been brief hand holding. Knees touched once while we sat on a bench by the Hudson River as the sun set or we sat waiting for the sun to set, and there were four long goodbye hugs—my face turned from hers, eyes wide, my heart beating in proportion to my perspiration. I'm an adult. I was thinking too much. It had been months since I'd kissed someone, and then years before I kissed someone different, kissed differently. A peck on the check. Mouth slightly ajar. Bottom lip in my mouth. Dry. Wet. Bad breath. It is a moment invested with superstition and drama, and almost utterly inconsequential—we learn to kiss our partners over time, in one long night. The first kiss is only to say, "Yes," "I want to kiss you," "I just kissed you," "What's next?"

It was middle school all over again. Beth Warner standing against the brick wall, yellow buses around the corner—it was awkward, pressured. We'd been dating since Christmas, maybe I bought her a charm bracelet from Woolworth's—I couldn't afford Macy's. It was quick. It was over. Her braces had been removed three days before and I watched her swipe her new teeth with her tongue. She didn't tell me it was good. Didn't congratulate me with a gold star or ever kiss me again. I was an adult now. I understood the basic mechanics.

Nina had first kissed me in the stairwell to my apartment, without warning. She was in the process of breaking up with someone and though we flirted via email throughout the workday the thought of anything happening hadn't entered my mind as a real possibility since the barrier of a relationship hadn't yet been removed, even if I knew its disintegration was imminent. Of course, I was quick with critical words towards her current boyfriend, providing a near constant litany of ways in which he was unappreciative, downright rude, and bordering on complete assholeness, whenever the opportunity seemed to naturally present itself. He wouldn't let her spend the night and called a cab at three in the morning. "Really, what kind of person would do that?" She told me both his parents were deaf and he'd never learned sign language. "Really, what kind of person wouldn't want to be able to communicate with their parents?" I was a passive-aggressive advocate for a more understanding partner—I was the new boy sending emails signed "xoxo."

I typed the following eloquent sentence into the IM box, because as with most things, it was easier than talking about it face to face.

ME: Hey, so is it weird we haven't, you know, like done anything yet?

BELLA: What are you talking about?

ME: I mean if you just think of me as a friend that is completely cool, and no pressure or anything.

BELLA: Oh, you mean, like made-out yet?

When she arrived at my apartment that night to watch *Deadwood*, I paused in the lobby and kissed her. Her lips didn't quite part, and my mouth was too eager. It never went further than that.

By the time I met Ingrid, I had recently shared nine first kisses (receptionist at a hair salon, two elementary school teachers, an architecture student, a bartender, a nanny, two librarians, an assistant at a PR firm), and the hurdle of crippling self-doubt about when and how and is this person actually attracted to me had become such a normal question as to be a question I allowed myself to ignore. On our first date, after three hours at the café on the walk back to my apartment, I leaned over and kissed Ingrid as we waited for the crosswalk light to change. The idea was to appear natural.

Dear Mom,

With these letters, what I find myself asking for or, rather, requiring, in order to even have a semblance of a relationship with you—more meaningful than opening your cards and jotting a thank you note, or phone calls every month and a half with a report on who is doing what and with who and where—is an apology. By an apology I do not mean a defense, an excuse, a life history of events crafting a psychological profile, but an acknowledgement of wrongdoing regardless of intent. "A fearless, moral inventory of wrongs, and a willingness to make amends."

I find this necessary to dwell on because we never have. I am not responsible. I won't be. I tell myself: *You cannot parent the parent.* I am responsible for myself. I've been sober thirteen years. As the estranged son, left with information passed from one brother to another like a game of whisper-down-the-lane, I hear information revised as each imagination interprets the events for the other. I mishear their reports as: "She must live with herself." I tell my brothers: "I never asked for much." They tell me: "Ask for less." You're unable to reach out to me. I should be bigger. "If she were sick with cancer you wouldn't turn your back."

I've never made it easy for you. I was distant, and on the phone I was short. I never asked: "How are Mittens and Professor Booty?" We could have at least talked about our pets. I never told you how I calculated the time it takes for my cats to follow me into bed. (On average, thirty seconds to a minute.) At any hour of day, they jump from the top of the bookcase or refrigerator, or drift from inside the closet to come lay beside me. I can't help thinking there is something pathetic in these calculations. I don't want to feel dependent and yet I am. On unlocking the door and walking up the stairs I anticipate their meowing behind the door. It provides comfort. On the phone you would ask: How are things? "Fine." Enter silence.

If, on the contrary, I had demonstrated any sign of openness, you might have made the first gesture. And now, I've moved forward in life without this relationship, and it's a defining element for how I've come to view myself in the world. The glass half-full and emptying, the disappointment around the corner. To that end, what would reconciliation entail? What if we sat down, face to face, and talked? Who would I be then?

Noah says your gestures of reconciling are like a meteor traveling through the atmosphere burning away its mass until it lands to earth as a pebble in a field unnoticed as part of the natural landscape. Simon tells me you asked: "Is he just not talking to the family?" I tell them: "Tell her I will not speak with her until she apologizes." They tell me, "Tell her yourself."

Love,
Brett

I don't know what I was looking for searching Nina's name online—an inevitable wedding announcement, a wedding registry? Each time I searched, I prepared myself, took the prerequisite deep breath for what I might uncover, for the moment of shock, my stomach finding new and unbearable ways to contort. I asked myself if it would be better or worse to discover that Nina ended up marrying Richard, by which I mean better or worse as to how I would interpret the event, the version of the narrative I would create and live with. I knew a marriage would serve to legitimatize her actions—that the pain and suffering she caused me and Richard's wife would now in some regards become justified: star-crossed lovers, soulmates who were meant for each other and found themselves in complicated situations but prevailed over their circumstances in order to experience true love. I wondered how they would tell any future children they might have or for that matter anyone, how they met. "We met at work." Would their children and colleagues know they were married before? Would their children care? And why did I care about their future offspring or cocktail party friends? I thought about the moments in which they might feel compelled to disclose their actions and how they had contextualized it to their loved ones, and hoped those moments were awkward for everyone.

If they were to get married, would it be a small wedding on a beach or at the courthouse? I wondered if my friends would tell me, if they would know, if they were still in touch with her. Maybe I was ahead of myself, I didn't even know if they were living with each other, if they had already combined their two homes with all the appliances and gadgets after our divorce. I went to the Macy's website and searched their names in the wedding registry—they would certainly need to replace some things, items get worn down, two-households-to-one or not. New sheets, for instance. Even if they weren't the jealous types and nothing lingered in the other's mind when one of them stayed at work late, it might just be common courtesy not to fuck on the sheets you fucked your previous husband or wife on.

I wondered if Nina would purchase items I hadn't been interested in. She had wanted Fiestaware dishes the first time we walked through Macy's with a price gun, giddy and scanning items to a virtual wish list. I wasn't a fan. The colors seemed particular to a California upbringing, and I wanted to resist this. I knew we were moving to California in a few months and thought I had conceded too much already and resisted embracing too fully the domestic landscape of a California kitchen, which the pottery came to represent. I'm sure Richard was a better man, or maybe they shared the same taste, or he didn't have a strong aesthetic vision for his life. Maybe he hated Fiestaware but would compromise: "You can have the canisters, but not the dish set." Maybe such compromise hinted at a long and healthy marriage.

When I moved into my apartment, I didn't think of it as a bachelor pad per se, but I did think there was the prospect, however far off, that someone else might stay the night there with me. I wanted the best of everything. I told myself I deserved it—that, having left almost everything in California, sleeping on cheap thin sheets would only add to my depression. I wanted small details of my apartment to combine with other small details towards a collective home. I wanted to feel like I wasn't a sad divorcé with mismatched items. I went to Home Depot to replace the plastic light switchplates and electrical sockets with a brushed metal variety. I bought a ceramic dish for the kitchen sponge, a device that stored all my grocery bags and attached to the door below the sink, and lavender-scented hand soap. More importantly, it was about feeling at home, creating a place with purpose rather than a place of necessity—i.e. a room I needed to rent because my wife no longer wanted me. These were items that displayed care, thoughtfulness. And in the end, I knew this wasn't for me. It was anticipating that someone would one day walk up the stairs and into the hallway, and see my apartment, superficially or not, as a reflection of who I was.

I told myself if I found a registry for Nina and Richard, I would purchase the most expensive item on it for them as a gift. I would start a Kickstarter campaign asking friends and strangers for donations in order to purchase a set of twelve crystal goblets, a Dyson vacuum. I wasn't sure it was worth the joke, but it might be how we should utilize the Internet: small donations and micro-loans for jokes. It is possible I only contemplated this not from real vengeance, but in order to have the story to retell later.

Ingrid had the best laugh, loud and long, pure and goofy. She was filled with a joy that was infectious—it was found in a cat in a brownstone window, paintings, old soul records, puns, lord did she love puns. All of this without being a Pollyanna—she had an edge and bitterness, but wasn't world-weary. She was the first person I dated whom I introduced to friends, who came to a work event. Why in the world did she allow me to ironically wear a pink trucker hat the first time I met her friends? Or ever? What was I thinking? What were they thinking? There are no excuses, and yet maybe she was too shy or possessed a certain sense of decorum that prohibited her mocking my fashion choices, or maybe it was some ridiculous quirk she found charming.

My friends began adding her to email chains almost immediately—I'm not sure they even asked me—inviting her to poetry readings, to kids' birthday parties, where incidentally all the children swarmed her, pulling her arms to show her a new doll, to create a new imaginary world. Even my neighborhood welcomed her. The men who were forever outside my door on a upside-down milk crate reading the paper, scratching a lotto ticket, observing our coming and goings, the neighbors who had renamed me "David Spade," now just pointed and said "Here come the movie stars." It was a welcome change for me; we laughed, and I gave a cigarette to anyone who asked to bum one.

One day when I entered the laundromat where I deposited my thirty-pound bag of clothes to be washed each week, the women working there became excited. They began laughing, talking to each other, and pointing towards me and then to the bag I'd come to pick up. Tied to the outside of bag, where once they had tied a key I had left in a pocket of a pair of jeans, were a few of Ingrid's intimate items, carefully folded. She had left them at my apartment. The women knew they weren't mine. They'd not only become familiar with me, but with my belongings. And now here we all stood, not sharing a common language, attempting to get to the bottom of this mystery. They were unclear if they had suddenly uncovered a secret habit or, as happens occasionally, an errant item left over in the dryer from the previous customer's load had mistakenly wound up with my items. I blushed; it is something with my pale skin that I excel at, blushing. I stammered "Oh! Oh, no. No," trying to string together an explanation. I stepped outside where Ingrid was waiting; I pulled her toward the open doorway and pointed at her. Ingrid raised her hand, an accounting for, a wave. The women immediately understood.

It was easy and it was natural with Ingrid. I don't mean "easy" in the sense that we both liked chicken pot pie and so unwrapped the frozen pot pie cellophane together and placed them in the microwave and settled down on the couch just in time to watch our stories, forevermore. And I don't mean "natural" to hint at the notion of soulmates locating each other in a world filled with unlimited choices and false turns. What I mean is that I felt like myself, that though maybe there is excitement and drama in playing roles, ultimately a life of such constant performance isn't sustainable. And the excitement she felt for the world didn't necessarily open my eyes, but it allowed me to remember those aspects of myself.

The first period of estrangement from my mother when I was a teenager concluded in classic subterfuge, with Noah employing the oldest trick in the book. It is a trick, I understand, only successful when both parties willingly, perhaps even subconsciously, allow themselves to be misled, from hubris and a stubborn unwillingness to admit their errors, and ultimately with the desire to be reconciled. "He would like to see you." "She would like to see you." He told me she had stopped drinking. Five years of relative silence ended based on misinformation. I walked down a corridor to a person standing in the doorway, as if nothing had transpired. We hugged. She said: "I'm glad you came."

I felt alienated from my brothers then, and that feeling seems even more pronounced for this latest go-round of refusing to speak to my mother. I imagine that they think I'm unwilling to accept or respect an opinion different than my own. I was the last to be born; a decade separates me from my oldest brother. It is the curse that the role of the youngest child is to be forever the youngest, and thus what's seen as being principled is interpreted as disdainful righteousness—the preserving and naive ideals of a teenager who believes he understands perfectly the complexities of the adult world. I was twelve when my parents' divorce was finalized and Simon was six hours away at college. We set patterns to be meticulously adhered to and here I am, like a teenager again, the only son not speaking to his mother.

It is possible—it is quite likely—that my brothers' memories are different than mine. It should go without saying. I asked Simon what his earliest memory of the family was. It was early in the morning. I told him I wanted to interview him. We were drinking coffee. He was doing *The Philadelphia Inquirer*'s Sunday crossword puzzle. I placed the recorder I purchased the night before between us. I started the recorder. "Philadelphia, December 15, 2007. What is your first memory?" He looked up. "Mom was crowning me." He turned off the recorder. He told me a different story about when I was born and he walked into my room, stood over the crib, and vowed to always take care of me. These days, I speak infrequently with any of my brothers. "Have you spoken to Dad? Have you spoken to Mom?" "I got nothing." "Yeah, me either." "Talk to you soon."

May 22, 2008
2:22 PM

ME: I saw you online on Nerve today. How is that working out for you?

INGRID: Ha!! Well, you were online too, then, weren't you?

ME: Yeah, I was. I went to check to see if you were. Right?

INGRID: Yeah right. I got an email that someone had messaged me.

ME: Was she cute?

INGRID: Ha! I felt bad, because it was someone I'd been writing before I met you, and he sent me a very sad "Why haven't you written me back?" email.

ME: Oh, those suck!

INGRID: Yeah. I feel terrible. I don't want to lead him on.

ME: How many emails back and forth did you have?

INGRID: Two each I guess?

ME: How many does it take to get you on a date?

INGRID: Depends. If I'm really interested I'll just go ahead and ask right away, but it depends on how the conversation is progressing. Like if the first email is one sentence, that doesn't really count for much. Do you remember how quickly I replied? I was all over that.

ME: I guess I do! So are you coming over tonight?

Dear Mom,

I will be turning thirty soon and next month would have been my third wedding anniversary. I should be shopping for the perfect gift made of leather. A journal bound in Italian leather, or luggage. A modern gift would be crystal or glass. A paperweight with a decoupage image of a French playing card, the ace of hearts frozen inside.

I won't attempt to draft an incomplete list of my likes and dislikes in an effort to get to know each other better. I'm unable to visualize the benefits; would we know what to cook if the other was coming for dinner? Too many days have come and gone, each one the same, each one slightly different, the weather on a yearly loop. It has rained for three straight weeks. It's strange the things I don't know about you. How many siblings did your mother have? I always forget. I know it approaches the double digits, maybe there were twins. Or what did you do the summer you lived in New York? Did you really work in a department store or have I invented that fact? I don't know when or how you met my father. I was never told. How many times can a history be repeated? I never asked. I was the fourth son, clearly the last hope for a daughter. By the time little league or piano lessons came around, both you and my father were exhausted with almost a decade of child-rearing. I would not be forced to play. I don't blame you. There is only so much stamina exerted before one gives in. It's these types of details I want, details that transform a character from a novel into someone almost real.

From my journal, October 1988: "Life at my house is painful. My brother Paul always picks on me because I am smaller. My brother Simon is my favorite brother, but he is away at college. My only brother left is Noah and he is never home or he is asleep. It's also hard because I hardly see my mom, but I sleep over at her house just about every weekend. But when I get home the only one I can do something with is my Dad but he is usually at a meeting or tutoring, but he is always there when I need him." We can return to the beginning, to follow how things progressed. I recently found this form from preschool filled out by you or my father. I can't distinguish the handwriting. I look at the cards you sent me over the years, filled with celebratory slogans: "Happy Birthday" and "Merry Christmas." There isn't enough handwriting to create a sample size to compare adequately. I tell myself though, that the handwriting on the form is yours—that we're sitting at the kitchen table, where my homework was done, where my school projects were glued together and sprinkled with glitter, where we lived together, an unhappy family similar to all unhappy families, hoping things could change, and waiting as they didn't. There shouldn't be anything special about it.

Dear Parents,

We are eager to get to know your child and have him feel important and happy coming to school. To foster this we would like you to discuss with your child these things of interest about himself/herself. Please write the response on this sheet. Do not feel pressured to fill in every blank. Do feel free to add any comments of your own or your child's.

Please bring this autobiography with you to the interview.

My name is Brett. I am 5 years old. My favorite toy is my boat. I like to eat cake and chicken. The other people who live at our house are: Dad, Mom, Noah 11, Simon 13, Paul 8, Logan (dog), fish, and the hamster.

Something else I want you to know about me is: I don't care.

At William Penn Center I hope I will be able to: Learn to read.

General Health: Brett is in excellent health, although slightly small for his age. He had a milk allergy as a baby and consequently will not drink milk. He does however eat milk products, i.e. cheese, ice cream.

General Knowledge: Brett has learned much from his brothers. He likes to look at books and magazines and can usually find someone to answer his questions. He also formulates his own theories.

Interest and Behavior: Brett seems to deal well with both peers and adults. He has begun to take the lead in playing with his friends. He likes to dig holes, build forts, set up army men and play super heroes.

Goals for This School Year: We'd like to have Brett make continued progress—learn his abc's and maintain his positive attitude toward school.

I can best describe my child by saying: He's a pretty good all around kid.

Comments: His older brothers are concerned about possible WWIII, talk army etc. a lot. Brett picks up their lead.

Can define:
  Ball: A circle.
  Lake: I don't know.
  House: Has a Roof.
  Ceiling: Where light is.
  Jumps from bottom step: Yes.
  Hops 2 times on 1 foot: Needs support.
  Balances on one foot for 5 seconds: Needs support.

Brett enjoys being independent. He has fit into our routine very well. He prefers speaking to grown-ups. He has a quiet voice and is difficult to understand at times. He is also reluctant to speak in group situations. He dresses for outdoor activities but needs help with buttons. He accepts responsibility, but cries easily. He needs improvement showing concern and sympathy. He has difficulty holding a pencil.

Love,
Brett

The summer my mother kicked us all out of the house, Noah was the first to make amends, to return to her a day or two later. It was the end of summer, he was returning to college in Washington, DC. He needed a ride, or my mother had previously promised him a coffee table or a dresser for his new apartment. Or he had other emotional reasons. And then at my wedding, Noah was the first to comfort her, to follow her to the gravel parking lot, to stop an immediate and stormy exit. She stayed through the first toast, in which Simon read a childhood poem of mine.

After my wedding, Simon didn't speak with my mother for a month, not an abnormal amount of time to pass in our family. I can't be sure if his distance was meant to pass judgment on her behavior or not. As a teenager, Simon had been my silent partner when she had kicked us out of the house. He went three years without communicating with her, and then one day he slipped a note under my bedroom door.

Dear Brett,

I'm sorry that you are so mad at me. I know you don't like what I'm doing and I understand your point of view and how you feel. I never meant to let you down or make you feel alone. It doesn't really matter if I talk to Mom now or five years from now. It's something I have to do. I know that may sound selfish to you. In the end, everyone must find their own happiness and do what they think is right—be an individual. One of the greatest things about you is that you are an individual and try to live by what you know is right in your heart. I totally respect that about you. But in my heart I know that I must at least talk to Mom again one day in my life. I know you don't understand me but that is honestly how I feel. Nobody is perfect. We all make mistakes, including mom and myself. No matter how hard we try, it is nearly impossible to make ourselves or anyone else perfect. Don't put so much pressure on yourself to be absolutely perfect. You have friends that care about you and a family that loves you, including your brother and Dad. I care about you so much and hate to see you so mad and upset. You are a great person. I know you try very hard to please everybody and to do the right thing. I am very proud of you and I love you very much. We will always be brothers (even if you wish we weren't). We may not always agree or have the same views, but as long as I'm around you will never be alone. I'll always be there for you and you can always trust me and count on me to take care of you. You are my kid brother and one of my favorite people in the world. I love you very much. Hang in there "little man."

Simon

Dear Mom,

It causes me great pain to confront you with this letter. None of this has been addressed since I was twelve and now I am thirty. I will feel guilt when you die, that you will die without your youngest son. But that guilt seems a selfish reason to speak with you.

I didn't want to accept your letters or your holiday checks. It was a weakness. I wanted to demonstrate an understanding of right and wrong, both to myself, and to you. Gestures are noticed in the world. Your monthly bank statement noted the check was cashed. By cashing them, I continued to have contact with a person I refused to have contact with.

I knew when I was twelve and I know it now, that it was unprincipled to allow you to reach me. I don't want to be found, located, and understood. I have given up trying to forgive you. Maybe I'm supposed to rise to the occasion. As a child, my observational skills were not yet enriched with the knowledge of the particulars of the disease and I was lucky that my own addiction ended without any serious or irreparable damage to myself or others. But now I should know better, should have the empathetic understanding that the rooms of addiction and recovery should have instilled.

Instead I will address this letter, seal it, and place it in the box beneath my bed.

I hear a pigeon cooing on the fire escape. If it is white, my luck will change. I will forget this all tomorrow or attempt to memorialize it.

Dear Mom, I got nothing. Talk to you soon?

Love,
Brett

June 3, 2008
10:35 AM

INGRID: I feel terrible about our conversation last night. You've been so lovely, and I'm totally happy with things as they are.

ME: You don't have to feel terrible about anything.

INGRID: I was just in a little bit of a mood yesterday and I'm sorry if I said anything hurtful or annoying.

ME: Nah, hold on.

INGRID: Ok, I'm going to keep typing anyway—I just feel dumb for being such a girl. You're not really being distant at all. I'm just feeling vulnerable because I like you, so I'm anxious for any kind of reciprocal "I like you, too" gesture. I just need to chill and I can. Ok. That's what I wanted to say.

ME: Well, a) I don't want you selling yourself short about what you want and expect because you are easy-going, passive, or "selfless" b) You shouldn't feel that you have to back-step after expressing yourself, I'm a big dude, a huge dude, and can deal with it.

INGRID: Meh, I was just thinking it over on my own. Plus, as I'm sure you noticed, I was so sleepy when we were having that conversation. I wasn't in the best state of mind.

ME: I actually think your points were valid.

INGRID: Well, what do you think about all this now? In the light of day.

ME: I am VERY angry.

INGRID: What? Really? At me?

ME: Oh come on!

INGRID: Well, I don't know. You said you didn't feel good about the conversation, that could mean anything.

ME: I'm concerned about certain things.

INGRID: Ok, what specifically?

ME: Your generation wants to deal with everything on chat . . . just kidding.

INGRID: We can wait and talk in person.

ME: My understanding is this: You want to feel secure with me, and I am a little distant, I will admit that, it is a way to protect myself from being vulnerable, yet in order for you to feel secure I will need to be vulnerable, and for me to be able to see and get to know the whole Ingrid package, I will need to be vulnerable so you feel secure expressing yourself.

INGRID: I'd say that's spot-on. So now what do we do? What do you want at this point? I don't want to feel like I'm forcing you to do something that makes you uncomfortable.

ME: I do have a question though.

INGRID: Yes?

ME: I'm looking for a working definition or clarification of how all these terms work. Would you say you are dating me? Seeing me? If you said it is "casual" what does that mean, if each person isn't seeing anyone else? And if each person isn't seeing anyone else, what is that?

INGRID: Oh. Yeah, I don't know, those terms are all so vague.

ME: Well, how do you use them?

INGRID: I think everyone has different definitions. I guess I would say I was either dating you or seeing you. I think of those as being basically the same thing. Meaning, we're not officially bf/gf.

ME: Now again, what does that "not officially" mean?

INGRID: Official = had a discussion about it, acknowledging that it's serious, not dating anyone else, etc. I think that's pretty standard. I think it just depends on what the two people agree on, it's always a gray area. I'd say not official means not fully committed or exclusive, like, right now, for instance, you could be dating other people, and that would be okay, because you'd be totally within your rights. That doesn't mean I'd be thrilled about it but it would be fine, morally. I'm sure other people feel differently about it.

ME: Gotcha. But shouldn't the fact that it would make you unhappy affect what you would want or ask for?

INGRID: Right, but at this point, having agreed to not be exclusive, I wouldn't really have any right to be upset. Of course I'm entitled to feel whatever I feel.

ME: Ok. Any questions for me?

INGRID: I guess I'm just wondering how you're feeling about all this in general? Are you freaking out? I don't want you to feel uncomfortable or like I'm putting any pressure on you.

ME: First, I don't think you are putting any pressure on me. I can handle that.

INGRID: Okay.

ME: But what are you asking me? How I feel about you? How I feel about dating?

INGRID: I meant the first one, but both I guess.

ME: I like hanging out with you. You make me feel good and comfortable and sexy. I want to spend time with you and get to know you better, and look forward to seeing you, and all those things seem like good signs. Is that bad?

INGRID: No! It's great.

ME: Is there something else you wanted me to be thinking?

INGRID: No! Not at all I just wanted to make sure I was interpreting things right. I feel the same way.

ME: So you know, I'm not seeing anyone else, and if you are that is completely fine.

INGRID: I'm not. Would you really be fine with that? I don't want to, I'm just curious.

ME: I'm not saying it would make me feel amazing, but since I have obvious commitment issues, I just expect that it is a very real understandable possibility that someone wouldn't want to stake that much interest in that arrangement.

INGRID: Well, I have no qualms about being serious and no qualms about not being serious.

We were in bed, looking at my high school yearbook. I was bragging. Ingrid hadn't believed I was voted "Best Dressed." We made a handshake bet. I forget what for. A fancy chocolate bar, or the loser would have to go downstairs to pay the delivery man when he arrived with our food. A car, even though I can't drive. I hadn't mentioned that the subtitle to the award was actually "Most Likely to Be Seen on a Paris Runway." That sounded better, obviously, but it also offered an explanation at how the student body had arrived on my name through the popularity contest that is any high school voting. The specifics of a "Paris Runway" twisted their arms into selecting a slight weirdo in a disco-era butterfly collar and bell-bottoms rather than the boy in a polo shirt and khakis with perfectly parted hair.

Ingrid asked if we had met in high school whether we would have been friends. She wished she had known High School Brett. She joked that she was going to write and post a Missed Connection for my teenage self. She thought I should keep writing them, and should start a website cataloging the fake Missed Connections I'd been writing. I told her how tired I was of writing them.

She told me about "Take Care of Yourself," a recent work by the French artist Sophie Calle that was based on a break-up email the artist received and named after the last words in the correspondence. For the work, Calle had gathered responses to the offending email by 107 females who were experts in their field—a copyeditor proofed the letter, a cruciverbalist created a crossword puzzle of the words, a scientist and Talmudic scholar offered analysis. We began to brainstorm together, and settled on the idea that we should ask others to write the Missed Connections. We knew artists, musicians, and writers who would be willing to join the experiment. My boredom wasn't necessarily with the idea, but with the private obsessiveness, the tunnel vision of my particular experience, which was exhausting and exhausted. But, as with Calle's work, what can be interesting is another's particular version of loneliness, or how they imagine loneliness is articulated. As with a theatrical production, each actor invents his or her own backstory and motivation for a new run of an old play.

I showed Ingrid more photos, showed her Beth Warner, who was my first kiss, the girls I had wanted to date, and the boys who at various moments wanted to beat the shit out of me. I showed her a page of thirty portraits, all in the identical formal garb of black dress or tux, and asked her to identify who she imagined was the most popular person based on their photograph. And confirming some deep truth about high school, she was never correct.

I am of the belief that most terrible news arrives with a phone call. I don't expect the alert of the death of a loved one to arrive via a text message, and yet I never answer my phone, since the entities that call these days are robot debt collectors, Sallie Mae, and the junior high school that erroneously believes I am the guardian of a boy named Alberto, and is concerned I didn't return their call about parent–teacher conferences. When my phone vibrates with an unknown number, I don't pick up, I google that number.

I was visiting my brother Noah in Oregon. Ingrid and I had been dating for a few months, and she was staying at my apartment cat-sitting. This time, when her name appeared on my caller ID, I did answer. I had been away for a few days and hadn't heard her voice. But the voice on the other end wasn't hers. It was a man. He told me he had dialed the most recently called number in the phone and that "Whoever's phone this is just had a seizure and the ambulance took her to the hospital." He worked at a grocery store in Park Slope and informed me which hospital the ambulance had taken her to.

There wasn't much I could do from across the country. I couldn't be there to comfort her, couldn't ask the doctors questions about whether she fainted or had a seizure, and what could have caused it. It had been 90 degrees in Brooklyn. Maybe she was dehydrated, had low blood sugar. I went online and messaged Ingrid's roommate. I called my friend Charlie so he could get on the train and head to the hospital. Ingrid hadn't mentioned having an illness or condition. My only information was secondhand from a grocery clerk and what I read on the WebMD entry on seizures and how long they lasted, what happened to the body, what were the causes. There was no real way of knowing what had happened. I sat anxiously on a couch states away.

A few hours passed before her roommate called me. He handed the phone over to Ingrid, who was resting in the hospital with a bandage on her head, stuck with an IV injecting salt- and sugar-rich fluid, and in my memory, this is the first time she told me she loved me. Her roommate quickly took the phone from her—knowing it was still early in the relationship and protecting her from woozy talk. I said it back. It was the first time I had said it in a long time.

And I hate to tell this story this way, fearing it sounds like a relationship created from the bond of crisis or trauma. I imagine two people who meet in shared grief at a funeral, or over an existential crisis about humanity, like the thousands who must have been brought together after September 11 all over the city, the two old lovers who called each other to check in, to say "I was a fool, I'm standing outside your apartment door right now. Please let me in."

This was different. Instead of calling into question my own fragility, my own grief at an unknown future alone, it cut the emotional distance I was maintaining. This wasn't about my own selfish concerns or existential dread. It sounds so simple, so obvious; it was about experiencing the care and love I felt for another in my life. After the end of my marriage, this was something I had been unable to allow myself—up until this moment.

■

A greeting card arrived from my mother with a remorseful cartoon bear wearing a blue shirt and red slacks and a maze between him and another bear.

"Here I am, there you are."

Dear Mom,

I don't know what to do. I'm not sure how to reach you. I searched last night and couldn't find your phone number. Is it possible I no longer have your number? I wonder if it is listed. We can go on like this forever, each searching for the other somewhere. Each asking Simon, Noah, Paul for information, facts, gauging the temperature of the other. And it is possible we might. I'm not sure what it means to have a mother, and by the same token, not to have one. You were always there, a phantom possibility things could be different. This is what absence taught me, that there is no absence. It will never be the same; it will happen all over again. Nothing grows fonder. It rots, it decays, is rebuilt over a burial ground. Now, as has always been the case, each morning begins where the night trailed off. There is no end. There is no beginning. The sun goes down and rises on the same set of grievances we invent and if nothing changes then nothing changes.

At a certain point I found myself standing in the line at Baskin-Robbins, wondering if the ice cream cake would fit the message I wanted to place on it. I brought it home to surprise Ingrid. Everyone loves cake. Everyone loves ice cream. I asked the person at the counter to write on the cake: "Will you be my girlfriend?" She looked at me and said: "Yes, if you brought me home this cake." And I brought home the cake, and that is how it started over. There has to be a moment—a grand or, in my case, a simple, ridiculous gesture, to say *Yes, I believe life with you will be better than life without you.*

And now, as I write this letter, Ingrid is asleep in the room to my left. She has read everything I have written so far in my memoir, copyedited, cut, insisted on changes and details, and it is better for it. I am better for the thinking she required of me. She knows everything now. One evening, as she slept, I saw a peaceful ghost-like figure hovering above her body as I sat here writing.

I've told myself it appeared again, after months, to investigate, to give the all-clear, to approve of my decisions. I haven't told her this yet. I've learned my lesson. Some things might be too early to reveal. There is a black cat resting on her chest. It is my cat. The cat's name is Kiki. Ingrid takes more photographs of the cats than I do. She is allergic and at the beginning of each week she must wake early before work and take a train to the allergist to receive a shot that they hope will make her immune. She does this for me. She does this for the cats. I love that her emotions show on her face when she is unhappy. That she can express them. That she can challenge me when I'm wrong and I want to apologize. She has asthma, and I've had to stop smoking in the house. I would never want to hurt her. I must quit smoking soon. I love that on the street a dog, almost any dog, can bring her happiness, and that she knows the breeds of these dogs, the names of flowers, and every answer to the 90s edition of Trivial Pursuit. I love that she told me, after the fact, that when she entered my apartment for the first time that it was as if she decorated it herself. She only objects to a single band of color on the kitchen arch-way, painted in the ridiculous color Hot Lips. I love that she understands I couldn't not paint it Hot Lips. I love that she doesn't flinch when my step-mom accidently calls her Nina, that later that night when we whisper in the guest room, she doesn't launch into a list of complaints about the event, which she would be completely justified in doing, and I would understand, but that we can commiserate about it, turn it into something funny. And I love that she is excited to meet you, even or especially knowing that it might not be the easiest homecoming—we are still planning to visit over the Christmas break when Noah and Simon will be in town. I love that she has told me she's already reserved the email address ingridhollylauer@gmail.com and that she says "autumnal" as the season is changing.

Love always,
Brett

PERMISSIONS AND ACKNOWLEDGEMENTS

. . .

The instant message conversation with Bella reprints my side of the conversation, with Bella's words being recreated by Jennifer Kronovet without any knowledge or reference of Bella's original writing. Thanks to my father, Simon, Daphne, Charlie, Cassie, Jess, Mary, and Ingrid who all graciously granted permission to reprint their correspondences and writings. Some correspondence was combined and edited for grammar.

Sections of this book have appeared in *A Public Space*, *The Rumpus*, and on the Happy Ending Reading Series website. Thanks to Anthony Brosnan, Rob Casper, Timothy Donnelly, Monica Fambrough, Matthea Harvey, Stefania Heim, Rachelle Katz, Jenny Kronovet, Dan McGehean, Travis Nichols, Fred Nicolaus, Elsbeth Pancrazi, Peter Pihos, and of course my family. All my thanks in the world to Brigid Hughes, Lynn Melnick, and Gretchen Scott, who have read this book too many times and provided me with unlimited advice and wisdom. And thanks to Lindsay Edgecombe and Dan Smetanka.

Ellis nodded. She didn't look happy. "Called a few minutes before I left. She said the locket in the picture looked like the same one to her and that Opal was curious about it, too. Said she was sure she'd seen one just like it."

Please don't let this be happening to Idonia! "What are we going to do?" I said. "Should we say anything to Idonia?"

"Say anything about what?" Nettie came out of my bedroom snapping the elastic in her long skirt. "This blasted thing's about to cut me in two. If you hear a loud pop, you'll know what happened."

The planners of the event had asked The Thursdays, as hostesses, to dress in period clothing and allowed me to bring several items home for Nettie, Ellis, and me. "Try that blue gingham. It might be more comfortable," I said, and while Nettie was getting into the dress, Ellis and I told her what we suspected about Idonia's locket.

"I wouldn't want to be the one to tell her," Nettie said. "This is not good! It might be better to speak directly to that rat Melrose." She finished buttoning her dress and tied an apron around her plump middle. "Ah, that's better! At least I can breathe."

We dressed in layers because, except for fireplaces in some rooms, the areas at Bellawood weren't heated. Ellis chose an ankle-length black skirt with a high-necked white blouse, and draped a blue knitted shawl about her shoulders. Her dark curls, now streaked with gray, looked becoming tied back with a black ribbon. "I'll be darned if I'm going to look like that woman in the *American Gothic* painting with my hair pulled back and parted in the middle!" she informed us.

I wore a mop cap to cover my short straight hair and slipped on a purple-flowered dress large enough to have room for all the layers underneath.

"Are we supposed to bring anything?" Ellis asked as the three of us climbed into her van.

"Nettie's punch bowl is already there and the docents are

taking care of refreshments," I said. "All we have to do is meet and greet."

"I wonder what the others are wearing," Nettie said, spreading her skirt about her.

"Idonia said she was going to borrow something for herself and Jo Nell from the high school drama department," Ellis said. "Her niece teaches over there, you know, and Zee told me she was wearing a dress she had in college."

"Not that Southern belle hoopskirt thing!" I said. "Bellawood's a farmhouse, not Tara."

Nettie laughed. "Didn't she wear that in some kind of pageant one time? Remember when Stone's Throw put on that bicentennial play? That dress was cut so low I thought surely her bosom was going to bounce right out of it!"

"Genevieve Ellison will have apoplexy," I said, but I couldn't help but feel a little jealous. There was no way I would be able to fit into a gown I'd worn in college!

It had turned dark by the time we arrived and someone had already lit the luminaries that lined the long drive up to Bellawood. A man dressed for the cold in muffler and cap directed us with a flashlight into the meadow across from the house where several other vehicles were already parked.

I parted reluctantly with my wrap at the door, while Ellis was whisked immediately to the building that housed the kitchen, and Nettie to the schoolhouse, where, we were told, Jo Nell waited. A quartet from the Baptist Church, scheduled to entertain guests with carols, was assigned there as well. I obediently took my place in the drafty entrance hall and watched them hurry away to spend a toasty evening in their allotted places.

The old house looked festive and welcoming from the wreath on the front door and banks of greenery on the mantel to the pungent smell of wood smoke and pine. I spoke briefly to Andy Collins, known to most of us as the Dulcimer Man, who was setting up in the parlor where candles glowed in hurricane lamps and firelight flickered on the hearth. Zee would be stationed in the upstairs hall, I learned, and Idonia in a second-floor bedroom, and every time I heard footsteps cross the porch, I braced myself for Genevieve's outburst when she saw Zee's revealing gown. I could hardly wait!

It served me right, I suppose, to be disappointed. The rose taffeta had faded over the years and Zee had even sewn a lace insert at her throat. Still, she managed to look trim and youthful with an antique brooch at her neck and her hair piled high on her head. Zee had chosen a dark auburn as her hair color for the season and it really was becoming.

"Zee, you look beautiful! Scarlett would be jealous," I said, ushering her into the hallway. "But where's the hoopskirt?"

She laughed. "I let Melanie borrow my hoop for a party one time and never saw it again." Melanie was Zee's daughter by her first husband—or maybe it was her second. "Anyway," she added, "can you imagine trying to *drive* in one?" She twirled, showing off dainty slippers. "Consignment shop—aren't they adorable? Of course, my feet are freezing! And how about this fancy brooch I found at a flea market? They have the most fascinating things in there."

Genevieve came along to hurry Zee upstairs before I could answer, and soon afterward a great swirl of frigid air ushered in Idonia stamping her feet and hugging her new suede coat about her.

"Good heavens, it's cold out there! And Zee just ran off and left me as soon as she parked the car. Had to hike all the way from across the road by myself in the dark, and I'd give my right arm for something hot to drink." Idonia pulled off her gloves and stuffed them into her pocket as she glanced upstairs. "I hope there's going to be some heat up there."

I told her Genevieve had put space heaters in some of the upstairs rooms and that Zee was probably in a hurry because she said her feet were cold.

"Well, of course they're cold since she insisted on wearing that sorry excuse for shoes." Idonia slowly unbuttoned her coat and passed it over to a waiting docent. She wore a prim gray silk with tucks down the front and a lace collar. The infamous gold locket was her only adornment.

"They're serving cranberry punch in the dining room," I told her, "but I don't think it's hot."

"What's Melrose doing with himself tonight? Is he planning to drop by?" I called after her as she made her way upstairs.

She gave me a backward wave of her hand. "He was going to, but his cousin needed him to help out at the funeral home, so I guess he won't be coming."

Fulton McIntyre, of course. Our minister announced in church that morning that Fulton had died, which was no surprise since the man was ninety-three and ailing. *So that's why Idonia's so crabby,* I thought. I knew something must have gotten her dander up. If Idonia was upset over playing second fiddle to a dead man, what would she think if she knew what we suspected about her locket?

I didn't have time to think about it, however, as guests began to arrive and I stayed busy guiding them from one room to another. From the parlor came the strains of "What Child Is This?" and "Away in a Manger" played sweetly on the dulcimer and for a second I thought I saw Augusta sitting in a corner by the fireplace listening. A closer look proved me right: it *was* Augusta and her expression was so blissful and serene it made me forget for a moment just how bossy she can be. I had mentioned to her earlier that the Dulcimer Man was scheduled to play, so I wasn't surprised to see her there. Augusta had attended one of Andy's concerts with me earlier in the year and I knew she was fond of his music. When I glanced in there a few minutes later she was gone.

"Augusta was in here a little while ago," Ellis whispered when I dropped by the kitchen during a break later that evening. "Didn't stay long…guess she came to hear the Dulcimer Man."

"I saw her in the parlor," I said, sipping gratefully on the hot spiced cider served from a pot on the hearth. "Aren't the Fiddlesticks coming back? I passed Albert and Miranda leaving with their instruments."

"Nope. I believe a flute trio from the high school band is next on the agenda," Ellis said as she added more ginger cookies to the tray on the table.

I turned in front of the fire to get thoroughly warm before crossing back across the yard to the main house. "Better let me have a cup of that punch to take back to Idonia," I said. "She was asking for something hot to drink."

Ellis laughed. "She's already been in here. Drank two cups in here and took one back with her."

"Did she seem upset?"

"No, just thirsty. I thought she was going to drink the punch bowl dry. Why?"

I told her about Idonia's earlier behavior. "I guess she's just disappointed that Melrose couldn't join her tonight."

"If there's anything shady going on about that locket he gave her, Melrose DuBois had better get a running start!" Ellis said.

In keeping with the period, we had been asked not to wear watches that night, but because long sleeves covered my wrists, I could keep mine well out of sight. It was almost eight-thirty when I returned to my post in the hallway, and every room in the old house seemed to be filled with visitors. It was easy to imagine the home as it had been in the past with friends, music, and laughter, and if a building has a spirit, this one must have been happy. Plans were for the open house to end at nine, but some of the musicians stayed longer, and several of the town's older citizens settled down to exchange tall tales by the dining room fireside, so it was closer to ten before everyone cleared out.

I was helping some of the docents clear away the clutter downstairs when Zee rushed into the room on the verge of tears. "Lucy Nan, something's wrong with Idonia! You've got to come quick! I can't wake her up."

We all raced upstairs behind her to find Idonia seated at a small writing desk in a rear bedroom, her head upon her chest. The room was close and warm because of the space heater, and Idonia, who was unaccustomed to late hours, had been out caroling the night before.

"She's probably just worn out," I said, calling her name. "Idonia! Wake up! It's time to go home." I got no response.

"I felt her pulse," Zee said. "She's breathing okay, but she seems to be out like a light."

By that time Nettie and Jo Nell had joined us. "She's not on any medication, is she?" Nettie asked. "Sometimes antihistamines can make you drowsy."

"Nothing but a low-dose thyroid pill," I said. Idonia was usually as healthy as a horse.

Jo Nell sniffed at a punch cup beside her. "What's she been drinking?"

"Just hot spiced punch, and so have I," I told her. "There's nothing in there to harm her."

"Wait a minute…I think she's waking up," Zee said as Idonia blinked her eyes.

"Is it time to get up?" she mumbled before closing them again.

"That does it!" I said. "Who has a cell phone? I'm calling nine-one-one."

TEN

"No, WAIT! DON'T!" Nettie said. "We might be able to catch Glen Smiley before he gets away. He was talking with somebody out front just a few minutes ago. Idonia would hate it if we made a big issue of this."

Genevieve rushed into the hallway and hollered downstairs in her loud demanding voice for somebody to run and find the doctor. Glen Smiley graduated from high school in the class just ahead of ours and has been practicing medicine in Stone's Throw for close to thirty years. Although his name is somewhat of a misnomer, as his bedside manner leaves something to be desired, you won't find a better diagnostician, so I was relieved to hear the doctor's monotone muttering in the hallway below.

"What's going on here, Lucy Nan?" he asked, taking the stairs in great loping strides. But I could only shake my head. I was too frightened to speak.

"Idonia Mae, I want you to look at me," he said, kneeling beside her chair. "Look at me and tell me where you are."

Idonia's eyelids fluttered and her head rolled to one side. "Don't feel so good…leave me 'lone." She sounded more like herself in spite of the slurred words.

"Have you had anything to eat or drink tonight?" the doctor persisted, examining her more closely. Idonia slumped forward until her head rested on the desktop. She didn't answer.

"She drank a lot of that spiced cider," I told him, gesturing toward the cup.

"Is this it?" He picked it up and sniffed it. "You-all didn't slip any vodka in there, did you?" He directed the question at Genevieve without so much as a flicker of a smile.

"Certainly not!" she answered, looking from one to the other of us. I could tell she wasn't quite sure about the rest of us.

"I can't do anything for her here," he told us, taking a cell phone from his pocket. "She needs to go to the ER, but first we'll have to get her out of that chair before she slides onto the floor."

"It'll take them about five or ten minutes to get here," Dr. Smiley said, after making his phone call. "Meanwhile, let's get her over on that bed so the EMTs can take a look at her."

I heard somebody gasp behind me and turned to find Genevieve with a fist rammed into her mouth. "That bed's almost two hundred years old," she said. I honestly thought she was going to faint.

"Then it oughta hold up a few minutes longer," the good doctor said. "And we don't need all of you in here, either," he added. "At least one of you can go outside and watch for the ambulance."

"I—I will! I'll wait for them out front." Jo Nell's voice trembled. "Only I'll need to borrow a flashlight. I don't—can't remember where I put mine."

"Take mine. I left it by the front door," I said. I could tell she was about a sniff and a swallow away from crying.

"And somebody needs to find Ellis," Jo Nell said. "Oh, Lordy! What if something's happened to Ellis, too?"

"Nothing has happened to Ellis. She's probably still straightening up out in the kitchen," Nettie assured her. "Don't worry, Jo Nell, we'll find her." And giving Genevieve's arm a jerk, she propelled the startled woman from the room.

Zee and I stayed to help Glen Smiley move Idonia to the bed, and I must say she didn't cooperate one bit.

"Like picking up a big sack of chicken feed," Zee said.

I couldn't imagine where that analogy came from because

as far as I know Zee St. Clair has never lifted a sack of chicken feed in her life.

"You better hope and pray Idonia didn't hear you say that," I told her.

The doctor frowned as he took her pulse. "Does anybody know how to get in touch with Nathan?"

Idonia's only son lives somewhere in Georgia but I couldn't remember the city. "Is it that serious?" I asked him. "What's the matter with her, Glen?"

"I'll know more about that when we get her to the hospital and have whatever's in that punch analyzed. Are you sure Idonia's not on any medication? Has she been having trouble sleeping lately? Look in her purse—see if you can find anything in there."

"She came with me. I don't even know if she brought a purse," Zee said.

"Yes, she did! I saw her take it upstairs," I said, "so it should be somewhere in here."

Zee found Idonia's gray leather handbag in one of the bureau drawers but there was no medication in there, only a comb, a package of tissues, and a tube of her favorite shade of lipstick, tawny rose.

"Is there anything you can do to help her?" Zee asked, kneeling by the bed.

"To be on the safe side, they'll probably have to do a gastric lavage," the doctor said.

I've watched enough medical shows on television to know that meant washing out the stomach and that Idonia wasn't going to like it one bit. Now she sighed as she shifted her position on the bed and made a face as if she smelled or tasted something bad.

"What's the matter with Idonia?" Ellis's breathless question accompanied her frantic footsteps on the stairs. "It's not her heart, is it?" she asked, grabbing Glen Smiley by the arm.

"I'm inclined to believe it's possibly something she ingested," he said, freeing himself from her grasp. "You were in the kitchen, weren't you? Do you know if anyone else suffered an adverse reaction to something they may have consumed tonight?"

Ellis looked at him as if he'd asked her if she'd served up rat poison. "Well, of course not! It was only spiced apple punch and ginger cookies. Idonia did drink a lot of it, though. Said she hadn't had time for supper."

"She's going to be all right, isn't she?"

"Glen thinks we should get in touch with Nathan," I said before he could answer. "Do you know where he's living?"

"No, but Jennifer should," Ellis said. Jennifer Cole is Idonia's niece, who teaches at the high school.

"Then I think you'd better call her." Glen moved to the doorway at the sound of a siren in the distance. "That must be the ambulance, so let's clear out and give them some room. You can follow us to the hospital if you like, but the sooner we get there, the better."

Taking his advice, I hurried into the hallway, but Ellis still stood in the middle of the room looking like she just remembered she'd forgotten to put on underwear. "Wait a minute!" she said.

"Wait for what?" Zee asked. "Hurry up, Ellis, we have to get out of here."

Ellis turned and walked resolutely to stand over Idonia's inert body. "It's gone," she said, turning to look at us.

"What's gone?" I said.

"The locket. Her locket's not here." Ellis's searching fingers traced Idonia's neckline, felt beneath her head and shoulders. "Did one of you take it off?"

"Of course not," Zee said. "That locket was the last thing on my mind."

"But not Idonia's," I said. "If that locket doesn't turn up, we'll have another emergency on our hands."

"She didn't appear to be wearing anything like that when I

examined her," Glen said, "but if she is wearing jewelry, they'll remove it at the hospital for safekeeping."

"WELL, IT WASN'T ANYWHERE on the floor," Ellis said as we followed the ambulance to the hospital. "I searched that room on my hands and knees."

"Genevieve promised they'd comb that whole area tomorrow," I said. "It might have fallen off somewhere between the house and the kitchen, so it would be almost impossible to see it in the dark."

"Right now that's the least of our worries," Nettie said. "I phoned Jennifer and she's going to meet us at the hospital."

"What about Nathan?" I asked. "Did she know where to find him?"

"She said she'd try, but he travels a lot in his work, and it's not always easy to catch up with him." Nettie whistled through her false teeth as she sighed. "Do-law! Won't we be a sight parading into the hospital in these long-tailed outfits? It must be close to midnight already."

"The drunks in the emergency room will think they're hallucinating," Ellis said in an attempt at humor.

But the three of us were quiet for the rest of the ride. I'm sure the others were hoping and praying, as I was, that our friend was going to be all right. We Thursdays made up a strange motorcade, I thought, noticing Zee's headlights following closely behind us, and Jo Nell's behind her. Because of the late hour, we decided not to call Claudia unless Idonia's condition worsened. After all, what could she do? What could any of us do?

Ellis's gaze met mine in the rearview mirror as we finally turned into the hospital parking lot, and I knew we must be thinking the same thing. *Where was Augusta when we needed her?*

THERE WAS A TIME WHEN I considered anyone in their forties to be ancient. Not anymore! If I remembered correctly,

Idonia's niece Jennifer was at least forty-three, and she still looked young to me in spite of her lack of makeup and red-rimmed eyes. She greeted us all with hugs as we filed into the waiting room and led us to an area that was comparatively unoccupied.

"They won't let me back there yet, but they sent a sample of whatever she drank to the lab for analysis," she told us, shoving a strand of brown hair from her face. "I guess all we can do now is wait. I'm so glad you're all here! It would be awful to have to go through this alone." She had left a telephone message at Nathan's home in Savannah, Jennifer told us, but he hadn't re-turned her call. "I left my cell phone number and asked him to get back to me as soon as possible, so he must be out of town," she said.

"He'll probably check his phone messages in the morning," I said, seeing her downcast face.

We had received curious stares from most of the people in the waiting area—at least those who weren't asleep—but it wasn't until Ellis rose to get coffee that Jennifer seemed to realize we were dressed a bit out of the ordinary. "Have you all been to a costume party or something?" she asked.

We laughed when Zee explained about the candlelight tour, and that seemed to help everyone relax at least for a little while.

Several of us wanted coffee so I volunteered to help Ellis with the errand, glad of a chance to do something other than sit and wait. The receptionist pointed out a small snack room at the end of a hallway and I saw Ellis, who walked ahead of me, hesitate in the doorway. "I should've known you'd be in here," she said to someone inside.

The room seemed empty at first until I noticed a lone figure drinking coffee at a small table in the corner. Augusta.

"Where in the world have you been?" I asked, taking the vacant chair across from her. "Idonia's really sick, Augusta. We don't know what's the matter with her."

"I know." She reached across the small table and took my hand. Her hand on mine was light and calming, and although it didn't relieve my anxiety about Idonia, I drew a sense of serenity from her touch.

"I became a bit chilled at Bellawood," she said, "and so I came on home. When you didn't arrive by midnight, I sensed something was terribly wrong."

"But how did you know where I was?" I asked.

"I saw all your friends' cars here in the parking lot." Augusta took a swallow of coffee and wrinkled her dainty nose. "This coffee is really quite dreadful!" she said.

"The menu is limited, so I'm afraid we don't have any choice," Ellis said. Inserting money in the machine, she waited for the cup to fill. "Augusta, can't you do something—*anything*—to help her?"

"I'm sure you're aware, Ellis, that I can't interfere in matters—" Augusta began.

Ellis filled another cup and set it down with a slosh. "Why not?"

"It's not in her contract," I muttered. I was fed up with platitudes. I wanted action.

"It has nothing to do with a contract, Lucy Nan. Your friend is under the care of excellent doctors who are doing their best for her. I am here for both of you, and will continue to be if you need me. And I will pray." Augusta's sea green eyes looked almost gray and she fingered her necklace as she spoke. The stones were a clear blue like a rain-swept sky.

"Well, if you see Idonia's guardian angel, I wish you'd tell her to get cracking," I said.

The angel spoke softly, slowly lifting her eyes to mine. "She already has," she said.

"I THINK WE HURT Augusta's feelings," Ellis said as we started back to the waiting area. "Lucy Nan, you're *crying*! And I feel awful, too. I think we should go right back in there and tell Augusta we're sorry."

"The coffee spilled over and burned my fingers," I told her. "It hurts—that's all." That wasn't true, of course, and Ellis knew it as well as she knew me. I hurt. I hurt all over from the inside out. My friend might be dying and I had been rotten and mean to my own guardian angel, who was as close as a sister to me. What was the matter with me?

I swallowed the knot in my throat, sniffed back the tears and put on a cheerful false face for the others. As soon as Ellis and I distributed the coffee I would go back and admit to Augusta that I was a royal pain.

But an intern chose that moment to summon Jennifer into the emergency room.

ELEVEN

"IT WAS SOME KIND of sedative," Jennifer explained later. "Starts with an e and sounds like a prehistoric animal, and it was in her punch."

We'd waited over twenty minutes wondering if Idonia was going to make it, and Jo Nell had already started making a list of the people we'd have to call if she didn't when Nettie marched up to the desk and demanded to know what was going on. Intimidated, no doubt, by a bunch of nutty women in long dresses, the clerk phoned back to the ER to explain the situation, and a few minutes later Glen came out to tell us they had pumped Idonia's stomach but she was going to be all right.

"But how did...whatever that drug is get in her punch?" Zee wanted to know.

"That's something we need to find out," Glen said. "The dosage was more than the amount needed to make her sleep. I doubt if it would've killed her, but at her age, it's best not to take any chances."

Beside me, Jo Nell drew in her lips and grunted. She always gets her hackles up at the mention of age.

Glen sat on the edge of a chair looking every one of his fifty-seven years with tired eyes and rumpled clothes. "I've phoned the police and they're sending someone right over to talk with all of you, so please don't leave until they get here."

"Surely they don't think one of us might've done it!" Jo Nell, who had been nodding off herself a few minutes before, grew wide-eyed and bushy-tailed at the thought.

Glen managed a feeble attempt at a smile. "Jo Nell, I'm sure no one would ever think that of you, although I'm not too

sure about the rest of this motley crowd. The point is, however, somebody did drug Idonia's drink and one or more of
you might have noticed something that would help us find out
who it was." He looked at his watch. "Now, after I fill out this
report, I'm going home to bed. As soon as you give the police
the information they need, I suggest you do the same."

"You won't have to twist my arm," Nettie said, covering
a yawn. "But why in the world would anybody want to hurt
Idonia?"

THAT'S WHAT KEMPER MUNGO wanted to know when he arrived a few minutes later. Idonia had been taken to a private
room where Jennifer planned to stay with her overnight. If her
condition improved as expected, we were told, she might even
be released the next day.

One of the residents at the hospital herded us into a small
meeting room on the first floor for our session with Kemper,
who kindly apologized for keeping us up so late. "It's imperative," he explained, "that we try to find the reason behind this
before too much time passes."

"You mean before we all forget," Zee said.

"The medication must have been in the third cup of punch,"
Ellis told him. "She drank two in the kitchen right there in front
of me. I would've noticed if somebody slipped something into
her drink."

"It could've happened in the main house where the Dulcimer
Man was playing," Nettie said. "I saw Idonia talking with somebody in there while I was taking a break from the schoolhouse
and I'm almost sure she had a cup of punch with her then."

"Good. Good." Kemper was silent for a minute. "Now, try
to remember if she set the cup down. Was there a table nearby?
And do you know who she was talking to?"

"It was a woman—one of the docents—can't think of her
name, but I've seen her there before…" Nettie smiled. "Now,
I remember! The docent offered Idonia some refreshments,

shortbread cookies, I think, and Idonia put her cup aside to serve herself from the table."

Kemper frowned. "And the docent? What did she do then?"

"Several people came into the room just then and she went over to speak to them." Nettie shook her head. "Oh, I wish I'd stayed around longer, but I had to go and give Jo Nell a break!"

Zee patted her arm. "How could you have known?" She turned to Kemper. "What's in this stuff that was in the punch? Where did it come from?"

"From what I understand it was a prescription drug for insomnia," Kemper said. "Dr. Smiley thinks it was probably dissolved in some kind of harmless liquid before being added to the punch."

"And the punch was hot, so that would probably make it even less noticeable," Nettie pointed out.

"But why Idonia?" I said. "And why would somebody want her to sleep?"

Ellis spoke out with the voice of reason. "So they could steal her locket."

"Her locket! Of course. I'd almost forgotten about that," Jo Nell said, shaking her head. "Why would anybody want Idonia's locket?"

"It might be a good idea if somebody would tell me about this locket," Kemper said.

"It was an early Christmas gift from Melrose," Jo Nell said. "It belonged to his grandmother, and Idonia's going to hit the ceiling when she finds out it's gone."

"Melrose is Idonia's gentleman friend," Zee explained, seeing the expression on Kemper's face.

We took time about describing the locket, and then, of course, Kemper wanted to know when we first discovered it missing.

"When was the last time any of you saw Idonia before the drug took effect?" he asked.

"I guess I saw her last," Zee said, "since I was hostess in the upstairs hall and she had that room up there in the back. She spoke to me as she came upstairs that last time."

"Can you remember what she said?" Kemper asked.

"She said I should go downstairs and listen to Andy Collins— he plays the dulcimer, you know—and…"

Kemper frowned. "And what? Anything else?"

Zee flushed. "Just that whoever made the shortbread cookies stinted on the shortening. Idonia's shortbread is always a bestseller at bake sales, you know. It's her grandmother's recipe."

Kemper tried to cover a smile. "Did you see anybody upstairs who might have had an opportunity to put the drug in Idonia's punch?"

"I went down a little while after that to listen to the dulcimer music," Zee said, "and I guess two—maybe three—people passed me on the stairs. Later, when it was time to leave, I couldn't wake her up."

"Can you remember who these people were?" he asked.

"Two of them were our minister and his wife, Pete and Ann Whittaker, and the other person was one of the docents, I think. She was wearing a sunbonnet and a long dress."

"Sunbonnet? Is that the usual dress for a thing like this?" Kemper scribbled something on a notepad.

"There were a few of them around," I told him. "They left it up to us about what we wore as long as it suited the period."

Kemper sighed and sneaked a look at his watch. "Tell me about this…what's his name…Melrose? Has Idonia known him long? Does anybody know where he came from?"

Nettie explained that Melrose was staying at the Spring Lamb and worked part time for Al Evans. "He seems harmless enough," she added. "Idonia brought him to our caroling party last night and he sings a pretty good tenor."

"And by the way," I added, "Idonia seemed to think someone was following her last night."

Zee frowned. "You mean while we were caroling? Wouldn't we have seen them?"

"Has anyone else mentioned this?" Kemper asked.

I shook my head. "Not to me. Of course we were all bundled to the nines and it was dark as pitch out there."

Kemper made a note of this, shaking his head. "Any of the rest of you notice an extra person?"

Nobody answered.

"I'll take that as a no," he said, covering a yawn.

"You don't think Melrose had anything to do with what happened to Idonia tonight, do you?" I said. "If he was working over at Evans and Son like Idonia said, he wouldn't have had the opportunity."

"*If* can be a big word," Kemper said.

"IF MELROSE DUBOIS WAS at Bellawood tonight, one of us would've seen him," I said after Kemper left.

"I'm sure Kemper will check with Al over at the funeral home to make sure he was where he said he'd be," Nettie said.

"And *who* he said he *is*," Jo Nell added. "He might not be kin to Al at all."

Zee's once-elaborate hairdo was tumbling over one eye and she shoved it back carelessly as she buttoned her coat. "Now that we know Idonia's going to be all right, I'm going home and sleep for a week!"

"I'm with you," Jo Nell said. "I can hardly keep my eyes open."

"Not me." Ellis stood and stretched, earning sleepy-eyed glances from stragglers in the waiting area. "I was so tired just a while ago I thought I'd drop, but now I've gotten a second wind." She looked around. "Anybody else for coffee?"

"Ellis Saxon! Do you realize what time it is?" Nettie pointed to the clock. "It's time to take me home—that's what time it is, and then you two can stay up all night if it suits you."

"I'LL BET I KNOW who has a pot going," I said to Ellis after we dropped Nettie off next door. And then I remembered: *Augusta!* I had meant to go back to the hospital snack room and apologize for being such a miserable creature, but Jennifer had been called to the inner sanctums of the ER and I had forgotten all about it.

"If I were Augusta, I'd tell us to brew our own coffee after the grief we gave her tonight," Ellis reminded me.

And that's what I was afraid of. A light shone from the kitchen window as we hurried up the steps and across the back porch, but I hesitated with my hand on the doorknob. *What if Augusta wasn't there?* The very thought of it made my insides turn to slush. I had lived for fifty-five years before Augusta Goodnight entered my life, and I could manage without her again, but it would be like saying good-bye to a part of me. A part that was sometimes direct to the point of being blunt, but was also warm and kind and endearingly funny.

"What's wrong with you? It's cold out here! Move it, will you, Lucy Nan?" Ellis stomped her feet.

The kitchen was empty except for Clementine, who looked up from her sleeping place on the rug and reluctantly came to greet us. The coffeepot stared at us with a cold eye.

I stooped and took the dog's big, shaggy head in my arms. I wanted to cry. "Hey, girl," I said, stroking the soft fur on her neck. "Where's Augusta?" But I wasn't sure I wanted to know.

"In here." She stood in the doorway of the sitting room wrapped in a ratty old throw I keep on the back of the sofa, only on Augusta it looked almost elegant. From the television behind her came familiar voices from one of those old movies she loves to watch. Augusta adores Cary Grant. She glanced at the kitchen clock and then at us with something akin to relief on her face. It was almost three a.m. "Idonia?" Augusta spoke softly.

"She's going to be all right," I said. "There was something in the punch she drank that made her sleep and they had to pump her stomach…Augusta, I meant—"

The angel nodded. "I stayed to hear what the physician said about your friend's condition, but didn't find it necessary to linger. Do they know how something like that happened to be in her drink?"

Ellis, with a yearning look at the coffeepot, told her about our conversation with Kemper. "It must have been put in Idonia's cup when she set it down for a few minutes in the parlor. I think Kemper believes it was Melrose.

"Lucy Nan and I are sorry we were rude and obnoxious to you back at the hospital," she added, "but does this mean you aren't going to make us any coffee?"

When Augusta Goodnight laughs, as she did now, it clears the air like an April breeze and makes you forget, at least for a little while, your nagging little doubts and fears. "Cinnamon or vanilla? Or how about a dash of chocolate?" she asked, adding coffee to the pot. Augusta never measures and it always tastes just right.

We all agreed on chocolate and I got out mugs and plates for the apple cake Augusta had made earlier.

"I hope Bennett won't wake up and look at the time," Ellis said, helping herself to the coffee. "I phoned from the hospital and told him I'd be late, but not this late."

Augusta sat at the table across from us turning her coffee mug in her hands. "Why Melrose?" she asked.

I swallowed a forkful of apple cake. It was warm, moist, and spicy. "Why Melrose what?"

"Why does your policeman friend suspect Melrose?"

"I don't know that he *suspects* him," I said. "It's just that we really don't know much about him. Melrose was supposed to be working at the funeral home, but I guess he could've mixed in with the rest of the crowd. Maybe he wore a beard or something."

"And Idonia's locket was missing," Ellis added. "Looks to me like whoever drugged her punch did it so they could steal the locket."

"It's beginning to look that way," I said. "She's worn it all over town since she got it, and last night she seemed to think somebody was following her while we were caroling."

"Do you think we should've told Kemper about the locket in that photograph at the Tanseys?" Ellis asked.

"I thought about that, too," I said. "But we're not really sure it's the same one, and Idonia would never forgive us if we got Melrose in trouble over nothing."

Augusta fingered the stones in her necklace. "Why not ask your friend Idonia if there might be something significant *inside* the locket—something the thief might consider important? I can't imagine why Melrose DuBois would give Idonia a special piece of jewelry like that if he was going to take it back."

Ellis shrugged. "Beats me, but I suppose anyone could have done it. Idonia made a big fuss over that hot spiced cider, said she'd be back for another cup later. Several people came in after that because Idonia told them how good it was."

She stood to take her plate to the sink. "And I didn't mention this earlier because I didn't want to get him in trouble, but there was somebody else there tonight who might want Idonia's locket."

"Oh, for heaven's sake, Ellis, just tell us who!" I demanded. It was too late and I was too tired for my friend's theatrics.

"I'm surprised you didn't recognize him, Lucy Nan. He was the one who showed us where to park the car. He was all wrapped up, of course, but I'm almost sure it was Preacher Dave."

"Dave Tansey? How could you tell? It was dark and that man wore a hat pulled down over part of his face." *But if the locket really had belonged to his daughter, Dave Tansey would naturally want it back,* I thought. Louella had said it was a family keepsake.

"I recognized his voice," Ellis said. "Besides, I've seen Preacher Dave do that kind of thing before. Remember when we went to that big wedding last summer when Claudia's cousin married and they had the reception at somebody's estate? He was helping to park cars then. Guess it earns him a little extra money."

Augusta hadn't spoken during this time and now she seemed to be regarding her empty cup as if she expected to find an answer there.

"So, what are you thinking, Augusta?" I asked, preparing for her quiet words of wisdom.

"It seems to me," she said with a whisper of a smile, "that both Melrose and this Preacher Dave have got a lot of 'splainin' to do."

Augusta has been watching entirely too many *I Love Lucy* reruns.

TWELVE

"MELROSE WAS A LITTLE out of sorts that you all didn't call him last night," Idonia said when I dropped by to see her the next day. "I really believe it hurt his feelings."

After observing her all night, the doctors had dismissed her with instructions for rest and diet, so I made my customary boiled custard run and found Jo Nell there ahead of me with the same. It must be a family thing, but as soon as somebody sneezed at our house my grandmother was already heating up milk in a double boiler.

We hadn't been there long before Zee popped in with some of her chicken noodle soup and a big bottle of ginger ale. "I didn't think you'd be in the mood for spiced apple punch," she joked. Idonia didn't think it was funny.

"Where is Melrose, by the way?" Jo Nell asked. "Did you tell him about the locket?"

Idonia nodded. "No way I could keep it secret. Everybody in town probably knows it by now, and the police have been all over me like white on rice. They seem to think somebody drugged me to steal it."

"So what did he say?" I asked.

"What did who say?" Idonia sprinkled nutmeg over some of Jo Nell's custard and took a tentative taste.

"Melrose. What did he say when you told him about the locket being stolen?"

"He was most upset, of course. Wanted to hurry right over, but to tell the truth, I'm not feeling up to snuff just yet—you know, to put on makeup and all that. Besides, Nathan's due in later this afternoon. I do wish you hadn't called him, though. It nearly frightened the poor boy to death."

Idonia's "poor boy" was close to forty years old. "Of course it frightened him, Idonia," I said. "You're his mother and he loves you."

"Well, I hope he doesn't start in on my going back to Savannah with him for Christmas. I've been rehearsing with the choir since October and I'm not about to miss out on Lessons and Carols next Sunday. Besides, dress rehearsal's tomorrow night."

"Do you think you'll be strong enough for that?" Zee asked.

Idonia smiled. "I feel stronger already. This boiled custard just hits the spot, Jo Nell. What kind of extract is that?"

"Oh, I put in a little of this and a little of that," my cousin said. I knew very well she used blackberry wine but what Idonia didn't know wouldn't hurt her.

"Idonia, can you think of any reason somebody would want that locket?" I asked.

"The police asked that same question, and the answer is no. It isn't especially valuable except in a sentimental way, of course, and Melrose is as much in the dark about it as I am."

"Maybe it will turn up yet," Zee said. "I know they planned to retrace your steps at Bellawood. Could've been a faulty catch or—"

"I don't think so, Zee, or they would've found it by now." Idonia set her empty bowl aside. "I think somebody wanted that locket for a reason. Remember when I said somebody was following me when we went caroling?" She shuddered. "Every time we passed along where those big oaks are on Heritage Avenue, I felt like somebody was waiting behind them, and I could've sworn I saw somebody dodge under the limbs of that magnolia in the Dorseys' front yard."

"If they meant to snatch that locket it would've been impossible to reach it under all those wraps you had on," I said, "unless…"

"Unless they intended to grab me along with it," Idonia added.

"Remember how dark it was that night? And we were all bunched together and bundled so, who would've noticed?"

"I'm sure Nettie would," I told her, in an attempt to put her at ease. My neighbor had admitted she couldn't follow the harmony unless she was standing next to Idonia.

"Maybe it wouldn't be a bad idea for you to go home with Nathan," Jo Nell said, with a look that had *trouble* written all over it.

"Fine, if he'll wait until after the program Sunday. Now, could I have a little more of that custard, Jo Nell?" Idonia held out her bowl.

"I DON'T HAVE a good feeling about this," Jo Nell said as we walked outside together. "If I were Idonia, I'd be scared to death."

"I guess she feels that whoever drugged her cider was after the locket and not her," Zee said, "but it makes me furious to think what could've happened. I certainly hope they'll hurry and find who did it."

But *whose* family keepsake? I wondered. In all the worry and excitement of the night before, none of us had thought to relate our suspicions about Idonia's locket to the rest of The Thursdays. And I'd rather have a root canal than mention it to Idonia just yet.

"Well, I hope Nathan will put his foot down about Idonia staying here through Sunday," Jo Nell said. "I just don't think it's safe for her here."

"You know good and well Idonia's going to do what she darn well pleases," Zee said. "And what makes you think it will be any safer when she comes home after the holidays?"

AUGUSTA AND CLEMENTINE were waiting for me on the back steps when I got home, and naturally Augusta wanted to know about Idonia.

"She's doing better than I thought she would," I told her, surprised to see her waiting in the cold. "You haven't been out here all this time, have you?"

"I took another little tour of your grandmother's old home," she said, following me inside. "They've boarded up the place to discourage intruders."

"Good. As long as it didn't discourage you," I said. "Find anything interesting?"

She smiled. "It's what I *didn't* find that seems curious."

"What do you mean?"

"I believe we've all been looking in the wrong places to discover where that music is coming from," Augusta said. "Everyone's been concentrating on those cabinets in one of the front bedrooms upstairs, so I did a little experimenting to find out if they're being tampered with."

"What kind of experimenting?"

"I strung a very fine hair across the area where there might have been a panel or other opening," she explained. "It was almost invisible to the eye, and if anyone disturbed it, it's doubtful they would have noticed it."

"And did they?" I asked.

Augusta curled up on the sitting room couch and took Clementine's head in her lap. "It hasn't been touched," she said.

"But where else could it be? It has to be coming from somewhere."

"I don't know," Augusta said, "but I intend to find out. I'm not ready to toss in the dishrag yet!"

"Uh-huh," I said, as her meaning sank in. "And where did you learn about that clever little experiment?"

"I have my sources," she said, reaching for the TV remote. "If there's nothing you want to watch right now, I really should catch up on my exercising. I'm afraid I've been remiss all week. Do you mind getting it started for me?"

"Of course not," I said, feeling a slight twinge of guilt for my own slackness in that area. Augusta had learned to insert a videotape, but she has yet to master the DVD, which she referred to as BVDs until Ellis told her that was an old-fashioned term for men's underwear.

I left her there, bending and swaying as gracefully as a ballet dancer to the tune of that old song, "The Continental," and went upstairs to change. Ben was picking me up for dinner in less than an hour and I hoped I wouldn't fall asleep at the table after getting to bed so late the night before.

I showered quickly, smiling as I thought of Augusta's method of detecting, learned, no doubt, from one of the many mysteries she'd read, and of her funny, upside-down expressions, and I wished I could share them with Ben.

Later, over dinner, I did tell him what Claudia had observed of the photograph in the Tanseys' living room. "The same pearls were missing in the locket their daughter wore as in the one Melrose gave Idonia," I said.

Ben hesitated with his coffee cup halfway to his mouth. "Surely you don't think the man gave Idonia the jewelry then drugged her to steal it back."

"Zee told me she heard his alibi checked out," I said. "Al Evans said Melrose was helping him at the funeral home until after ten o'clock. Idonia was already deep in 'la-la land' by then, but somebody did it, Ben. They did it deliberately."

His hand reached for mine across the table. "My God, it might've been you, Lucy Nan."

"I don't think so," I said. "I wasn't wearing the locket. Idonia thinks somebody was following her the night we went caroling…somebody who wanted that locket!"

During dinner I had toyed with the pork tenderloin, a favorite of mine, and then refused an offer of dessert. The red carnation in a bud vase on the table began to blur in front of my eyes and the room seemed much too hot.

Ben called for the check. "Time to get you home. Guess I shouldn't have ordered that wine."

"And tired as I am, I should've had better sense than to drink it." Thankfully, I let him help me with my coat and practically crawled into the passenger seat of the car. Afterward, at home in bed, I remembered something else I meant to tell him. I was going to ask Ben if he thought I should mention to the police about Preacher Dave being at Bellawood the night before.

I wasn't surprised when Idonia showed up at dress rehearsal for *Lessons and Carols* the next night looking, as my grand-daddy used to say, like she'd been jerked through a knothole backward. Nathan had personally escorted her into the church and promised to return for her as soon as rehearsal was over.

"He's going to stay with me tonight, then come back for the service on Sunday," she told us, beaming. "And Sara and Millicent are coming, too!" Sara and Millicent are Nathan's wife and teenaged daughter who, much to Idonia's distress, rarely visit Stone's Throw, so at least something positive came of our friend's ordeal.

Although we customarily wear black choir robes, Cissy Sullivan, our choir director, had decided white would be more fitting for the occasion and the small choir room was filled with the flurry of flapping sleeves as we tried them on.

"I look like Moby Dick in drag," Nettie whispered as she studied her reflection in the mirror. "I'm sure angels don't look anything like this."

Ellis looked at me and grinned. "I think you can take that to the bank," she agreed, which naturally reminded me of Augusta and what she had suggested the night before.

"Has anyone thought to ask Idonia if she looked inside the locket her friend gave her?" I asked. "Somebody might be after what's *in* the locket instead of the locket itself."

It hadn't, of course, because up until the night we discovered it missing, most of us admired it for what it was—an interesting piece of jewelry and a thoughtful token of affection. After that, Idonia's alarming experience at the hospital and our concern for her welfare took precedence over everything else.

I had promised Augusta I would ask Idonia at the first opportunity, and that opportunity was now. I found her sitting at the back of the alto section studying her music. "I hope I can still hit that low F," she said, looking up. "My throat's still a little froggy."

"Just fake it," I said. "Who's to know?"

She made a face. "Cissy."

She was right, of course. Our choir director can zoom in on a false note as if she has built-in radar.

I sat beside her. "Idonia, do you mind telling me what was inside that locket Melrose gave you? It might have something to do with why it was taken."

She shook her head. "I don't see why. It was just an old picture, a photograph of a man and woman. Looked like it might've been made back in the twenties sometime. It was rather sweet, really. Melrose said they were his grandparents."

"Was there anything else?"

"No. I don't know why there should be."

"I don't suppose you've heard anything more about it," I said.

"Nothing encouraging, and Lucy Nan, the police have even been questioning poor Melrose—as if he might have something to do with it. Can you imagine? The man wasn't even there that night!"

"I guess they have to cover all their bases," I said. "I'm sure he understands."

At that moment we were interrupted by Cissy banging several loud chords on the piano, our signal to take our places, and we spent the next hour or so going over the music for the following Sunday.

When Cissy was more or less satisfied we were as good as we were going to get, we were told to line up to rehearse the processional.

"I wish we didn't have to process," Zee complained as we walked through the Fellowship Hall and up the stairs to the back of the sanctuary. "Cissy always puts me between two sopranos and I can't hear my notes."

"That's called harmony," Ellis reminded her as we lined up to process. Ellis, one of our stronger sopranos, took her place to lead us down the center aisle to the choir loft in the front of the church, and I stepped in line between Idonia, an alto, and R. G. Strickland, a tenor, and tried to remember to start off on the left foot—and the right note.

Large white candles in feathery wreaths of evergreens were arranged beneath the stained-glass windows on both sides of the sanctuary and a graceful swag of magnolia leaves intertwined with burgundy and gold ribbon scalloped the choir loft behind the pulpit. I thought of all the Christmases the century-old building had marked, of faithful hands, long gone, that had decorated as we still did with magnolia, holly, and pine; of voices, silent now, that filled the church with praise and song. The place smelled of dust and candle wax and cedar, and a little of the spicy scent of R. G. Strickland's aftershave, and I basked in the warmth of just being there.

I knew Augusta planned to attend the service Sunday and was looking forward to the music. I hoped she wouldn't be disappointed.

Cissy took her place at the great pipe organ and the first few bars of "Hark the Herald Angels Sing" resounded through the empty sanctuary. I felt a thrill as I always do at the joy and excitement of it and took a deep breath to begin.

Ahead of me Idonia took one step into the sanctuary. *Glory to the newborn King!* we sang. And then somebody screamed.

It had to be a soprano because it was shrill enough to shatter glass, and it seemed to go on forever.

And—oh, God, it was Ellis!

THIRTEEN

HAD SOMETHING HAPPENED to Ellis? I pushed my way down the aisle through a flock of white-robed choir members to find a knot of people hovering over something or someone in the center of one of the back pews.

"Is she breathing? Let me through!" Margaret Moss demanded, and we parted like a billowing white sea. Margaret has been Glen Smiley's nurse for as long as he's been in practice and we meekly bowed to her authority. I saw Ellis's face as she stepped aside to make room for her and if she hadn't blinked, I'd have thought it was carved in marble.

"She's not moving." Zee reached out a tentative hand.

Who's not moving? I couldn't see over the snowy mountain of shoulders.

"Don't touch her! Somebody call nine-one-one!" Margaret barked, and I maneuvered my way to a pew in front of her to see the nurse feel for a pulse on a limp wrist. Behind me I heard Cissy calling for help on her cell phone. Margaret soon abandoned the wrist and began CPR by breathing into the patient's mouth. It wasn't until she tilted the injured person's head back that I saw who was lying on the pew in such a twisted manner. It was Opal Henshaw!

Jo Nell crowded against my shoulder. "Oh, my goodness! What happened? She's not dead, is she?"

By the way Margaret, her face set in a grim expression, continued with her chest compressions, I thought it very likely that was the case.

White-faced, Cissy hurried toward us. "The rescue squad

is on the way," she said, and then caught sight of poor Opal knotted pretzel-like in the pew. "Dear God in heaven! What happened to Opal?"

Ellis glanced at the balcony above us. "She must've fallen from the balcony. You know how she is about having everything just so. The swag up there is way off-center. Opal probably went up there to put it right."

"But it was perfect yesterday when I was here going over the music," Cissy said. "Opal was putting on the finishing touches and she seemed pleased with everything then."

"Do you suppose somebody moved it?" Jo Nell asked in a small voice.

Why would anyone do that? No one spoke it aloud but I could guess what the others were thinking. Although Opal Henshaw wasn't well liked, I couldn't imagine why anyone would wish her dead.

Nettie turned away from Margaret's attempts at resuscitation. "That's a long way to fall. If only Opal had just left well enough alone! She probably went up there to make one last adjustment and lost her balance—bless her heart."

"Looks like it was her last adjustment, all right," Zee muttered.

"Isn't she breathing *yet*, Margaret?" somebody asked, breaking what seemed like eons of silence. But Margaret didn't answer.

In one of the pews across the aisle I saw Opal's familiar green jacket and the large wicker basket she usually carried that contained extra ribbon, tape, wire, and scissors among other items used for decorating.

Somewhere somebody started to cry and I moved as far away as I could get and sat near the front of the church. My legs gave about as much support as those pine boughs in the window and I didn't feel so pert myself.

"Maybe we should pray," Jo Nell suggested. That made

sense to me, but at the sound of the approaching EMTs Margaret looked up and bellowed for us to clear out and wait in the choir room.

"POOR OPAL!" Ellis sighed, plopping down beside me. "I can't imagine how helpless she must have felt when she fell."

"She was usually so careful," Cissy said. "Opal always had someone with her when she was decorating the balcony. It doesn't make sense that she would go up there and try to adjust things on her own."

"Who?" Ellis asked.

Cissy frowned. "Who what?"

"Who was with her when she hung the swag in the balcony?"

"Oh…different people." Cissy paused for a minute. "This time I believe it was Preacher Dave."

"Opal's seemed a bit despondent since Virgil passed away so suddenly from that heart attack last summer," Idonia said. "You don't suppose she—"

Zee pulled off her choir robe and tossed it over the back of a chair. "If Opal Henshaw wanted to kill herself, I doubt if she'd jump from the church balcony.

"Besides," she whispered, "everybody knows that sorry husband of hers flirted with every woman in Stone's Throw. She had to have known it, too."

"Virgil Henshaw was annoying, but harmless," I said. "Still, I doubt if Opal would deliberately end her life over him."

"At least not until she'd straightened that lopsided swag," Ellis said.

Jo Nell dug in her purse for a tissue to stem her tears. "I don't see how you all can be so catty and hateful with poor Opal squashed like a melon out there in our own church—and right here at Christmas, too!" And she blew her nose with a loud blast.

Cissy sat facing us on the piano bench, her cell phone still open in her hand. Now she flipped it shut. "She used a cane," she announced. "Opal used a cane."

I had never noticed her needing one. "I didn't know she'd been injured," I said.

"No, no! I mean she sometimes used a cane to reach down from the balcony and center the swag on the hooks," Cissy said. "That was how she made adjustments without having to lean over so far."

"Then where is it?" Nettie asked.

"Maybe we should look for it," Idonia suggested. "Not that it matters now."

Margaret came in a few minutes later to tell us the medics hadn't been able to save Opal Henshaw. "Her neck was broken. They said she'd probably been dead several minutes before we found her." Margaret shook her head and eased into a chair on the first row. "I was afraid of that all along, but I had to try... I just had to try."

We all sat silently for a while, not knowing what to do or say, and I, for one, was depressed. *What would Augusta do?*

Tea, of course. In emergencies like this one, Augusta would brew hot, bracing tea. We kept a large electric percolator and a supply of coffee and tea bags in the choir closet. At least I could do that much. I rose abruptly and almost stumbled over Ellis's feet.

"Where are you going?" she said.

"To make tea, of course."

"Good," Margaret said. "We had to notify the police about Opal, and I look for them any minute. I expect we'll be here for a while."

"What about Opal?" I asked. I would never be able to look at that pew again without thinking of Opal Henshaw's unfortunate tumble.

"Well, they couldn't move her yet—not until the police get here," Margaret said. "We had to leave her where she fell."

"I don't suppose you noticed a cane?" Cissy said, explaining about Opal's method of decorating from the balcony.

Margaret nodded solemnly. "You're right. I've seen her use that, too, but I didn't notice it anywhere around. I think she usually keeps it in that little alcove behind the last pew in the balcony."

A couple of the other choir members who had served on the decorating committee with Opal said they, too, had seen her put the cane away in there.

Then why hadn't she used it today?

I was dismayed a few minutes later to hear the grating voice of Stone's Throw's Police Chief Elmer Harris, and the irritating squeaking of his shoes as he approached from the hallway outside the choir room. Thank goodness Ed Tillman, a childhood friend of Roger's and a lieutenant in the Stone's Throw police, came along as well.

"Miss Lucy Nan, Miss Ellis, Miss Nettie," Ed began, acknowledging most of us by name, "why don't we step into the classroom next door for a few minutes while Chief Harris talks to some of the others?"

We clamored to follow him, leaving the chief to growl his questions to the remaining choir members. And I must admit, Ed didn't seem at all surprised to see us there.

As Ed made notes, Ellis began by telling him how she had first discovered Opal's body, when she led the procession down the aisle.

"And prior to this, did any of you see or hear anyone in the balcony or anywhere else in that area?" Ed asked, pausing in his scribbling.

"I guess we were so busy rehearsing—and talking, too," Jo Nell admitted, "we probably wouldn't have heard anyone if they'd been there." She frowned. "Why? Surely you don't think somebody *pushed* Opal from that balcony, do you?"

"For heaven's sake, Jo Nell, he's just being thorough," Zee said. "I mean, I suppose you have to cover all possibilities, don't you, Ed? And I for one find it the tiniest bit peculiar that nobody's seen hide nor hair of that cane Opal used!"

Ed, of course, was not aware of the cane or its purpose, and everyone tried to explain it to him at once until he insisted, rather sharply I thought, that we speak one at a time, and then only when called upon.

After Ed was satisfied with our answers, we were told to wait in the choir room while he and Chief Harris searched the balcony and the sanctuary for any sign of the missing cane. Meanwhile, we were relieved to learn that Opal Crenshaw's body had been removed.

"This is awful!" Ellis said as we sat sipping a second cup of tea. "It's hard to believe this is really happening."

Zee groaned. "Leave it to Opal to take all the joy out of Christmas."

"I'm sure she didn't die on purpose, Zee," Jo Nell said. "But at least she's gone to a better place."

I supposed that was true; at least I hoped it was, but to tell the truth, I couldn't think of a better place than Stone's Throw, South Carolina. I had been raised in this church and Charlie and I were married here, as were my parents and grandparents before me, and now Opal Henshaw had gone and bashed herself in the very pew where my great-aunt Edith and great-uncle Davis had worshipped for at least forty years.

Finishing my tea, I was startled by the sudden racket of three loud chords on the piano. "Come on, everybody and take your seats," Cissy directed. "We might as well use this time to go over the music."

We had just finished the "The Cherry Tree Carol," our third selection, when Chief Harris squeaked back to announce they had been unable to find Opal's cane.

"Could this be it?" Hugh Dan Thompson, our baritone solo-ist, returned from the men's room just then waving a wooden walking stick with spiral carving.

"Sure looks like the one," Cissy said. "Where did you find it?"

"It was propped behind the john in the men's room." Hugh Dan passed the stick along to the chief. "I remember Virgil Henshaw using this cane or one like it when he had that knee surgery a few years back," he said. "This must be the one Opal kept in the balcony."

Chief Harris turned the cane in his hands. "Then what in tarnation was it doing in the men's room?"

"Looks to me like somebody didn't want Opal to find it," Nettie said.

"IDONIA'S BEEN AWFULLY quiet," Jo Nell said as we hung up our choir robes before leaving. "I wonder if she's feeling all right."

"I saw her go into the restroom a little while ago," I said. "Maybe I'd better go and check on her."

Only a couple of days ago Idonia had been close to literally sleeping her life away, and for all I knew she might have passed out in there. I hurried down the hallway and pushed open the door of the ladies' room, dreading what I might find. Our church had recently benefited from improvements to our kitchen and bathroom facilities and as a result just about everything in the ladies' room was mauve. I found Idonia sitting in the room's one upholstered chair, a somber figure against a floral pattern of mauve and green, clutching her pocketbook on her lap. She looked as if she'd been told to make her own funeral arrangements and not to take too long about it.

"Idonia, what's going on? Are you all right?" When I drew closer I noticed the tearstains on her face. "Do you want me to call Nathan?"

She looked up at me with eyes as bleak as the dark December sky. "I don't know what to do, Lucy Nan. I just don't know what to do."

"About what?" I knelt beside her and took her hand. It was

cool and trembled at my touch. "Idonia, I'm afraid this has all been too much for you. You'll feel better when you get home where you can rest." I wondered if there was any hot water left in the percolator. "Do you think you might be able to get down some tea?"

She shook her head and threw aside my hand. "There's nothing wrong with me! It's not that—I'm fine."

"Then what?" I stood and rubbed the cramp in my leg. She didn't seem fine to me.

"It's... well, it's Melrose."

"What about Melrose?" I wet some paper towels and passed them along to her. "Here, maybe you'll feel better if you wipe your face. I really think you're trying to do too much too soon, Idonia."

She accepted the towels and made a couple of token dabs. "He was here. I saw him."

"Melrose? When?"

"Earlier, when we first got here. I saw him leaving as Nathan and I were walking into the building, and I thought maybe he'd come to watch us rehearse and changed his mind." Idonia wadded up the paper towels and aimed them at the trash can. She missed. "I called to him, but he didn't answer. Pretended like he didn't even see me."

"Maybe he didn't," I said.

"You should've seen him, Lucy Nan. He couldn't get away from us fast enough." Grim-faced, Idonia looked up at me. "And what in the world was he doing here in the first place?"

FOURTEEN

AUGUSTA WAS WAITING up when I got home.

"I kind of halfway expected you to drop in on rehearsal," I told her.

She smiled. "I'd rather wait and be surprised."

"You would've been surprised all right if you'd been there tonight," I said, and told her what had happened to Opal Henshaw.

Augusta's hand went immediately to her necklace, which caught the light from the fire, and I felt as if I could lose myself in its shimmering twilight depth.

"And how is Idonia?" she asked, setting down a tray with two glasses and a bottle of red wine.

"Close to being a basket case, I'm afraid." I poured a glass for both of us and took a sip. It tasted of wood smoke and cherries and late summer sun—not at all like the inexpensive wine I usually buy at the supermarket, although the label was the same. "Why did you ask about Idonia?" I said.

"Because this all seems to center around her." Augusta's loose garment trailed the floor as she sat on the hassock, glass in hand. "Think about it, Lucy Nan: Idonia's gentleman friend, Mr. DuBois, is living in Opal Henshaw's home. The locket he gave her, which may or may not have belonged to the Tanseys' daughter, has been stolen and Idonia drugged. Now Opal herself has been killed." She paused to study the contents of her glass, turning it so that it, too, caught the fire's light. "But that's not where the trouble began." Augusta looked up at me as if she expected an explanation.

"I suppose it began at Willowbrook when that vagrant fell

from the balcony," I said, "but I don't see how that could possibly have anything to do with Idonia."

Augusta went to the kitchen and returned with a small plate of gingersnaps. Now she broke one in two, gave part of it to Clementine and ate the other.

"Now, why did you do that, Augusta?" I asked. "You're always telling me not to feed her and you've gone and broken your own rule. Clementine will be begging all night."

Augusta laughed. "No, she won't, will you, Clementine? Be a good girl now and lie down."

The dog did as she was told without so much as a beseeching look.

Augusta took another cookie and passed the plate to me. Clementine put a paw over her eyes and whimpered but she didn't move. Augusta ignored her.

"I'm afraid your friend, however innocent, has been caught up in a dangerous web of wickedness and deceit," she said.

"Idonia had nothing to do with whatever's going on!" I said. "And now Opal Henshaw's death has everybody scared. I'm worried, Augusta. I'm beginning to think this Melrose DuBois isn't all he's cracked up to be. Idonia admitted she saw him leaving the church tonight before Opal fell from the balcony…and frankly, we're not all that sure Opal's death was an accident." I told Augusta where the missing cane was found.

"Still," she said, "we have to consider the possibility that Mr. DuBois might have had other reasons for being there. Perhaps he only wanted to hear the choir rehearse."

"Then why didn't he stay? And why did he pretend he didn't see Idonia when she called to him?" I shook my head. "No, I think there's something fishy going on there, and I'm afraid poor Idonia's going to be the one who pays for it."

"You said the police were there tonight. Did she mention this to them?"

"You see…that's another thing. She admitted that she didn't, and now she's all upset for keeping quiet about it," I said.

Augusta cupped her wineglass in both hands. "There must have been other people about as well," she said.

"Zee said she saw Preacher Dave cleaning in one of the Sunday school rooms, but that's not unusual. He often works there at night and had been helping Opal with the decorations earlier. Chief Harris was talking with him when we left."

"Preacher Dave...his daughter wore an identical locket in that photograph on the Tanseys' piano..." Augusta sat quietly for a while, wondering, no doubt how Miss Jane Marple or Hercule Poirot would approach the situation. "Do you think the authorities believe Opal Henshaw's death was deliberate?"

"It looks that way," I told her. "And so do I."

"It would help," she said, "if we knew more about the man who was killed out at Oakcreek."

"Huh?" Maybe I had missed something.

"Your family home. Isn't that what you call it?"

I laughed. "I think you mean Willowbrook. And I agree it all seems to stem from what happened there. The police aren't talking, but I'll see if I can't get Weigelia to find out if Kemper knows any more about it."

"Do you know where the Tanseys lived before they came here?" Augusta asked.

"No, but I can find out," I said. "The deacons are in charge of buildings and grounds so I'm sure they did some kind of back-ground check before they hired Preacher Dave to fill in for Luther. Claudia's husband Brian is on the Board of Deacons. I'll give him a call tomorrow." I yawned. "Right now I'm going to bed...and you might as well go ahead and give Clementine that other gingersnap you have in your hand. I know you're going to do it as soon as I leave the room."

Augusta only smiled.

"LUCY NAN, TELL ME it isn't true about Opal falling from the balcony!" Claudia called the next morning before I had a chance to finish my first cup of coffee. "You were at choir rehearsal last night, weren't you? I heard Ellis was the one who found her."

"The answer is yes to all of that," I said. "Are you still at home? I was going to call Brian later to ask if he might have any information on where the Tanseys lived before they came here."

"I'm just getting ready to leave, but Brian's in the shower. I'll tell him to give you a call." Claudia works several days a week in the dean's office at Sarah Bedford, our local college. "Oh, Lord, Lucy Nan! Do you think this has anything to do with what happened to Idonia and the locket the Tanseys' daughter wore in that picture? And I know I should feel awful about the things I said about Opal Henshaw, but I can't help it. I just plain didn't like her!"

"I don't guess we're supposed to like everybody, Claudia. And let's face it, Opal didn't make it easy."

"Have you talked with Idonia this morning?" Claudia asked. "I called a little while ago to see if she was okay, and she wouldn't give me the time of day. Sounded pretty upset."

I didn't doubt it. "I'll check on her later," I said. "And don't forget to ask Brian to give me a call."

I WAS PUTTING AWAY the breakfast dishes when Brian phoned a little later. "That was quite a shock about Opal Henshaw," he began. "Police have been questioning Preacher Dave, I hear, and I understand he's kind of upset."

"I can see why," I said. "This has shaken everybody up. Brian, weren't you on the committee that hired him when Luther fell and broke his hip? Do you happen to remember where the Tanseys lived before?"

"You'll have to ask your cousin about that, Lucy Nan. The family was already living out there on his property when he came with us. I do remember he gave us a written recommendation, though, from some little place in Georgia."

"Do you know where it was?"

"No, but it's in the files. I can look it up, or you can ask Frances."

Frances Smith was secretary of the diaconate and one of the few people I knew who wouldn't be embarrassed if she were hit by a bus and strangers came to poke about in her refrigerator.

"Sure," Frances said, when I phoned her at home a few minutes later. "I remember exactly where Preacher's from because it's such a peculiar name for a town. He comes from a little place in Georgia called Soso—worked for a lumberyard there." She paused. "I suppose you were at the church last night when they found poor Opal. Preacher Dave's all torn up about it. Blames himself for not going up in the balcony to help her, and from what I hear, that idiot Elmer Harris isn't making him feel any better grilling him like he did."

I agreed with Frances's opinion of Stone's Throw's police chief, but I didn't think it was out of line to question anyone who might have been in the church when Opal was killed. "He was probably in another part of the building when that happened," I said. "Preacher Dave shouldn't feel guilty about something he couldn't help."

Unless he had reason, I thought.

Augusta began looking up Soso in the encyclopedia as soon as I got off the phone. "I wonder why they named it Soso," I said, looking over her shoulder. "Guess they decided it wasn't all that great, but it wasn't too bad, either—just soso."

"Here it is, right below Milledgeville. Is that very far from here?" Augusta held a finger in place on the map.

"If we started early we could probably make it in a day," I said. "I'll ask Roger to drop by and let Clementine out while we're gone, but first I want to see if Weigelia's learned any more from Kemper."

But Weigelia Jones was more interested in what she could learn from me.

"What about that Henshaw woman they say fell from you-all's balcony?" she bellowed. "Sounds like somebody done pushed her to me!"

I told her I suspected pretty much the same thing and had she managed to learn from Kemper any more about the dead man we found out at Willowbrook.

"I believe I'm gonna be staying away from any balconies," she said. "Getting to be downright dangerous if you ask me—bodies falling all over the place! Why you so bent on knowing 'bout that man?"

"I have my reasons," I said. "Just tell me, Weigelia. Do they know what he was doing there or not?"

"Not," she said. "Kemper did say somebody had seen him on a motorcycle when he stopped at a convenience store somewhere in North Carolina the day before he was killed, but ain't no motorcycle turned up around here." She frowned. "That's all I know. Besides, I don't think I'd tell you if I did know anything more. And don't you and those Thursdays you run around with go poking your noses where you got no business! It would just plumb ruin my Christmas if I had to go to your funeral this week!"

I thanked her for her thoughtful concern and promised to remain upright and breathing.

It was a little after nine before Augusta and I got on our way, and we had been on the road for about an hour before I remembered I had meant to go by and check on Idonia.

"You brought that funny little folding telephone along, didn't you?" Augusta said. "I happen to have a Thermos of hot chocolate, and my strawberry muffins are still warm. Why don't we stop up there on the other side of that bridge and you can call her?"

Augusta is fascinated by the tiny size of cell phones but I can't get her to use one to call me. She says her fingers are too big. "My old friend Mr. Bell would be amazed if he could see what has come of his fascinating invention!" she'd exclaimed when she first saw one.

"You mean Alexander Graham Bell?" I said.

"The very same."

"You *knew* Alexander Graham Bell, the inventor of the telephone?"

"And why ever not? That gentleman had his problems the same as everyone else. More than his share, in fact." Augusta got almost testy.

"You've never mentioned that before," I reminded her.

"I don't like to brag," she said.

THIS MORNING THE IDEA of hot chocolate and muffins sounded tempting and it *had* been a long time since breakfast. I parked under a large pine tree in a grassy area beside the road and punched in Idonia's number while Augusta poured steaming chocolate into two Christmas mugs. It smelled wonderful!

The phone rang four times before she answered, and Idonia's voice sounded muffled.

"Are you all right?" I said. "I'm worried about you, Idonia. Did you get any sleep last night?"

"Not much," she said. Or at least I think that's what she said.

"Is Nathan still there?"

"Had to leave for some kind of meeting," she said. "No reason for him to stay anyway."

I took a sip of chocolate. And then another. "I don't guess you've spoken with the police."

That was met with silence. "Idonia," I said, "why don't you just phone Melrose and talk with him about this instead of letting it worry you this way? I'm sure he must've had a reason for being at the church last night."

"Can't. He's gone." If a voice were a color, Idonia's would've been black.

"Gone? Gone where?"

"I don't know, Lucy Nan. The police were here asking about him earlier. Somebody told them they saw him leaving the church last night. They couldn't find him at Opal's and Al Evans said he hasn't seen him since yesterday."

This didn't sound good. "I'm going to call Ellis," I told her, "so don't do anything until you hear from her. And, Idonia? Lock your doors!"

"We might have to turn around and go back home," I said as I explained the situation to Augusta. "I don't like leaving Idonia alone, and if I can't reach Ellis or one of the other Thursdays, we'll have to leave Soso for another day."

But Ellis picked up on the first ring. "North Pole," she said. I could hear carols playing in the background.

"You sound awfully chipper after your gruesome discovery last night. What are you doing?"

"I know. I'm awful, aren't I? But everybody's coming here for Christmas and I'm getting ready to make Susan's favorite cookies…I found the prettiest little Christmas dress for Beth, and that game she's been asking for…and, oh, blast it, Lucy Nan, don't ask me not to be merry! I'm not letting Opal Henshaw ruin the holidays for me!"

I laughed. Ellis's granddaughter, Beth, was almost seven and her daughter, Susan, was expecting her second child, a boy, the first of the year. "Do you think you might share some of that Christmas cheer with Idonia?" I told her about Melrose's conspicuous absence.

"That little jerk! Don't worry, I'll get her over here if I have to drag her, and I'll call Zee and Jo Nell, too. Good excuse to bring out the wine."

"You know Idonia doesn't drink wine," I reminded her.

"Well, maybe it's time she started." The music in the background shifted into secular with "Santa Claus Is Coming to Town." "Say, what are you and Augusta up to anyway? Where are you, Lucy Nan?"

"Tell you when we get back," I said, and helped myself to a muffin.

"Idonia will be in good hands with The Thursdays," I told

Augusta, "but we'd better get a move on if we plan to get to Soso and back in one day."

She packed the remaining muffins away. "I do hope we're not just running around in pursuit of wild ducks," she said.

FIFTEEN

Augusta drew in her breath sharply as we drove through a small country crossroads before turning onto Interstate 26. "Dear heavens, what is that?" she asked, staring at a large looming figure in one of the yards to our right.

I laughed. "An inflatable snowman," I said. "It's made out of vinyl."

"Why?" Augusta continued to look over her shoulder as we passed.

"It's a Christmas decoration," I explained. "See, here's a big Santa on the lawn up ahead."

"My goodness." Augusta sighed, and adjusting her cape about her shoulders, took needlework from her huge tapestry bag to begin working what can only be described as magic. I glanced at her from time to time to see what looked like a winter landscape emerging as she drew threads in glorious colors in and out of the fabric. I've never seen her use a pattern nor have to remove a stitch.

I turned the radio to a station that featured semi classical holiday music and Augusta turned up the heater. Almost every house we passed had some token of the season: wreaths on doors, swags along fences, mailboxes decorated with evergreens and red ribbon. If our trip to Soso had been for some other reason, I would have felt positively festive, but in spite of The Thursdays and all their TLC, I couldn't help worrying about Idonia. Someone had deliberately shoved Opal from that balcony, and if they felt it necessary, I didn't think they would hesitate to kill again.

"Oh, dear," Augusta moaned when we turned onto Interstate

85 at Spartanburg, South Carolina. It was as close to complaining as she would allow herself and I knew she preferred to observe the scenery from the smaller side roads but today we needed to reach our destination as quickly as possible.

"They have good barbecue in Georgia," I told her. "We'll stop somewhere for lunch."

Augusta perked up considerably. "And Brunswick stew?"

Barbecue and Brunswick stew are two of Augusta's favorite things. "Of course," I assured her. "Where do you think Brunswick stew got its start?"

But it took longer than I had remembered to reach the state line and by the time we crossed Lake Hartwell into Georgia it was after one o'clock and my stomach was growling. "If you can wait until we turn off at Commerce," I told Augusta, "there used to be a good place to eat between there and Athens."

She looked up briefly from her needlework. "I'm not the one with the noisy stomach," she said.

Less than an hour later I turned onto Highway 441 and hurriedly purchased our late lunch to go at a place called Pig in a Poke, eating my barbecue sandwich as I drove. The two of us rode in companionable silence as we passed the little towns of Madison and Eatonton before branching out onto the two-lane road that would eventually take us to Soso. On either side of the road, winter-bare trees stretched dark limbs against a gray sky, and now and again a strong wind swept dry brown leaves across the road in front of us. In the pasture on our left, white-faced cattle huddled together, looking up to stare as we passed by. I glanced at my watch to find it was three-fourteen. Soon we would lose daylight and a storm was coming up.

"Here! Turn left!" Augusta suddenly directed, pointing to a sign a few miles down the road. "Soso must be over this way."

"Don't blink," I said a few minutes later as we came into a smattering of stores and houses scattered along both sides of the road.

"Why not?" Augusta asked.

I laughed. "It's just an expression. It means the place is so small, if you blink you might miss it."

Augusta didn't answer. Her attention seemed to be fixed on something on the opposite side of the street and she turned to look back as we drove past.

"What is it? Did you see any sign of the lumberyard?"

She shook her head. "No, it's just that for a minute I thought—"

"Thought what?"

"It's nothing, really." Augusta waved her elegant hand. "Now what are we supposed to be looking for?"

"We need to find the lumberyard. Sandy said Preacher Dave had a recommendation from a man named Martin Shackelford of Shackelfords' Lumber."

"Perhaps we should ask—" Augusta suggested.

"No need. Can't you smell it?" The pungent scent of raw pine and sawdust grew stronger as we came to the end of the third block. "There it is, just down the road on the right."

"It appears to be closed," Augusta said as we drew up in front of a head-high chain-link fence. "The gate's locked."

I parked and got out of the car to see if I could find a sign of life, but the only living being I aroused was a mutt about half as big and ten times more ferocious-sounding than Clementine, which came bounding out, teeth barred. This dog was not in a good mood. I backed quickly away.

"Come now, we're not here to harm you…that's a good fellow." Augusta spoke calmly from somewhere behind me and the dog grew quiet and sat, tail thumping. He seemed to be smiling.

"Well, I'll be doggone! I ain't seen nothin' like that since Christ was a corporal!"

I turned to find a middle-aged man in sweat-stained overalls and a John Deere cap approaching from across the street. He snatched off the cap as he drew nearer. "Old Skeeter here must've taken a likin' to you, ma'am. He acts like he's gonna eat most folks fer supper."

I smiled and introduced myself. He couldn't see Augusta, of course. "I was hoping to speak with a Mr. Shackelford. Martin Shackelford. Do you know where I might find him?"

He scratched his head before replacing the cap. "I reckon he's done gone on over to the church. Tonight's the Christmas covered dish and Martin always helps them set up fer it. We've done closed for the day, but if there's anything I can help you with, ma'am, name's Buster—Buster Shackelford. I'm Martin's cousin."

We shook hands. "Our church has hired a sexton who, I understand, used to work here, and I just wanted to get some information about his background," I said. "Maybe you knew him—Dave Tansey?"

He frowned. "Don't know as I did, but I haven't been back long. Just retired from the army last summer, and it sure is good to be home!" He grabbed his hat as the wind picked up. "It's a-fixin' to come up a pretty bad storm, and we need to get out of this weather. Why don't you come on over to Aunt Eula's where we can talk without gettin' wet?" He pointed to the house across the street.

WHAT WAS I going to do? I hated to turn around and go home after having come this far. "Is there any place I can stay tonight?" I asked. "Maybe I can come back and speak with your cousin tomorrow."

"Lord, don't you worry none about that! I'll bet you could use a good hot cup of coffee about now and Aunt Eula always keeps a pot on. She just took her lemonade cake out of the oven, too, and I reckon she might even spare us a piece." And with that Buster Shackelford turned and started back across the street, expecting me to follow. As I stood there wondering what to do, a large woman in a big pink apron waved to me from the porch and motioned for me to come on over, so I did. Augusta, I noticed, followed at a distance.

As soon as I introduced myself and began explaining the purpose of my visit, Aunt Eula whisked me into the kitchen, sat me at the table, and served me coffee in a mug with gingerbread men painted on it. "My grandson did that in kindergarten," she said proudly. "Harry's almost seven now."

I told her I had one the same age and we became instant friends. The coffee was almost as good as Augusta's and not only was the cake warm, moist, and tangy, but the slice she gave me could have fed the entire state of Georgia. Augusta, I noticed, lingered in the doorway with a pitiful look of yearning, and I knew she was practically tasting that cake and coffee, but there wasn't a thing I could do about it. When Aunt Eula wasn't looking I broke off a good-sized chunk of cake, wrapped it in a paper napkin, and stuck it in my purse.

Buster finished his cake in double time, washed it down with coffee, and helped himself to another cup. "Bet you never tasted cake as good as this," he said, and I took one look at Augusta and said it was even better than my mother made. I'll bet my mother hasn't made a cake from scratch in thirty years, and even then they weren't anything to brag about.

"I hate to intrude on your family at a busy time like this," I said to my hostess, "but I was trying to get some information on a man who was hired to fill in temporarily with maintenance at our church. His name is David Tansey but everybody calls him Preacher Dave."

"Oh, sure, I knew Preacher Dave, but they lived out a good ways and we didn't see a whole lot of him in town—at least I didn't, but I think he was a good, hard worker over at the lumberyard. I never heard anything against him. It was sad, though, about their daughter. Dinah was a friend of Carolyn, our youngest, and such a pretty girl."

The chair creaked as Aunt Eula plopped down beside me. "Lord, it's good to take a load off! Been on my feet all day."

She fanned herself with the bright apron. "Made two chicken pies, two pecan pies, that lemonade cake, and a couple of loaves of dilly bread, and honey, I'm about done in!"

I told her I could certainly understand why. "Your daughter Carolyn," I said, "does she live nearby?"

"Oh, honey, I wish she did! Carolyn and her husband moved to Florida last year, but they'll be here for Christmas. They have the sweetest little girl now—just learning to walk, and we just can't wait to see her!"

I said I didn't blame them, thanked her for the refreshments, and rose to go. I wanted to ask her more about the Tanseys' daughter, but I could see this wasn't the time. "I really must go, but do you think it will be all right with your cousin Martin if I come back and talk with him in the morning?" I asked Buster.

"Go? Go where?" Aunt Eula clamped a big red hand on my arm. "You gotta eat somewhere, honey, and you're not going to find anything half as good in one of those fancy restaurants in Milledgeville or Macon as what we'll be serving up tonight. And then, you'll *have* to stay for the pageant afterward. Our Harry's one of the wise men."

Now, how could I refuse an offer like that? I glanced at Augusta, who waved a few fingers and disappeared.

It was beginning to rain when I went across the street and moved my car into the Shackelfords' backyard. Augusta joined me there and I gave her the cake I'd saved for her.

"So you're going?" she said, pinching off a crumb to taste.

"To the church supper?" I shrugged. "I don't think I have a choice, and then there's the pageant afterward. We'll have to find some place to stay tonight."

Swaddled in her endless emerald green cape, Augusta leapt from the car and lifted her face to the rain. She did a quick pirouette, skirt whirling. "I do love Christmas pageants!" she said.

"Maybe I'll have a chance to talk with Martin Shackelford or someone else who knew the Tanseys," I said.

I rode to the church with Aunt Eula and her husband, Ed, along with Buster, his niece Mae Edna, and two of the Shackelford cousins Annie Lou and Fannie Sue. Annie Lou, who wore her graying brown hair in a bun on top of her head, was freckled and tall and so skinny you'd have trouble seeing her if she turned sideways. Her cousin Fannie Sue was as round as a beach ball with a rollicking laugh and a head full of short red curls. All had the surname Shackelford, and all, including me, balanced a cake, pie, or casserole on their laps. The car smelled so good I think I gained weight on the ride over alone.

Martin Shackelford was up to his elbows in flour when we stepped inside the fellowship hall of the Light and Life Baptist Church a while later. "Be sure and try his biscuits," Buster advised. "But you better get in line because they go fast. Makes them with whipping cream."

Earlier I had phoned Roger to let him know I wouldn't be home until the next day and asked him to please take care of Clementine. Of course, he wanted to know what I was doing in Soso, Georgia, so I told him I was there for a little last-minute Christmas shopping at the outlet in Commerce. Now, to stay honest, I would have to stop and buy something on the way home.

Aunt Eula introduced me to so many cousins, nephews, nieces, and siblings I lost track after the first three or four. Everyone had brought something to eat and the women scurried about placing the food on long tables and setting out dinnerware while the men set up tables and chairs for the meal. I was glad when one of the women (I think it was Mae Edna) accepted my offer of help and allowed me to place red candles and freshly cut evergreens on every table. A cedar Christmas tree surrounded by wrapped gifts stood in the corner of the room. The gifts, I was told, were for the children and would be given out later.

I sat during the meal with Aunt Eula and Ed, Ed's sister

Ruby, Buster, and Mae Edna, and although we take pride in our fare in Stone's Throw, I'll have to admit, these people had us beat. They had chicken cooked every way imaginable, plus casseroles, bread, cakes, pies, and pickles of just about every kind.

During dessert, I managed to ask Mae Edna, who sat on my right, if she knew anything about Dave Tansey.

"Not much," she said, after finishing a generous wedge of apple pie. "They didn't belong to our church, but their son... Joshua, isn't it?"

"Jeremiah," I said.

"Well, he was a couple of years ahead of me in school, and it seems like he stayed in trouble most of the time."

"For what?" I asked.

"Oh, just different things...smoking pot...cutting class... stuff like that."

"What about Dinah, his sister?" I said. "She must've died awfully young. What happened?"

"From what I heard, she married the wrong man. Just ran off without a word. It was awfully hard on the Tanseys."

"But what hap—" Before I could learn anything more, somebody came around to ask if we wanted coffee, and people started moving tables to the side to make room for the pageant to follow. Somebody turned out the lights except for those in the front of the room illuminating a small makeshift stage. The room grew quiet as the minister began to recite the familiar passage from Luke: *And it came to pass...*

The pageant had begun. Everyone had turned their chairs to face the stage and there happened to be an empty one next to me. It didn't stay empty long. I soon felt the light touch of a hand on my arm and knew Augusta was beside me.

Watching the scene unfolding in front of me I forgot about what had happened to Opal Henshaw the night before; forgot about the elusive Melrose; and forgot about Idonia's brush with danger. And when we rose at the end to sing "Silent Night,"

Augusta sang as well. And this time she almost managed to stay on key.

Afterward, the kitchen was filled with the crinkle of plastic wrap and the crackle of aluminum foil as people hurried to cover what was left in their dishes for the trip back home. I grabbed a sponge and helped Ruby Shackelford wipe off the tables, then overwhelmed, tried to stay out of the way. But as the bustle died down, I grabbed the chance to jump in to renew my conversation with Mae Edna.

"You were telling me about Dinah Tansey's husband," I began. "What happened? Why did she die?"

"I'll tell you why she died."

I turned to find Martin Shackelford standing behind me. "She died because that worthless man she married didn't get her to a doctor in time," he said.

"Tubal pregnancy," Mae Edna whispered. "Tube ruptured and the poor thing died from internal bleeding. I've heard it near about destroyed her husband. They say he hadn't been the same since."

"Huh! Crocodile tears if you ask me! All that caring came a little too late for that poor little gal," Martin continued. "And what's more, he didn't even have the decency to tell her folks what had happened until she was dead and in the ground.

"Dexter Clark!" Martin spat out the name as if it left a bad taste in his mouth, and looked at me sharply. "Not worth killin', if you ask me. You're not kin to him or nothin', are you?"

Without waiting for an answer, he began lining up empty containers on the table. "Mary Lynne, this one's yours! Got your name on it. And, Elaine, I know this pan belongs to you. I seen you when you come in with it."

"Did you say, Dexter *Clark*?" I asked, dogging the man's heels. "The man Dinah married was Dexter Clark?"

He nodded. "She married him, all right, but he wasn't much of a man."

I looked around for Augusta and saw her standing close by.

It was obvious from the expression on her face the angel had heard every word.

Dexter Clark was the name of the man who had died at Willowbrook.

SIXTEEN

By THE TIME WE STARTED back to Soso, the temperature had dropped and an icy wind blew in gusts that chilled me to the bone. We didn't waste any time crowding into the family van, and Ed Shackelford drove slowly to avoid sliding on black ice in the road.

"There is no way I'm gonna let you drive in this mess tonight to any hotel," Aunt Eula informed me when I brought up the subject of a place to stay.

"You've already been so kind, I don't want to crowd you," I said—although I really didn't relish the idea of driving on slick, wet roads, especially since I didn't know where I was going.

"Honey, one more is nothing to me. I won't even know you're there. You can have Arabella's room. She's not due in until the weekend." Arabella, I learned was the Shackelfords' oldest daughter, who taught at an elementary school in Covington.

"Hope you don't mind sharing with Cousin Fannie Sue," Eula continued. "She just drove down from Atlanta to see Harry in the pageant tonight. She'll be leaving in the morning."

Fannie Sue and I had worked together clearing tables earlier that evening, and although she seemed pleasant enough, the woman must have weighed over two hundred pounds. I hoped we didn't have to share a bed, but I was so tired, I felt I could probably sleep anywhere.

But that seemed out of the question just then because the Shackelfords wanted to discuss the events of the evening and all of them began to talk at once. Naturally everyone thought Harry was the star of the show. We congregated in the kitchen, where Aunt Eula heated a big pot of spiced apple cider and passed around a tray of fruitcake and sugar cookies. I didn't see how anybody could possibly eat another thing after what we had put away at the covered dish supper, but the refreshments soon disappeared. I sipped the cider slowly, grateful for its warmth, and wondered if I should bring up the subject of the Tanseys again, but decided it would be best to wait until the next day when I could speak with Martin Shackelford alone.

Just as I finished my drink one of the cousins suggested a game of charades. This was met with boisterous approval and the whole family filed into the living room where they gathered in front of a huge Christmas tree and began to choose sides. I hung back in the kitchen, hoping I wouldn't be noticed.

"I hate to be a party pooper," I told Aunt Eula, "but I have a long drive ahead of me tomorrow so I'd better get some sleep."

"I guess I should've warned you about these folks," she said. "They'll stay up all night sometimes, and be no worse for the wear for it the next day." She patted my arm. "I expect you're tired, as well. Come on upstairs and I'll show you where you can sleep."

"Count me in, too. I have an early day tomorrow." Overnight bag in hand, Cousin Fannie Sue followed along behind us.

To my relief, Aunt Eula opened the door to a pleasant, inviting room with crisp white organdy curtains, colorful hooked rug, and *twin beds*. I thanked her and said my good nights, then washed my face, and slipped into the soft flannel gown she left out for me. I was asleep as soon as my head hit the pillow.

I didn't even think about Augusta until I woke the next morning at a little after eight, but she usually takes care of herself in situations like this, so I wasn't worried. The house was quiet when I came downstairs, Fannie Sue having risen earlier, and the charade-players still asleep. And although I had thought I couldn't possibly be hungry again this soon, I found myself devouring crisp bacon with coffee and orange juice and the best waffles I've ever put in my mouth.

Because I hadn't planned to stay overnight, I had nothing to leave with Aunt Eula as a hostess gift to thank her for her hospitality. I would stop at the outlet in Commerce on my way home and have something sent from there, I decided. I was rinsing my dishes at the sink when Aunt Eula came into the kitchen and planted a kiss on my cheek.

"Guess what I just found on the hall table—and with my name on it, too? Lucy, are you sure you want to part with this? Please tell me you are, because I can't bear to give it back!"

I tried not to act surprised when she held out Augusta's beautiful hand-stitched needlework of a small country church in the snow. It looked amazingly like one we had passed during our drive over the day before.

"Of course I want you to keep it," I said. "I can't think of another person I'd rather have it than you."

"Well, I'm going to take it over to Milledgeville this very morning and have it framed. I don't believe I've ever seen anything like this—it's absolutely perfect!"

Of course it was. "Why, thank you, Aunt Eula," I said, and smiled.

I found Augusta waiting in the car when I left a few minutes later. "Thanks for leaving the needlework, Augusta. It was a thoughtful thing to do and a perfect gift for Aunt Eula. She loved it!…And by the way, where were you all last night?"

"I found the sofa most comfortable after the Shackelfords finally tired of their game. Have you ever played charades, Lucy Nan? All those signals—it was most enlightening."

I laughed and assured her that I had as I drove across the street to the lumberyard. This morning the gate was open and the unfriendly dog was nowhere to be seen.

"I wonder if I might find a cup of coffee in there," Augusta said.

"I'll bring you some if they have any, but on second thought, maybe you'd better come with me, just in case our friend Skeeter is anywhere about," I said as I got out of the car. A man who looked vaguely familiar—probably one of the cousins—pointed the way to Martin Shackelford's office and I found him at a makeshift desk covered with blueprints and a disarray of papers.

He didn't seem to recognize me at first glance so I introduced myself again, reminding him we had met briefly the night before.

"Right. You were asking about Dave Tansey. Might I ask why?"

"My cousin hired him to take care of the family property just outside of Stone's Throw, and he's also filling in for our church sexton for a while. I understand you wrote a recommendation for him, and I wanted to find out a little more about his background." Taking the chair he offered, I told him there had been several puzzling incidents since the family's arrival.

He frowned. "Like what?"

I told him about finding Dexter Clark's body at Willowbrook and what had happened to Opal Henshaw at our church. I really wanted to learn more about the Tanseys' daughter Dinah but couldn't think of a way to approach the subject tactfully.

"Dexter Clark? So he's dead, huh? Well, I hate to say it but that ain't no great loss!" Martin Shackelford threw back his head and laughed. "You don't think Preacher Dave had anything to do with all that, do you?" He shook his head. "Ugh-uh. That dog won't hunt! I wouldn't be surprised if Dexter was mixed up in selling drugs or something. Ran around with a bad bunch. Now, Dave Tansey—he's a good man and a hard worker. I hated to see him go."

"Then why *did* he leave?" Nothing ventured, nothing gained, as Mimmer used to say.

Martin Shackelford stood and poured coffee for himself in a thick white mug and some in a Styrofoam cup for me. I took a sip before I remembered to save the rest for Augusta, who was sending frantic signals from across the room.

"He never came out and said so, but I think he just wanted to get away from bad memories… The Tansey boy got into some trouble in school here, and then the girl married that sorry son-of-a—Sorry, ma'am—and then her dying like that. It like to broke her mama's heart. Poor woman! Louella Tansey was always quiet, shy, you know. Wouldn't say boo to a goose, and this girl's death like to done her in."

"When Dinah married, did they live around here?" I asked.

"No, he took Dinah to live somewhere in North Carolina if I remember right. Far as I know, they never came back here, and I was glad to see the back of him. Some say he changed, tried to turn his life around, but he sure as hell had a long way to go."

The telephone on his desk rang just then and I took the opportunity to thank him for his time and excused myself. He stood and shook my hand before picking up the receiver. It was good to know some men still had manners.

I waited until we got back in the car to give Augusta the coffee. "I guess that settles it," I said. "The man who died at Willowbrook was the Tanseys' son-in-law Dexter Clark. But the Tanseys claimed they didn't know him, and if the family disliked him so, what was he doing out there?"

Augusta drank her coffee before answering. "It does seem suspicious, but it could have been a coincidence, I suppose. Perhaps the Tanseys didn't know he was there."

I drove slowly through the town of Soso and turned right toward Eatonton. "Martin Shackelford said Dexter wasn't worth killing," I said. "Obviously, somebody thought otherwise."

Augusta was quiet for a while and I knew she was thinking. "Did Mr. Shackelford plan to go hunting this morning?" she asked finally.

"I don't think so. Why do you ask?"

"He said the dog wouldn't hunt."

I laughed. "Oh, Augusta! That's just an expression. It means the same thing as barking up the wrong tree."

Augusta shook her head and turned up the heater. "Never mind," she said.

Just before getting back on the interstate, we stopped at the outlet mall in Commerce. Weigelia needed some decent gloves and Julie had been asking for pajamas. For her main present I was giving my daughter a check to buy clothes. She works for a small newspaper in north Georgia, and although she loves her job, I know she has a hard time making ends meet on her small salary.

I made my purchases and was taking my time browsing in the boys' department considering just one more thing for Teddy when Augusta caught my attention. I looked up to see her standing by the window waving both arms. Her honey-gold hair had slipped over one eye and her long necklace danced and bounced in the sunlight.

"What is it?" I asked, hurrying over. Did angels ever have fits?

Augusta pointed out the window. "It's him! At least I think it is. See…he's going into that store over there."

I looked over her shoulder. "Who? Where?"

"Idonia's gentleman friend. What's his name? Melrose! Isn't that him just down the street?"

I shoved aside a display of toddler-size holiday dresses and pressed my face against the glass to see where she was pointing, and was just in time to catch a glimpse of a man's back as the door of a shop closed behind him. The man was of similar shape as Melrose: sturdy and round and a little less than medium height, and the coat looked vaguely familiar, but I couldn't be certain. "Are you sure?" I asked Augusta. "What would Melrose be doing here?"

She gave me a not-so-angelic push toward the doorway. "That's what we want to find out, but you'll have to move faster than that or we'll lose him."

Clutching my shopping bags in one hand and my purse in the other, I careened out the door and skidded wildly into a stunned group of elderly women who were trying to decide where to meet for lunch.

"So sorry. P-please excuse me!" I stammered, giving Augusta the look I usually reserve for people who talk on cell phones during a movie.

Racing down the sidewalk, I followed my impatient angel into a store that sells cookware and kitchen gadgets to find her waiting for me behind a display of spatulas. "Well?" I demanded. "Where is he?"

She nodded toward the back of the room. "He was looking at those aprons back there. He can't have gone far."

"*Aprons!* How can the man possibly be interested in aprons at a time like this?" I said. "Weigelia says the police want to talk with him about what he might have seen at the church the other night, but if he's made Idonia unhappy, they'll have to get in line after me!" I hurried to the area Augusta had pointed out, but Melrose DuBois wasn't there.

Parting an array of dish towels, I glimpsed the back of a Melrose-like head hotfooting it up the coffeemaker aisle. "I'll head him off at the pass," I whispered to Augusta. "You keep watch at the door."

She smiled and nodded, moving quickly into position. I knew Augusta had watched enough cowboy movies to understand the vernacular. Unfortunately, a very large woman who was obviously shopping to equip several kitchens for a school of the culinary arts picked that moment to wheel her loaded cart in front of me, blocking both my view of Melrose and the aisle.

I was getting out of breath by the time I reached the checkout counter and Augusta, who simply shook her head and shrugged. Melrose, or the man who looked like Melrose, was nowhere to be seen.

To tell the truth, at that point I was just about ready to give up. After all, we really weren't sure we were on the trail of the right person, and I had spied a couple of fascinating kitchen aids

I was certain would turn me into a gourmet cook and wouldn't have minded spending a little more time in the shop.

But that was not to be. "There he is in the parking lot!" Augusta said, grabbing my arm. "Oh, do please hurry, Lucy Nan!"

I gave the bewildered cashier an apologetic smile and rushed out the door behind her.

Weaving in and out among parked vehicles, I followed Augusta, who followed Melrose. Now and again she paused to wave me on with a swirl of her cape until we ended up on the other side of the mall. Cheeks flushed with excitement, and possibly from the cold as well, Augusta posted herself in front of a bookstore. For once, I noticed, the cold, damp December wind didn't seem to bother her in the least.

It bothered me. "It's freezing out here, Augusta! I don't see anybody out here that faintly resembles Melrose DuBois."

"That's because he's in the bookstore," she said, calmly folding her arms. "All we have to do is wait."

"Well, I'm waiting inside where it's warm," I told her. "And I suggest you do the same."

"But what if he sees you? We don't want him to slip away again."

"I know he can't see *you*," I said, "but do you think he's aware that *I'm* following him?"

"I wouldn't want to take a chance." Augusta shaded her eyes against the glare of the window and looked inside. "He seems to be taking his time browsing among the books. Let's give him a little time, Lucy Nan. He'll have to come out again soon."

"If I have to stand out here in the cold, at least I'm going to be sure it's worth the wait," I said, looking in my purse for dark glasses.

Augusta shivered the slightest bit and tried to pretend she hadn't. "What do you mean?" she asked.

I put on the glasses, pulled my hat over my ears and wrapped a muffler around the bottom of my face. "I just want to be sure it's Melrose DuBois in there," I said, trying to peer through the window without being obvious.

"But, Lucy Nan, I told you it was."

How could I put this gently? Augusta looked so crestfallen I hesitated to mention that she had been becoming more and more nearsighted in the past few months. Why just last week she'd mistaken our neighbor for a mailbox. Nettie had been standing at the corner in her long blue winter coat waiting for the traffic light to change when Augusta, who was watching out the window, drew in her breath.

"What's wrong?" I asked.

"Oh, nothing," she said. "It's just that for a moment, I thought I saw the mailbox move."

But as it turned out, I didn't have to remind her, because Augusta Goodnight was right. One quick glance was all I needed to assure me that the man in the bookstore was indeed Idonia's slippery "gentleman friend," Melrose DuBois.

SEVENTEEN

"DON'T LET HIM SEE YOU LOOKING," Augusta warned. "Perhaps we should step over there and wait. It's out of the wind and we'll still be able to keep an eye on the door."

I followed her to a sheltered spot in front of a nearby shop where we huddled miserably, eyes on the bookstore next door. Augusta wrapped herself mummy-style from head to toe in her limitless velvety cape and I stuck my gloved hands under my arms and stamped my feet to keep them warm, ignoring the curious looks of passersby.

"How many books is the man going to buy?" I complained at last. "Seems he's been in there for an eternity!"

Augusta laughed. "Not quite, but maybe we'd better take another look." She gave my arm a comforting pat. "If you're up to waiting a few more minutes I'll go in there and see what's holding him up."

It didn't take her long. When Augusta emerged from the store, I knew with one look our quarry had given us the slip again. The angel looked so disappointed I almost forgave her for making me stand outside in the cold. "He must have left by another door," she said. "I couldn't find him anywhere."

"Then he knows I was following him," I said as we hurried back to the car and blessed warmth. "But what in the world is he doing here? Do you think Melrose might be following *us?*"

Augusta waited until the heater warmed up before answering. "I think it's possible he was there ahead of us," she said.

"Where?"

"In that little town—Soso. When we first arrived yesterday I thought I saw him coming out of a building there."

"What building?" I asked.

"The post office, I think, but I didn't get a good look at him."

Taking my life in my hands, I merged into the traffic on the interstate heading north and home. "Why didn't you say something?" I asked when I was able to breathe again.

"I only got a glimpse and I wasn't sure it was the same man I saw at the caroling party." Augusta fingered her necklace as she watched the landscape rush past. "It puzzles me, Lucy Nan. What was he doing in that town? And if he means well, why did he avoid you back at the shops?"

I thought about that for a minute. "He must be aware that the police in Stone's Throw want to talk with him, and that doesn't stack up too well in his favor. It's all beginning to seem suspicious to me." I gripped the wheel as if it were Melrose DuBois's neck. "What I wouldn't give to have just five minutes with that little snake!"

"Let's wait and cross that stream when we come upon it," Augusta said primly. "After all, we don't have enough evidence yet."

"How much evidence do you need?" I asked.

"Right now what I *need* is another cup of coffee. Perhaps I'll be able to think more clearly then." Augusta loosened her wrap and tucked a stray strand of reddish-gold hair into place. "The cup I had earlier seems to have left me wanting."

I laughed. "My sentiments exactly. There's a place this side of Spartanburg where we can stop for coffee and pick up a couple of hamburgers, too. I'll be ready for a break by then."

I tuned in Christmas music on the radio and both of us were quiet for the next hour or so, Augusta with her thoughts, I suppose, while I concentrated on the traffic and wondered how The Thursdays were dealing with the situation back in Stone's Throw.

Later, we ate our burgers in the parking lot of a fast-food restaurant and shared an order of fries, while reviving on steaming coffee.

"About Melrose DuBois," Augusta began after I returned from disposing of the wrappers. "He and the people who live on your family's property—the Tanseys—seem to be key figures in this series of unfortunate events in Stone's Throw."

"Right," I said. "We just need to find the connection."

Augusta finished her coffee before speaking. "It's beginning to be plain that the connection is the locket."

I nodded. "I think you're right on the money there, Augusta. The locket belonged to the Tanseys' daughter, then Melrose came in possession of it somehow and gave it to Idonia. *Somebody* wanted it badly enough to drug Idonia and steal it that night at Bellawood. Dexter Clark, who had been married to the Tanseys' daughter, ended up under the balcony at Willowbrook with his neck broken, and Opal Henshaw, who rented a room to Melrose at the Spring Lamb, died in a suspicious fall from the church balcony. Melrose DuBois seems to be in the middle of all of this." I started the car and eased back onto the highway. "What is it that's so important about that locket? I wonder if Melrose knows?"

"If he doesn't, he must have guessed by now," Augusta said. She turned to me solemn-eyed. "And didn't your friend Claudia say that Opal Henshaw seemed unusually interested in it? Lucy Nan, I believe it's imperative that we find that locket—and soon."

But how will we do that if we don't even know who has it? I wondered. *Why would Melrose give Idonia the locket only to steal it back and risk her life in doing it?*

Augusta must have come to the same conclusion. "I think we should begin with the Tanseys," she said, almost as if she were thinking aloud. "Didn't you say Dave Tansey was helping to park vehicles at Bellawood that night?"

"Yes, but one of us would have noticed if he came upstairs—unless it was while we were taking a break in the kitchen."

"If he were in costume, however, he'd be less conspicuous," Augusta said.

Somehow the idea of Preacher Dave dressing up in period clothing made me laugh. Tall and lanky with a timeworn face, he would certainly suit the concept of a hardworking farmer of the 1800s, but I couldn't imagine him going to the extent of securing the proper costume, then scurrying to change into it after a night of directing parking.

"What about Louella?" I said. "Some of the women wore bonnets that night. It would've been easier for her to go unnoticed than either of the men. But how are we going to find out where she was during that time?"

Augusta smiled. "Where there's a will, there's a...well...a course of action," she said.

A perfect challenge for The Thursdays.

I FOUND SEVERAL OF THEM keeping Idonia company at her place when we arrived in Stone's Throw later that afternoon. While others in the group watched *A Wonderful Life* on television, I snatched Ellis away for a whispered conference in the kitchen.

"Where in the world have you been?" she asked. "We were getting worried."

"Never mind! I'll tell you about it later. Has Idonia heard anything from Melrose?"

Ellis shook her head. "Not a mumblin' word, the little twerp! What do you think that old fool's up to, Lucy Nan?"

"I'm beginning to think it's nothing good." I told her about Melrose giving us the slip at the outlet mall. "And Augusta says she saw him in Soso yesterday, too."

Ellis laughed when I told her about our adventurous stay with the Shackelfords, but grew serious when she learned the man whose body we had found at Willowbrook had been married to the Tanseys' daughter, Dinah.

"But didn't they tell the police they didn't know him? And

Preacher Dave made no bones about how he felt about the man she married. Do you think one of them gave him a shove?"

I shrugged. "Beats me, but it all seems to center on that locket. Augusta and I believe one of the Tanseys has it and that it's important for us to find some way to get a better look at it."

Ellis helped herself to an apple and polished it on her sleeve. "And how do we do that?"

"That's what we have to discuss. Who's not here? I didn't see Nettie or Claudia."

"Nettie's over at Claudia's helping her make a Japanese fruit-cake for the staff party at Sarah Bedford tomorrow."

"That's quite an undertaking! I think I'd volunteer for something simpler than that," I said.

Ellis laughed. "She probably didn't have a choice being the new kid on the block. Remember, Claudia's only been working at the college a few months."

"Do you think everyone might be able to get together for a little while tonight? Maybe we can put some of these pieces together."

Ellis swallowed a bite of apple. "I guess so, but what are we going to do about Idonia?"

"What's this about Idonia?"

For a few seconds I froze, then turned to find Idonia standing in the kitchen doorway.

Ellis and I stood there looking at each other for what seemed like minutes, waiting, I suppose, for the other one to speak. "Oh hell, Idonia, I guess the jig is up," Ellis said with a backward glance at me. "Maybe you'd better sit down. We have something to tell you." Ellis steered her back into the living room and switched off the television set.

"I guess we'd better start with the locket," I said after we settled Idonia in her favorite chair. "We're almost sure it's the same one the Tanseys' daughter is wearing in that photo of her on their piano. It even has the same seed pearls missing."

Idonia twisted her hands in her lap. "Then why would Melrose tell me it belonged to his grandmother?"

Ellis sat on the arm of our friend's chair and put a hand on her shoulder. "Maybe he thought it would make it seem even more special," she said, forcing a smile.

"Do you think he was the one who—who stole it?" Idonia bit her lip. "*Somebody* drugged my punch, but it wasn't him! I know Melrose wouldn't do that to me. Besides, he seemed most upset when I told him what had happened."

"It couldn't have been Melrose," I assured her. "Al Evans confirmed that he worked until after ten that night at the funeral home."

Zee frowned. "Then who?"

"Probably one of the Tanseys," I said, and told them what I'd learned from Martin Shackelford. "Remember that man we found out at Willowbrook? Died from a fall from the balcony out there? Well, he had been married to the Tanseys' daughter, Dinah."

Ellis made a rude noise. "Fall nothing! I'll bet one of those Tanseys pushed him."

"But which one?" Jo Nell asked. "I can't imagine Preacher Dave or that mousy Louella doing anything that bold."

"What about that boy—that Jeremiah? I wouldn't put much of anything past that one!" Zee said.

Idonia sat up straighter. "Seems if Jeremiah Tansey was at Bellawood, one of us would've seen him."

"Wait a minute!" I said. "Somebody had a video camera that night—remember? Genevieve wanted to get a record of the festivities and it seemed that every time I turned around, they had it in my face."

"Ralph Snow. He filmed for a while in the schoolhouse, too, until Nettie had enough of it and ran him off," Jo Nell said. "If any of the Tanseys were there, maybe they'll show up on film."

"I'll give Ralph a call," I offered, "if one of you will get in touch with Nettie and Claudia." I looked at my watch. "It's a little after five o'clock now. I'll be serving up soup and corn bread in a little over an hour for anybody who's interested."

"Sounds good," Idonia said. "But how can you manage, Lucy Nan, in such a short time?"

Ellis looked at me and smiled. She knew who would be making the soup and corn bread.

"RALPH'S GOING TO DROP his camera by in a little while," I told them as we all gathered around my kitchen table later that evening. "Of course I had to swear in blood I'd have it back by tomorrow."

Idonia, who had barely touched her food, shoved her plate aside. "It's not that old locket I worry about, it's Melrose! I haven't heard from him since day before yesterday, and it just isn't like him not to call. I'm so afraid something's happened to him."

Something *would* happen to him if I had my way, I thought, but instead, I said, with some conviction, that I was sure Melrose was just fine.

"I expect he'll show up before too long," Zee said. "After all, it's only been a couple of days."

Nettie stood as we heard a car in the driveway. "I'll bet that's Ralph with the camera now. I can't wait to see what's on that film."

Jo Nell frowned. "What if we don't find anything there? Then what?"

"Then we'll have to figure out some way to get our hands on that locket," Ellis said.

EIGHTEEN

"Now, WHAT DO YOU CALL this apparatus?" Augusta asked the next day, inspecting Ralph Snow's camcorder without daring to touch it. We had eaten an early breakfast of oatmeal, cinnamon toast, and freshly squeezed orange juice and the camera sat on the kitchen table ready to be returned to its owner.

"A video camera," I said, "only it records sounds and voices as well. I promised Ralph I'd have it back before noon as he'll be going out of town for Christmas."

Augusta laughed and clapped her hands. "Mickey Mouse!"

"What?"

"Mickey Mouse. Cleveland Tarver."

I shrugged. "I guess you're going to explain that," I said.

"Cleveland Tarver. I was assigned to him for a brief period during the war. He was a widower going through some difficult times just then. His only son was in the service overseas and his daughter-in-law and grandson came to live with him for a while— sweet little boy about three—Sonny, they called him. The son's wife was constantly worried, of course, so Cleveland bought this camera—a movie camera they called it then. With it she recorded Sonny's activities so his father wouldn't miss so much of his childhood, and once in a while they would show cartoons on their home screen—most were about Mickey Mouse." Augusta smiled. "How Sonny loved watching them… and so did I!"

"What happened?" I asked, expecting the worst. I knew Augusta was referring to World War II as that had been her last period on assignment as a guardian angel until recently.

"What happened to whom?"

"To Sonny's father, and to—Cleveland—what's-his-name?" I asked.

"Sonny's father came home after the war and went on to become a physician, I believe. Cleveland eventually married again and lived well into his nineties." Augusta examined her cup and seemed surprised that it was empty. "Any more of that coffee?"

I rinsed our dishes in the sink and put them into the dishwasher. All this chasing around and worrying was starting to get to me. I could use a little Mickey Mouse myself. "Augusta, what are we going to do? We seem to have come up against a brick wall and I don't know where to go from here. Ellis is right. We have to find out who has that locket!"

Augusta wiped off the table in one wide, circular swoop, and it gleamed as if it were new. "I was hoping something would turn up on that camera last night, but that doesn't mean any of those people weren't there."

"We know that Preacher Dave was in the vicinity, and Ellis was going to phone the fabric shop where Louella works and make up some story to find out if she was working there that night, but then we realized the drop-in at Bellawood was on a Sunday and they wouldn't have been open then," I said.

"Then where do you think she might be on a Sunday night?" Augusta asked, teasing Clementine with a doggy treat.

"Well...I suppose she could've been at her church, especially since her husband's the minister. But he was at Bellawood parking cars, so they must not have had a service."

"Maybe not a proper service, but there could have been choir rehearsal or some other kind of meeting," she said. "Do you know anyone who belongs to that congregation?"

"Not right offhand," I said, "but I'll ask around. Frankly, Jeremiah's the one who concerns me. I wish I knew where he was the night Idonia's locket was taken."

Augusta stood at the window as if she might find an answer somewhere in the clouds. "I'm sure the boy keeps company with someone. Perhaps some of his companions might be able to help."

"According to Kim who does Nettie's hair at the Total Perfection, Jeremiah hangs out with that bunch at the Red Horse Café and I'm not about to go in there! And even if I did, I doubt if they'd tell me the truth."

I remembered how Kemper had reacted when I first mentioned Jeremiah that morning at Willowbrook. "We've heard nothing more from the police about their investigation into what happened to Idonia. I guess Opal's death sort of put it on the back burner, but I think I'll give Kemper Mungo a call. They may or may not know about the Tanseys' connection to Dexter Clark, but I have a feeling the police know a lot more about what goes on with Jeremiah Tansey than they're letting on."

Augusta rode with me to return the camcorder to Ralph Snow, and afterward I dropped by the library to return a couple of her books and check out enough mysteries to last her until after the holidays. "I don't know what to do about Idonia," I confessed on the way home. "She's worried about Melrose DuBois—afraid something's happened to him, when I know good and well he was alive and kicking when we saw him in Georgia yesterday."

Augusta was reading the jacket copy on one of the mysteries. "If it were you, would you want to know the truth?" she said, setting the book aside.

I considered the question. "Yes, I think I would. But Idonia's been through a rough time, Augusta. She seems especially fragile just now. Do you really think I should tell her?"

"She seems an intelligent person to me, and she's certainly mature enough to deal with adversity. I believe your friend might consider it an injustice to be treated in any other manner."

"In other words, you think it's insulting to protect her?"

"Idonia's free to make choices just as you are, Lucy Nan. I'm sure she's capable of facing the situation if necessary."

I wasn't so sure about that, but I didn't have time to think on it longer because we reached home to find two cars parked in our driveway, and Nettie, wrapped in her old brown sweater, scuttling over from next door, house shoes flapping.

My first thought was that something was wrong with Idonia. "What's going on?" I asked Zee, who happened to be the first person I reached.

"Have you seen *The Messenger* this morning?" she asked.

"Not yet," I said. "Has something happened to Idonia?"

"No, no! Wait until you see this!" Claudia rattled the weekly newspaper in my face. At the same time, Nettie called out something I couldn't understand, probably because she was still putting in her teeth, and I ran to help her recover the fuzzy slipper she'd lost under the azalea bush.

"I had a feeling there was something peculiar going on there," Nettie said, panting to keep up.

"What? Where? Will somebody please tell me something?" I trailed after them into my house where Claudia spread the newspaper on the kitchen table, smoothing it with her hand.

"Read this," she demanded, poking her finger on what was obviously the lead story on the front page. I didn't need my reading glasses to make out the bold headline: LOCAL MATRON DIES IN FALL FROM BALCONY.

Silently I read the first few paragraphs describing what had happened at the church that night. I didn't see anything new.

"Well, we knew this already," I said, wondering why they were so excited.

Zee leaned over my shoulder. "Skip to the obituary information at the end," she said.

Services will be held, Sat., Dec. 22, at Stone's Throw Presbyterian Church... I read aloud. "Gosh, that's tomorrow!"

"Never mind that," Zee said. "Check out where it tells about her family."

I cleared my throat. *Mrs. Henshaw was preceded in death by her husband, Virgil Henshaw, and a sister, Maisie Clark*

of Raleigh, North Carolina. She is survived by a brother, Ter-
rance Banks, of Knoxville, Tennessee, and a nephew, Dexter
Clark…

"Dexter Clark! Do they mean Dexter Clark as in *dead* Dexter Clark?"

Nettie nodded. "One and the same."

"Whoever put this in the paper obviously didn't know he wasn't still alive," Claudia said.

"So Opal's nephew was married to the Tanseys' daughter, Dinah," I said. "That's why she was so curious about the locket Dinah wore in the photograph. But wouldn't she have known about the marriage?"

"Not necessarily," Claudia said. "We were talking about families, holiday customs, things like that, the day we delivered the fruitcakes and Opal told me her only sister died several years ago and she rarely spoke to her brother. She didn't mention a nephew."

Zee frowned. "Even if Dexter married the Tansey girl after his mother died…still, you'd think Opal would've been invited to the wedding," she said.

"Maybe they eloped," Nettie suggested.

"Wait a minute!" Claudia, who had been sitting, suddenly jumped to her feet. "If Opal didn't know about her nephew's marriage, why did she take such an unusual interest in that picture while we were at the Tanseys' place that day—especially about the locket Dinah wore? Wanted to know all about it."

"Do you remember what she said?" I asked.

"Something about her mother—or maybe it was her grand-mother—having one like it. Louella told her it was a family heirloom. She hurried us out of there right soon after that. You could tell she didn't want to talk about it."

"Melrose must have shown the locket to Opal before he gave it to Idonia," Zee said. "Do you remember if Opal mentioned Idonia having one like it?"

Claudia nodded. "I'm pretty sure she did…Yes, I'm positive

because Louella said she guessed there must be more than one."

"But not with two seed pearls missing in the exact places," I said. "And that very night somebody drugged Idonia's drink and stole it."

"But they must've known about Idonia's locket earlier," Zee pointed out. "She swears somebody was following her while we were caroling."

That didn't surprise me because Idonia had taken every opportunity to show off her gift from Melrose. "It had to have been one of the Tanseys," I said. "Do any of you know somebody who goes to their church?"

"I think Helen does," Claudia said. "Helen Harlan. She's a student at Sarah Bedford, works part time in the office to help with her tuition. Helen's kind of quiet and serious—keeps to herself, but she mentioned going to Chandler's Creek. I think she sings in the choir."

"Do you know how to get in touch with her?" I asked. "Maybe she could give us an idea where Louella Tansey was last Sunday night."

"Sure. I'll probably see her tonight at the staff Christmas party…but what'll I *say?*"

"You'll think of something," I told her, "just let us know what you find out—"

"As soon as you can!" Zee added. "And shouldn't somebody check with Al Evans about Idonia's slippery boyfriend? After all, Melrose is supposed to be working there."

"And claims to be related, too!" Nettie clicked her teeth. "You reckon Al knows what that little varmint's been up to?"

There wasn't but one way to find out, and I was about to volunteer when Ellis came bursting in, almost tripping over Clementine, who was stretched out in her usual place.

"I've left two messages! Don't you ever pick up?" she said, then realizing we were all gathered around the story in *The Messenger,* pulled out a chair and joined us.

"You're just in time. You're nominated," I told her after the others took time about telling her what we had discussed.

Ellis stooped to pet Clementine as an apology for almost stepping on her tail. "Nominated for what?" she asked.

"To see what you can find out about Melrose from Al Evans," I said. "Surely he must have some idea what the man's about."

I could tell by her expression Ellis was going to balk. "You want me to go to the funeral home? By myself? And I can never tell when Al's looking at me. He has a glass eye, you know."

"Oh, for heaven's sake, I'll go with you, but we'd better get on with it," I said. The day was over half gone, I realized, and I still hadn't spoken with Kemper Mungo although I had left a message earlier asking him to get in touch. No doubt he thought I wanted to bug him to tell me what he knew.

"Has anybody seen Idonia?" Ellis asked as we left. "I've been trying to reach her all morning."

Nettie suggested she'd probably gone to the grocery store and Zee promised to check on Idonia on her way home, but I still felt uneasy as Ellis and I drove the few blocks to Evans and Son. If the person responsible for the other two deaths thought Idonia might know too much, our friend could be next.

Al Evans greeted us cordially and seated us on a Victorian love seat upholstered in purple velvet. Now he shook his head and fastened his gaze on the huge decorative vase in the corner—at least that's where he seemed to be looking. "I wish I could help you, but I declare, I don't know what Melrose has gotten himself up to. I'm sure the police would like to know, too, but unfortunately, he didn't see fit to tell me."

"Do you know where Melrose lived before he came here?" I asked.

Our host pondered that silently for a minute. "Melrose spent most of his life in a small town in Mississippi working in his father's hardware store, then later, for somebody else. After his wife died a few years ago, he moved from here to there—didn't seem to know what to do with himself."

"Did they have children?" Ellis asked, and Al shook his head. "No, and I think it might've made a difference if they had. He's been lonely, I know, and I expect that's why he came here to work with me. As far as I know I'm the only relative Melrose has left. Our mothers were sisters, you know. I just wish I knew what was going on."

Suddenly he rose and went to a large metal urn-like vessel on the table behind him. "My goodness, where are my manners? Can I offer you ladies some coffee?"

I could feel Ellis stiffening beside me. "Um—no, thank you," we chorused.

Ellis leaned forward. "He didn't leave any word at all?"

Al Evans shook his head. "That incident with his friend Mrs. Culpepper really bothered him, I could tell. Seemed to blame himself. Of course I tried to tell him it wasn't his fault…I just wish I knew where he was."

I looked at Ellis and she nodded. "I know where he is—at least he was there yesterday," I said, and told him about my experience seeing Melrose DuBois at a north Georgia outlet mall.

"Well, if that doesn't beat all!" Al sighed. "I shouldn't be too surprised, though. Melrose seems to have developed some strange habits lately."

"Like what?" Ellis wanted to know.

"Secretive little things—like he'd go off by himself and not bother to say where he was going, what he was doing." Al shrugged. "Not that it really mattered. He's a grown man and it's his business how he spends his time. But I guess you could say Melrose made an issue out of not making an issue."

"I GUESS WE'LL HAVE TO tell the police about your seeing Melrose at the mall," Ellis said as we left.

I agreed. I was sort of holding out for Idonia's sake to see if he turned up. I had left another message for Kemper earlier, asking him to call my cell phone number, and when it rang, I thought the policeman was getting back to me. But it was Zee on the other end and I could tell she was trying to sound calm. It didn't work.

"Lucy Nan, I can't seem to find Idonia. Do you have any idea where she might have gone?"

NINETEEN

"WHAT TIME IS IT?" Ellis asked when I told her what Zee had said.

The clock on my dashboard said four o'clock, but then it always says four o'clock since it stopped running two years ago. I looked at my watch. It was a little after one.

"Has Zee gotten in touch with Idonia's niece Jennifer?" Ellis said when I told her the time.

"She didn't mention it, but surely Jennifer would know if Idonia has decided to take off to Savannah or something."

"She wouldn't go to Savannah. You know she wouldn't," Ellis said.

I did know it and so I didn't even bother to phone Jennifer at the high school but drove straight there. Luckily, Jennifer was on her lunch break when we arrived and when we explained the situation to the school secretary, she paged her right away.

"She assured me she was all right when I phoned her yesterday," Jennifer said when she met us in the office, "but frankly, I thought she sounded pretty stressed out. Are you sure she's not at the house?"

"Zee rang the bell and pounded on the door and she's tried to reach her by phone several times," I said.

Jennifer hesitated briefly then spoke with the secretary. "I have a key to Aunt Idonia's house. Just give me a minute to get my purse," she told us, hurrying back to her classroom. Fortunately, we learned, the secretary had been able to find someone to take her last class.

Ellis phoned Zee as we followed Jennifer to Idonia's and

told her to meet us there. I wasn't surprised when Jo Nell and Nettie showed up as well.

"Did you check to see if her car's here?" I asked Zee when she skidded to a stop out front.

"Of course, but she always keeps it in the garage and I couldn't see inside," she reminded me.

"I told Idonia she was doing too much too soon," Jo Nell announced as we waited for Jennifer to unlock the door, and although my cousin is the world's greatest worrywart, this time I tended to agree with her. I tried not to think of our friend lying cold and still across her bed or crumpled on her kitchen floor, and I must've had Ellis's arm in a death grip because she cried out that I was cutting off her circulation.

A lopsided spray of drying evergreens tied with a red plastic bow rattled as Jennifer opened the door and stepped inside while the rest of us hovered briefly on the threshold as if our entering would bring the news we didn't want to hear. The house was quiet and dim except for the light from a table lamp Idonia always kept burning in her family room. A holiday edition of a popular women's magazine lay open in the seat of the worn green recliner where Idonia liked to sit. A pink poinsettia drooped in its pot on the coffee table and I stuck my finger in the soil. Idonia had over watered it as usual.

"Aunt Idonia!" Jennifer called, softly at first and then more urgently until the rest of us began to take up the cry as we made our way through the house. There was no answer.

"She must have gone somewhere," Zee muttered, and nobody answered, probably because we were all thinking the same thing: *I hope she's gone somewhere.*

Idonia's bed had been neatly made and a still-damp towel was tossed over the shower curtain rail as if she had left it there in a hurry, which was most un-Idonia-like. The kitchen was clean and uncluttered except for a fat red candle surrounded by a wreath of pine cones that Claudia had given her for Christmas the year before on the kitchen table and a tin of cookies on the counter. Nettie lifted the lid and looked inside. "Charleston squares. Mattie Durham," she said. And we all nodded in agreement because Mattie always brought Charleston squares when anybody was sick.

Although I knew our friend had been there as recently as the day before, or even later, the house had an abandoned, neglected look, and it made me sad.

"Car's not here," Jennifer called out, looking into the connecting garage, and I felt weak with relief.

"Do you suppose she's just out running errands?" Zee said. "Lord help us if she is when she finds we've invaded her house!"

"No, here's something on the dining room table," Jo Nell called. "Looks like she's left a note."

Jennifer's name was on the outside of the envelope and she hurriedly ripped it open and read the contents, then silently held it for us to see. Idonia's usual neat handwriting could pass for an example in penmanship, but this note was written hastily on one of those greeting cards you receive unsolicited in the mail, and we sighed in unison when we read it: *Gone to meet Melrose. Don't worry. Be back soon.*

Jennifer sank onto a nearby chair. "Has she lost her senses? She doesn't even say where she went."

"Or why," I said.

Ellis and I exchanged looks before she spoke. "I don't want to alarm everybody, but Al Evans said Melrose has been acting kind of strange lately, and he didn't seem to know what to make of it. I don't like the idea of Idonia going off to meet him like this."

I agreed that Al had seemed worried about his cousin, and now I was worried, too, especially when I remembered that Idonia had seen Melrose hurrying from the church the night Opal was killed.

Jennifer's face was white. "Good Lord!" she said when I told them. "Why didn't she say something? Do you think he might have had something to do with what happened to Opal Henshaw?"

"He could've had other reasons for being there," Nettie reasoned. "Still, I think it's time we talked to the police about this."

Jennifer was already calling the number.

GUILT RODE WITH ME like a specter all the way to the police station. From what Al Evans had told us, Melrose might be unstable, and now Idonia had gone rushing off to meet him and we had no idea where she'd gone. I also wanted to wring her neck for making us worry like this.

Beside me, Ellis echoed my very thoughts. "I'm going to kill Idonia if that Melrose doesn't get to her first!" she said.

I shuddered. "Ellis Saxon! Hush your mouth!" It sounded awful when somebody spoke it aloud. I wished Augusta were with us, but just then it was more important to speak with the police.

"And I'd like to jerk a knot in that idiot Elmer Harris as well," Ellis added as we pulled into the parking lot behind the station. "That man doesn't have the sense God gave a billy goat!"

The chief had told Jennifer that because Idonia was a grown woman and had left of her own volition, he couldn't issue a missing person's bulletin. Besides, he added, he wasn't sure she'd been gone twenty-four hours yet. He did perk up when we told him she'd gone to meet Melrose, and asked us to let him know if we heard from her.

"Let's hope Kemper's here or Ed Tillman," I said as the six of us marched inside, an avenging army brandishing purses.

"There he is!" Jo Nell shouted, ignoring Paulette Morgan, the dispatcher who sat at the front desk, and I knew news of our arrival would be all over town in less than an hour.

Kemper seemed to cringe when he saw us, then immediately put up a bold front. "We need to talk," I said as we gathered around his desk. And supported by the others, I told him about seeing Melrose at the outlet mall in Commerce and how Idonia had glimpsed him hurrying from the church the night Opal Henshaw died.

"I'm beginning to think Idonia's gone off the deep end," Zee added. "She's completely bonkers about this man and she doesn't know a blessed thing about him."

Kemper sighed. Well, really it was more of a groan. He rubbed his face and then rubbed it again as if he could hide from us behind his hands. "Sit down, please," he said. I noticed someone had brought the required number of chairs, and so we did.

"It really would have been helpful if you had come to us with this earlier," he said, and he seemed to be staring straight at me.

I tried to explain that I *had* left a couple of messages for him earlier and that I didn't know Melrose had left town until I spoke on the phone with Idonia on my way to Georgia a few days before. That's when Kemper told us several choir members had seen a person of Melrose's description at the church the night Opal Henshaw was killed.

"Don't forget to tell him about the locket, Lucy Nan," Nettie urged me.

Kemper picked up a pencil and put it down. "I'm assuming you're talking about the locket that went missing the night your friend was drugged."

"Right," I said. "I don't suppose you've found it."

He shook his head. "What about the locket?"

"We think it's the same one the Tanseys' daughter, Dinah, is wearing in a photograph on their piano," I began.

Kemper leaned back in his chair and folded his hands over his stomach. He seemed to relax for the first time since we arrived. "Just because it looks like that doesn't mean they're the sa—"

"The Tanseys' daughter was married to Dexter Clark, the man who was killed out at Willowbrook," I said.

"Just how do you know this?" Kemper sat upright so fast I thought he might catapult over the desk.

I didn't answer. *Just let him stew a while,* I thought.

Ellis spoke quietly. "And Dexter Clark was Opal Henshaw's nephew," she said, meeting his gaze.

"It's in Opal's obituary in today's *Messenger,*" Jo Nell said.

Kemper picked up the phone. "Paulette, see if you can round up Captain Hardy—and you'd better put on another pot of coffee, too."

"You have several messages on your answering device," Augusta told me when I finally got home later that afternoon.

"Do you know who they're from?" I asked. (Of course I knew she did. I don't want to say Augusta's nosy. Let's just say she's extremely curious.)

"Two are from your friend Ben. I think he wants you to call him, and your daughter-in-law, Jessica, phoned to ask how much fabric she would need for the curtains *you're* going to make for her." Augusta didn't even try to hide her smile as she poured some of her wonderful apricot tea into the fragile violet-flowered cups that had belonged to my grandmother. I turned on the tree lights in the living room and we sat on the sofa to drink it.

"I'm too tired to answer them now," I said, kicking off my shoes. "And you know very well I have no idea how much fabric she'll need."

Augusta patted her lap and Clementine came up and laid her big head there. "She gave her window measurements and I wrote down the yardage she'll need and left it by the phone," she said, stroking the dog's soft ears.

"Augusta Goodnight, you're an angel!" I said, raising my cup in salute. She flushed, but I know she likes it when I say that. "I just wish you could tell us where we could find Idonia," I added.

Augusta listened quietly as I told her about finding the note from Idonia and our subsequent meeting with several of Stone's Throw's finest. "Have they changed their minds about trying to locate Idonia?" she asked. I could tell she didn't want me to know she was worried, but the stones in her necklace turned cloudy when she touched them.

I told her I had heard Kemper tell Captain Hardy he was going to talk with Al Evans again and try to get some idea about where Melrose might have gone. The captain was heading out to Willowbrook to speak with the Tanseys.

"Melrose must have phoned Idonia sometime yesterday," I said, "and Kemper even suggested trying to trace the call, but Melrose had obviously used a cell phone.

"Jennifer has left a message for Idonia's son, Nathan, in case she turns up there but I seriously doubt if she went to Savannah. Poor Nathan! He must be a basket case by now. I wouldn't be surprised if he showed up on our doorstep tomorrow."

"You said yourself Idonia was looking forward to singing in Sunday's musical program at your church," Augusta reminded me. "I fully expect her to be back before then."

I wish I could've believed she meant it.

BEN AND I HAD discussed going out that night and taking in a movie, but after all my running around in search of Melrose, then Idonia and our talk with Al Evans, I was more inclined toward a quiet night at home. Ben picked up a recent comedy on DVD and we ordered a pizza and spent the evening in front of the television.

"I'm dying to find out what the police learned from the Tanseys but I know they won't tell me," I said, polishing off my second piece of pepperoni with extra cheese. "I'm sure it must have been one of the Tanseys who took Idonia's locket, but why do you suppose it's so important? I wish I knew where it really came from."

Ben poured another glass of wine. "There's one person who might be able to help you."

"I can't imagine who. We've questioned just about everybody we could think of."

He picked up my copy of *The Messenger* and turned to the article that included Opal's obituary. "Not everybody. What about Opal's brother, Terrance Banks?"

"The one who lives in Tennessee? I don't think they were especially close. How do you think he could help us?"

"Don't forget, this Dexter Clark was his nephew, too," Ben said. "He might know more about the relationship between Dexter Clark and the Tanseys' daughter than you give him credit for, including how she came by the locket she wore. After all, Opal's sister, Maisie, was Dexter's mother, and the boy's parents are both dead. This uncle seems to be the only one left to ask."

"Knoxville's a big city," I said. "How am I supposed to find him?"

Ben finished the last wedge of pizza before he spoke. "Opal's funeral's tomorrow, isn't it? Surely her only brother will be there."

TWENTY

I WAS TRYING TO DECIDE what to wear to Opal Henshaw's visitation when Claudia phoned the next morning. "Sorry I didn't get back to you last night," she said, "but I was late getting home from the staff party. What's all this I hear about Idonia going off like that?"

I told her what Idonia's note had said and how we had gone to the police.

"Where in the world do you reckon she went? Have you heard anything more?"

"Not yet, but I'm hoping she'll get in touch with Jennifer or Nathan," I said. "Did you have a chance to talk with that girl who goes to the Tanseys' church?"

"Helen Harlan. She said Louella was at choir practice when Idonia's locket was stolen. They had an extra rehearsal that night to get ready for Christmas."

"So much for that theory," I said to Augusta, after assuring Claudia I'd let her know if I heard any more. "I was sure Louella Tansey was the one who took that locket."

Augusta clicked the remote and put her video exercise on pause. "Why Louella?"

"You saw the film from Ralph Snow's camera the same as I did," I said. "Remember how he focused on people in the entrance hall toward the end of the evening? The only men who even came near those stairs were our minister, Pete Whittaker, and Andy Collins, the man who plays the dulcimer, and I can't imagine why either of them would snatch Idonia's locket. The rest were women."

Augusta resumed her ritual, bending to touch one foot and

then the other. "Perhaps, as Ben suggests, Opal Henshaw's brother will be able to explain the significance of the locket. I hope there will be an opportunity for you to speak with him at the service this afternoon."

"Or even earlier," I said. "Ellis and I will be on the lookout for him at the visitation this morning, and some of us will be staying to serve lunch to out-of-town friends and family who show up." I had taken one of Augusta's pound cakes out of the freezer and Jo Nell was bringing her "Joyed-It" jam cake to serve with the fruit and sandwich trays we'd ordered.

I saw Ellis's car pull up out back before I even put on my makeup and glanced at the clock to see if I was running late. "You're early," I said as she breezed in through the kitchen, stopping to drop the latest Sarah Strohmeyer mystery on the table.

"This is such a good read, I thought Augusta might like it," she said, helping herself to a slice of banana bread left from breakfast. "I know I'm early, but thought maybe you might've heard something from Idonia."

"Nothing yet but it's still early. I'd give anything to know what went on out at the Tanseys' yesterday."

Ellis plopped on the side of my bed and examined her leg. "Damn! I've got a run in these blasted pantyhose. Got an extra pair?"

I tossed her one of several I had invested in at the Budget Shop and she kicked off her shoes and shimmied into them. "I'll bet I know somebody who might tell us something," she said.

"If you mean Weigelia, there's not enough time in the day to drag it out of her."

She grinned. "Not if you have the right bait. She's been after me for ages for that old photograph my great-uncle Pruitt made of one of the first black schools in town way back when he had a studio here. I'll have a copy made for me and let her have the original. She ought to have it anyway since a couple of her grandparents went there."

I blotted my lipstick and found some simple gold earrings I thought suitable for the occasion. "Go for it," I said, hunting for my purse. "But don't take long. We want to have plenty of time to track down Opal's brother Terrance."

I brushed my hair and changed shoes three times before Ellis finally hung up the phone. "Well?" I said.

"I don't think she knew much more than we do, but Weigelia said Kemper seemed kind of upset about it. He went out there with Alonzo Hardy after they talked to Al Evans and it sounded like the Tanseys were pretty torn up over it. From what Kemper said, she—Louella—got all weepy, and Preacher Dave just turned kind of pale and clammed up."

"What about Jeremiah?"

Ellis shrugged. "I don't think Jeremiah was there at the time."

"Are they planning to arrest anybody?" I said.

"Doesn't sound like it. I doubt if they have enough evidence— yet, but Weigelia thinks something's brewing."

I hadn't been to Willowbrook since the morning Ben and I went there for my Christmas tree and were greeted by ghostly music. "I know they've boarded up the house, but I'm still curious about those hidden stairs. Wonder if the police ever checked that out again."

"If they didn't, I'll bet they will now," Ellis said.

OPAL HENSHAW AND HER late husband Virgil had belonged to Stone's Throw Presbyterian Church for as long as I could remember, and I was baptized there, so the line to pay condolences had already snaked out the door of the fellowship hall and people were clustered on the walkway by the time Ellis and I arrived. I passed my cake along to one of the circle members in charge of today's lunch and turned up the collar of my coat to wait along with the others, waving to Nettie and Jo Nell who were ahead of us in line.

As we shuffled slowly along I caught snatches of murmured conversation about the circumstances surrounding Opal's death, and since most people knew we were in the choir, Ellis and I received several sympathetic pats and words of condolence for having experienced the trauma of finding her.

Oohs and aahs of approval rose when Geraldine Overton passed us on her way in the fellowship hall with an arrangement of daisies and white chrysanthemums for the table, and Ellis poked me from behind. "Opal will be whirling in her grave when she finds out that's not artificial," she whispered.

Out of the corner of my eye I saw Myra Jennings and her daughter Alice working their way up to where we stood and wasn't surprised later when I felt a firm grip on my arm.

"I heard Idonia Mae had a frightful scare the other night out at Bellawood," Myra bellowed loud enough to wake those in the cemetery behind the church. "Is she going to be all right?"

I saw Ellis bite her lip and look quickly away. "Yes, thank you, Myra. She's doing fine."

Alice stuck her face so close to mine I could tell she'd had sausage for breakfast. "What was the matter with her? I heard she was *poisoned*!"

"It was something she ate, but Dr. Smiley says she's going to be okay," I said. Thank goodness the line surged forward just then and Ellis and I were able to inch inside the hall and leave them behind. If these two heard Idonia had disappeared, we'd never see the last of them.

"I think somebody's trying to get your attention on the other side of the room," someone ahead of us said, and I looked up to see Nathan Culpepper waving to us from the table by the kitchen where coffee was being served.

"Maybe he's heard from Idonia," Ellis said as we hurried

over together, but as soon as I saw his face, I knew the news wasn't good.

"Any word?" I asked, trying to shield him from curious eyes.

"Nothing." Nathan sighed. "I don't know what else to do. I'm about ready to get in my car and start scouting the countryside." He poured coffee for Ellis and me and offered it silently. "The police told me you saw this Melrose fellow in Georgia. What was he doing there?"

"Beats me, unless he was doing the same thing we—uh—I was, which was trying to find out more about the Tanseys. I believe he was in Soso about the same time I was there. That's where the family lived before they came to Stone's Throw, and later he turned up at the mall in Commerce."

Nathan frowned. "And why, if I might ask, did you decide to go there?"

I took my time stirring sweetener into my coffee before answering, wondering all the while if Idonia had told Nathan there were doubts about the locket's origin, but as Nettie would say, the shit had already hit the fan. There was no holding back now.

"We think the locket Melrose gave your mother for Christmas might have originally belonged to one of the Tanseys," I began.

"You mean the man *stole* it?" Coffee sloshed as Nathan set down his cup.

"I don't know about that, but Dave Tansey was helping to park cars at Bellawood the night your mother was drugged and we believed there was a possibility a member of his family put that sleeping mixture in her drink," I said. "I thought if I talked with some of the people who knew them in Soso where he lived before, we might find out something about their background. After all, they're living out there at Willowbrook where a man died recently from a suspicious fall from a balcony." I didn't go into the fact that Dinah Tansey had been married to him.

"And Preacher Dave was seen at the church the night Opal died," Ellis added.

"Then, by God, why don't they arrest the man?" Nathan spoke so loudly several people turned to stare and Ellis and I hustled him into the kitchen where a couple of women from our circle arranged food on platters. I noticed that Anna Caldwell had brought her cream cheese salad with pineapple, apples, and pecans and hoped there might be at least a smidgen left for us.

We assured Nathan that the police probably didn't have enough evidence to arrest anyone yet but we had it on good authority (Weigelia's) that it would only be a matter of time.

"Meanwhile, my mother is who-knows-where with a man who might be not only a thief but a murderer as well!" he said.

Ellis was trying to convince Nathan to go back to Idonia's and wait in case his mother returned or tried to contact him there when the people who had been in line behind us signaled to tell us they had almost made their way to the front. As we hurried over I looked back to see him disappear through the door to the main part of the church and hoped he didn't intend to find Dave Tansey and confront him.

Ellis looked over my shoulder as we waited to speak to what was left of Opal Henshaw's family. "Which one do you think is her brother?" she whispered.

I shook my head. There were only a few people in the receiving line and none of them looked familiar to me.

I introduced myself to a matronly woman who looked as if all she wanted to do in this world was to sit down, and I didn't blame her. She turned out to be the sister of Opal's husband, Virgil, who died the summer before, and the younger man standing next to her, I learned, was her son. The son's wife, a teenaged boy, and two smaller girls comprised the family.

"Can you believe Opal's own brother didn't even come to her funeral?" Ellis said as we made our way back to the kitchen to help with lunch. "We'll have enough food left over to feed the multitudes."

And enough of Anna's salad left for us, I thought, eyeing the creamy squares on a platter of crisp green lettuce. But how were we going to get in touch with Opal's brother in Knoxville?

I kept an eye on the door the whole time we served the family, hoping that Terrance Banks would put in an appearance, but he didn't show. Ellis and I stayed after the meal to divide what was left of the food to take to some of the shut-ins in the community so the main sanctuary was full when we arrived for the service and we were directed to the balcony. Thank goodness we didn't have to sit on the first row because the only thing I could think of was poor Opal Henshaw tumbling over the railing.

Ellis nodded toward the area where Opal would have been standing, bending over the railing to reach the lopsided swag. "Can you imagine being shoved from behind like that?" she said under her breath. "Poor unsuspecting Opal!"

A shiver came over me as I looked involuntarily over my shoulder for some wicked unseen hand. Thank goodness Cissy, our organist, began playing softly, and since the hymn was "Nearer My God to Thee," I thought, *Maybe being in the balcony might have an advantage. Of course, I didn't want to be quite as near to God as Opal was, just yet.*

I was reading the memorial program when the family was ushered down the aisle to sit in the first pew so I didn't pay much attention to them until Ellis nudged me. "There's seven," she whispered.

I frowned. "Seven what?" All I could think of was that old tale, "Seven in One Blow," about a man killing flies, and I didn't see what that could possibly have to do with Opal's funeral.

"Seven *people*," she said. "There were only six for lunch."

I shifted to get a better look, and sure enough there was

an extra man down there. *Oh, please, let him be Terrance,* I thought. He looked to be about the right age with graying hair and a slight balding spot in the back. A brief graveside service was scheduled for immediately after this one and in spite of the rising winds and falling temperature, I was determined to see Opal Henshaw all the way to the end.

"Let's sneak out the side door," Ellis suggested as the service ended, and I nodded in agreement. If we could get to the cemetery ahead of the others maybe we could station ourselves to head off Terrance when it was over before he could get away.

"Listen," I said as we stood for the family to recess. "Cissy's playing 'Oh, Come All Ye Faithful,'" and I felt tears welling in my eyes in spite of myself. Opal might have been aggravating at times, but nobody could ever say she wasn't faithful.

TWENTY-ONE

HUDDLED TOGETHER IN the sparse protection of a large syca-
more in the corner of the Henshaws' plot, Ellis and I waited
for the family to be seated under the green canopy with Evans
and Son in white lettering on the side. Al Evans, who didn't
have a son, or at least any he was claiming, had been using the
same awnings since his father died at least ten years ago and
they were beginning to show the effects of the elements.

Al himself escorted the family of Virgil Henshaw's brother,
carefully holding the arm of his wife as she made her way
down the graveled path from the sleek black limousine, and I
wondered if he had heard any more from his cousin, Melrose.
As the town's decorous undertaker, Al Evans would hardly
take to the idea of having criminal kin, and if Melrose *had*
been responsible for what happened to Idonia or Opal, he might
be inclined to cover it up, I thought. After all, isn't covering
things up what undertakers do best? The more I pondered the
idea, the more I suspected that Al might even have been the
reason his cousin left town. But if so, why had they involved
Idonia?

"What are you frowning so about, Lucy Nan?" Jo Nell said
as she joined us. "I noticed your scowl two plots away."

"Tell you later," I said, keeping a watchful eye on Al, who
seemed to be looking back at me, or I thought he was looking
at me. It was hard to tell.

"We're going to try and have a word with Opal's brother
when this is over," Ellis told her. "He's the one in the gray
overcoat sitting on the end. It's important, so don't let him get
away."

"Good grief, you talk like he's going to make a run for it or something." Jo Nell drew a fluffy white beret from her coat pocket and pulled it over her ears. "What's so important that you need to speak with him?"

We didn't have a chance to answer as everyone grew quiet when the minister began reading a passage from *Psalms*.

I looked at the people gathered around the grave site to see if Nathan Culpepper was among them but he wasn't there. I hoped he had taken our advice and gone home instead of tearing off on the warpath as he seemed inclined to do.

Beside me Jo Nell was standing first on one foot and then the other and I supposed she was either trying to keep warm or she had to go to the bathroom. Mercifully, the service was brief and those attending paid hurried respects to the family before rushing to the warmth of their nearby vehicles.

The cemetery emptied quickly but the three of us stayed behind while Opal's brother held a quiet conversation with Al Evans.

"I wish I knew where Al was going when he leaves here," I whispered. "He looks like he's hiding something, don't you think? Kind of like he has a guilty secret."

"I guess he'll be going home to get warm like everyone else. The poor man can't help it if he has a glass eye," Jo Nell reminded me.

Just then the two men turned and noticed us there, pausing as if they expected us to join them, so we did.

"I wonder if we might have a few minutes of your time," I said to Terrance Banks after the three of us introduced ourselves. I looked pointedly at Al but he stood there as if he had no immediate plans to leave until Terrance offered him his hand.

"I'll drop by before I leave," Terrance said. "And thank you again for taking care of things."

"It's freezing out here," I said after Al finally left us. "Why don't we go inside where we can be more comfortable?"

Terrance nodded, looking puzzled. "You knew my sister Opal, then?" he said, walking along beside us. The wind lifted his scarf as he glanced back at the open grave. His face looked lined and sad.

"Oh, my, yes!" Jo Nell said. "And Virgil, too. It's not going to seem the same without them."

"I'm a good five years older than Opal," Terrance said, "so we weren't very close growing up, and I regret that. My sister was probably around fourteen when I left home, and frankly, we didn't have a lot in common." He sighed. "I wish I had made more of an effort to stay in touch."

I thought about my own brother, Joel, whom I adored but hadn't seen in months and promised myself I would phone him in Oregon as soon as I got home.

We found the church parlor empty and quickly shed our coats in the warm confines of the room after coming in from the cold. Terrance settled on one end of the mauve-striped love seat and leaned forward, hands on his knees. "If any of you have any idea about the circumstances of my sister's death, I'd like to hear it," he said. "The police seem to think it might not have been an accident, but they haven't been able to pinpoint a motive or give me any kind of explanation." He drew in his breath. "I'd like to get to the bottom if this."

"And so would we," Ellis said. She told him how we had found Opal the night of our Christmas choir rehearsal and how Margaret had tried to revive her.

His voice was bleak. "But it was too late. She was already dead. What in God's name was she doing up in the balcony?"

"Straightening an evergreen swag," Jo Nell said. "It was crooked, you know."

"I see." A smile played on Terrance Banks's lips. "She would, of course. I realize my sister could be a bit—uh—overbearing at times, but I don't understand why someone would want to kill her."

"Neither do we," I said, "but there seems to be some kind of connection to a family here, the Tanseys, and a locket that belonged to their daughter."

Disbelief was obvious in his face. "What does a locket have to do with it?"

"That's why we wanted to talk with you," Ellis said. "Opal told the girl's mother that a locket identical to the one belonging to her daughter had been in her family for years. We thought you might remember it."

He frowned. "Do you know what it was like?"

"Gold with a raised design of a dogwood blossom—" I began.

Terrance nodded. "Set with six small pearls. It belonged to my grandmother, but Mother passed it along to the older of the two girls, my sister Maisie. I remember Maisie wearing it when she married, but I don't know what happened to it after that."

"I think I do," I told him. I hesitated to bring up the subject of Terrance's nephew, Dexter Clark, especially since I would have to be the bearer of bad news, but it couldn't be avoided.

Noticing my hesitancy, Ellis jumped in. "Your sister Maisie's son, Dexter, was married to the Tanseys' daughter, Dinah. Dexter must've given her the locket as a wedding gift."

Terrance nodded. "Or his mother did—probably as an engagement gift. That sounds like something our Maisie would do. She died several months before the two married." He frowned. "My sister spent the last years of her life worrying about Dexter, and I don't doubt for one minute that his behavior hastened her death." Terrance paused as if weighing his words before continuing. "It's a terrible thing to say about my own kin, but Dexter always was a sorry sort, reckless and rebellious—didn't give a damn about anybody but himself. What happened to his young wife was a senseless tragedy! I didn't even know it had happened until months later when I learned about it from a friend, and well…I just couldn't believe it."

"Believe it," I said. "He didn't even bother to tell her own parents until she was dead and buried."

"God only knows what Dexter's up to now," Terrance said. "I heard he got religion after that happened to his wife, and I hope it's true—we'll see. Called me not too long ago, left a message he wanted to get together, but I hadn't had a chance to get back to him. I reckon he just wants money. Far as I'm concerned, it's just as well Maisie's not around to worry about it."

Ellis and I exchanged glances, hoping Jo Nell would volunteer to deliver the grim news, but she was preoccupied with folding her scarf in neat accordion pleats and wouldn't even look up.

"I don't think you're going to have to deal with Dexter anymore," I said, and told him what had happened at Willowbrook.

Terrance Banks didn't speak but sat for a minute with his hand supporting his forehead. Despite his harsh words about his nephew, he seemed to be genuinely upset. Maybe he was thinking of happier times when Dexter was small. Had he read to him from *Winnie the Pooh*? Given him a tricycle for Christmas? Probably not, I thought. The man hardly seemed the cuddly uncle type.

"And you think this locket might have had something to do with my sister's death?" he said finally. "Why?"

"I'm sure you knew about Opal's bed-and-breakfast?" Ellis said, and Terrance nodded, wondering, I'm sure, what connection that might have with Opal's quick descent from the church balcony. "One of her guests," she continued, "a fellow named Melrose DuBois, somehow came by that locket and gave it to a friend of ours for Christmas…"

"We can't be sure," I said, "but there's a possibility that he showed the locket to Opal before making a gift of it to—"

"And don't forget to tell him about Opal's fruitcake run," Jo Nell offered.

I frowned at her. "I was getting to that," I said. "A few days before Opal was killed, she and another member of our church circle took fruitcake and cookies to Dinah Tansey's family. You see, Dinah's father, Dave Tansey, is the sexton at our church. During the visit Opal noticed a studio photograph of Dinah on the piano, and she was wearing that locket in the picture."

"Did Opal ask the woman about it?" Terrance said.

"Yes, of course," I said, "but she was told that the locket in the photograph had been in the Tansey family for years and that it was probably one of several."

"Not so!" Terrance rose abruptly and walked to the window where he stood looking out at the playground where empty swings swayed eerily in the wind. "We were told our grandfather had that locket made especially for our grandmother for their wedding day with the date of their marriage inscribed on the inside." He turned and looked at us. "The woman was obviously lying, but why? Her daughter came by the locket honestly. It's not as if she stole it."

I didn't have an answer for that because it puzzled me as much as it did him.

"But that same night somebody did steal the locket from Idonia," Ellis said, and told him how our friend's punch had been doctored during the open house at Bellawood.

When Terrance spoke it came as a growl deep in his throat. "And a few days later my sister *accidentally fell* from the church balcony. And what, may I ask, are the police doing about this? I assume they've questioned these people—these Tanseys."

I replied that they had and I thought the police probably had a suspect in mind.

Apparently tiring of the view from the window, Terrance began to walk, making a circuit of the sofa, three chairs, and a table holding the ugly glass lamp Opal Henshaw herself had donated a few years before. I had to look away to keep from getting dizzy.

"It looks like an open-and-shut case to me," he said. "This family holds my nephew responsible for their daughter's death, and he ends up dying under suspicious circumstances on the property where the Tanseys live. When Opal identifies the locket as the one worn by our grandmother, they deny any connection to their daughter's marriage to Dexter. Seems to me they didn't want anybody else to know about it either— especially the police."

"But they know now," I said.

"And what about this Melrose you spoke of? Has anyone asked him how he came by the locket?"

Jo Nell spoke up. "Guess they would if they could find him," she said.

"OH, LORDY! I THOUGHT we'd never get away from there!" Ellis wailed as we finally left the church. "First Nathan and now Terrance! Maybe between the two of them, they'll track down whoever's responsible for all this."

More power to them, I thought, circling the cemetery where Terrance had gone to inspect his sister's grave, now heaped with the fresh flowers she had considered a frivolous expense.

"Where are you going?" Ellis looked at her watch. "The day's almost gone and I need to run by the store."

"Thought maybe I might see Al Evans here but I guess he's gone on back to the funeral home," I said. "Ellis, I wonder if he knows where Melrose is."

"Why would he?"

"Well, think about it. If Al's cousin Melrose had anything to do with what happened to Opal, it wouldn't do a whole lot for his professional image."

Ellis dug in her handbag for a notebook and pen. "Maybe not, but I don't know how you could prove it. Could we stop by the market? I need to pick up oranges and coconut for the ambrosia."

So much for that notion, I thought. Idonia had been gone over twenty-four hours and all Ellis could think about was her Christmas menu. Yet I knew I needed to do the same. Julie would soon be home for the holidays and she would expect all her favorite goodies.

I was making out a grocery list in my mind when Ellis interrupted my thoughts. "Do you still have a key to the Green Cottage?" she asked.

"You mean the house where the Tanseys live? I think there's one in that box of things that belonged to Mimmer, but surely you're not suggesting—"

Ellis shrugged. "How else are we going to look for the locket?" she said.

I felt the same sensation in my stomach I remembered from the summer we were ten and she assured me it really wasn't that far to jump from the pear tree to the garage roof. I had to wear a cast on my ankle until September and missed out on swimming the rest of vacation.

"And how do you plan to make the Tanseys disappear?" I asked.

"Tomorrow's Sunday, isn't it? And I happen to know the congregation at Preacher Dave's church is having their Christmas program tomorrow night."

"What do we do about Jeremiah?" I asked. "He might not be the church-going type."

She shrugged. "I guess we'll have to cross that bridge when we come to it."

And maybe it was my imagination, but I could swear I felt a pain in my ankle.

"I'm not going unless Augusta comes, too," I told Ellis as we loaded groceries into my car.

She wedged the last bag in the trunk and slammed the lid.

"She isn't going to like it—poking about in somebody's house when they're not there. You know how straitlaced Augusta can be."

"However, I sometimes make exceptions," Augusta said from the backseat. "Did you remember to get cranberries? I thought I'd make that salad Julie likes so much."

TWENTY-TWO

"ARE YOU SERIOUS?" I asked Augusta as the three of us drove the few blocks to drop off Ellis and her groceries. Searching someone's home without permission is frowned upon in most earthly tribunals, so I could only imagine how it would go over in even *higher* courts.

"I can't think of any other way," Augusta said, speaking in a matter-of-fact manner. I glanced at Ellis, who chewed her bottom lip, a sure sign she was reasoning we might have jumped in over our heads. I thought of my two children and six-year-old grandson coming to visit me in the penitentiary and almost ran a red light at the corner. It surprised me that Ellis and I seemed more concerned about our planned illegal venture than our virtuous guardian angel.

"Of course, there's no need for the two of you to be involved at all," Augusta continued. "I could go there tonight—or even sooner. I see no reason to wait."

I pulled into Ellis's driveway and threw on the brakes. "Now, just hold your heavenly horses!" I said. "I'm the only one who's ever been in that house, and I know the layout. Besides, whose idea was this, anyway?"

"I do believe it was mine," Ellis reminded me. "And I agree with Augusta, the sooner we find out about that locket, the better. We haven't heard from Idonia since day before yesterday, and for all we know she could be locked up there somewhere, or even worse—"

I didn't want to hear the "even worse" part. "But how do we know the Tanseys aren't there? What if one of them walks in?"

"I've thought about that," Ellis said. "It would seem reasonable for you to have a key since your relatives own the property, and you could always give some excuse or other like…"

I waited. "Like what?"

"Like—uh—well…measuring for new countertops or something," she said. "Maybe the sink drips or the toilet runs. Can't you just make up something?"

"I'd rather not," I said.

"And you shouldn't have to," Augusta assured me. "Not when you have me to do your recon—reconnais—preliminary survey of the area."

I smiled. "I'd hate to be the one to lead you into a life of crime, Augusta."

This time the angel didn't smile back. Her words were solemn and her voice, sad. "You must be aware there is someone in this town who holds human life in little regard. This person has killed twice, and I don't believe they would hesitate to do it again. If I have to make this choice to prevent another such loss, then so be it."

"Hooray, Augusta!" Ellis applauded. "Just give me time to put away my groceries."

ALTHOUGH IT WAS ONLY six o'clock, it was dark when we started out a short time later, which wasn't surprising since the day before, I remembered, had been the shortest day of the year. At Augusta's urging we stopped at a fast-food drive-in for milkshakes, although nobody seemed to be hungry but her.

"Your body needs fuel to go on," she reminded us.

The plan was for Augusta to find out if any of the Tanseys were at home. If not, using my grandmother's key, Ellis and I would enter and search for the locket we were almost certain was somewhere inside the house while the angel kept watch.

This time, Ellis drove and I sat in the passenger seat beside her holding an untouched milkshake in my lap. Augusta had ordered fries with her strawberry shake and sat in the backseat dipping each one in ketchup as she ate. Although I enjoy junk food as much as anybody, the greasy smell of the fries was causing a small uprising in my stomach.

"I don't see how you can sit back there and eat like we don't have a care in the world," I told her. "Aren't you even the least bit nervous?"

Augusta finished the last fry and dabbed her lips daintily with a paper napkin. "Think blue, Lucy Nan," she reminded me. "Take a deep breath, close your eyes, and think of a calm and beautiful place—a summer sky, a peaceful lake, a gentle stream."

Well, I tried, I really did, but all I felt was a tornado forming somewhere in my middle, and the closer we got to Willowbrook, the more I hoped we would find the Tanseys at home.

We didn't. The yellow-painted cottage sat bordered by huge oaks at the end of a lonely road, and the only thing that stirred on our approach was a gray squirrel scurrying across the grass in search of something to eat. The garage that housed the family's two vehicles was empty.

Ellis brought the car to a stop and parked boldly out front as if we had a right to be there. "Maybe you should go to the door and knock—just in case," she said, turning to me.

But holding up her hand, Augusta signaled for us to stay and silently slipped from the car. We watched as she walked up to the front door, hesitating for only a second before she disappeared inside—at least I assumed she was inside, although the front door never opened to admit her.

What would we do if any of the Tanseys drove up just then? What would we say? A hundred explanations came to mind but none was believable. I might be able to lie convincingly to Preacher Dave or Louella, I thought, but what could I say to Jeremiah?

The cottage, the yard, the car where we waited was shrouded in darkness now and I felt the bleakness of it creep into my head and inch its way down. I was afraid of Jeremiah Tansey.

"I guess they've all gone to church to rehearse for tomorrow's program," Ellis said, looking over her shoulder. "I hope it takes a long time." She shivered. "Why is Augusta taking so long in there?"

As if in answer, the angel suddenly slid into place in the backseat. "There's no one there now," she said, "but I wouldn't take too long if I were you. And it might be wise to move the car somewhere out of sight. Is there anywhere nearby where we could conceal it?"

"You mean so we could make a quick getaway?" I said. For some reason I wanted to giggle.

"What about that old shed just down the road? We could walk from there," Ellis suggested.

Or run, I thought, thinking more of the return trip. Mimmer had said the shed had once been used to weigh and store cotton, back when the fields were planted with cash crops, but now the sagging building contained only rusting pieces of outdated farm machinery and extra salt blocks for the cattle.

I watched for lights approaching the whole time Ellis turned back onto the road and drove the few yards to park behind the shed. In warmer weather weeds surrounding it would be so high it would be difficult to walk, but now dry grass only whispered under our feet. Ellis used a flashlight to find the narrow pathway through a thicket of trees and underbrush to the back of the Tanseys' cottage. Preacher Dave and others before him often used it as a short-cut to the shed and the cattle gate to the pasture across the road.

"I haven't the faintest idea where to start looking once we get inside," Ellis said as we made our way through the sparse woods Indian style. The moon was obscured by clouds, which was an advantage in a way because it gave us the cover of darkness, but it was difficult to see where we were going. I walked behind Augusta, keeping my eyes on the golden gleam of her hair.

"I suppose it depends on who took the locket as to where

they might hide it," Augusta said. "Or, if they believe no one will come looking for it, they might not hide it at all."

I hoped we would be that lucky. A glance at my watch told me it was almost seven o'clock already and I didn't want to spend any more time in that house than necessary.

With Augusta stationed out front to alert us if anyone approached, Ellis and I let ourselves in the back door and stepped into a small laundry room that opened onto the kitchen. I felt like the guilty intruder I was and resisted the impulse to turn and run, but I knew Ellis would never let me forget it. "Okay, I'll take Jeremiah's room and you search his parents'," I said, feigning bravery.

"Be sure to leave everything the way you found it," she warned me, knowing some of my more careless habits. "We don't want them to even suspect we were here."

I had brought a container of Augusta's homemade candy—divinity, of course—and hurried to slip it among the packages under the family's small artificial tree just in case we were caught. If we were lucky, however, the Tanseys would never know who brought it.

The cottage was built in the Cape Cod manner with a half story upstairs, which I assumed to be Jeremiah's, and as it turned out, I was right. The enclosed back stairway off the kitchen led to a long, narrow room with two dormer windows facing the front of the house. At least, I thought, from here I would be able to see the lights of an approaching car.

Jeremiah, it seemed, lived a rather Spartan lifestyle if it could be judged by the furnishings in his room, which contained a single bed, dresser, small table, and straight chair. On the wall across from his bed, shelves held a large television set with all the electronic attachments including a DVD, CD player, and speakers. But from the looks of my surroundings, I didn't think he spent much time there, and who could blame him? A computer sat on the table next to the bed and I was tempted to turn it on to learn if there was anything of interest there, but I'm just now getting accustomed to the one I use at Bellawood, and I didn't want to take a chance on messing with this one.

I didn't dare turn on a light so I used a flashlight to look through Jeremiah's dresser drawers which I found to be surprisingly neat. I don't even pretend to know a lot about current fashions for men, but I recognized some expensive brand-name clothing in Jeremiah Tansey's closet. For someone who worked as an unskilled laborer for a fencing company in nearby Rock Hill, he seemed to spend more on his wardrobe than my professor son, Roger. But being single and living at home, I reasoned, why shouldn't he?

Downstairs I could hear Ellis moving quietly about and when I was sure the locket couldn't possibly be in Jeremiah's room, I took one more look around, closed the door behind me, and went downstairs to help.

A glance out the living room window showed Augusta still keeping watch out front, wrapped to the teeth in her cape, and hugging herself for warmth, and I reminded myself to hurry as I knew she hated being cold.

"I found a box with a few earrings and a necklace or two in there but not much else," Ellis said, stepping from the couple's room. "I hope Santa Claus brings Louella a gift certificate for some decent clothes for Christmas. The contents of that woman's closet is just plain dismal."

"Sounds like she could take some pointers from Jeremiah," I said, and told her what I'd observed upstairs. Of course I knew I'd be the very last person appointed to snoop for the fashion police, I told myself as the annoying virtuous part of me waggled a finger, but I couldn't help what I saw.

It took the two of us several minutes to examine the contents of the curio cabinet in the dining room, being careful not to drop the souvenir cups, plates, and doodads from various vacation spots. I didn't dare to touch the lovely hand-painted cake plate that was displayed on the top shelf or the dainty china teapot beside it. Besides, it was obvious the locket wasn't here.

"What now?" I asked after a search of the buffet drawers proved disappointing. "Guess there's nothing left but the kitchen."

Ellis frowned. "Isn't there a small room on the other side of it?"

"You mean the pantry?"

"No, behind that," she said. "Looks like it's been added on."

"Oh, right! I forgot about that. One of the former tenants built it for his mother, but lately, I think it's just been used for storage."

"Sounds like a likely spot to hide a locket." Ellis pushed open the swinging door from the dining room and hurried through the kitchen, stopping abruptly at the closed door of the added room. "Damn! It's locked!" She tried the knob again, shaking it. "Well, this should tell us something. Now we'll never know if it's in here or not."

"Of course we will. We might not be able to get inside," I reminded her, "but I know somebody who can."

Augusta was so happy to be invited in out of the cold, she practically rushed inside in a blur and didn't even hesitate to debate the issue when Ellis told her we wanted her to let us into a locked room.

Ellis snatched up the jacket she had cast aside earlier. "I'll keep watch until it's open," she said, hurrying toward the front of the house. "Just try to hurry, please!"

But that last admonition proved unnecessary because Augusta had the locked door open before Ellis had crossed the room.

"Dear God!" I sighed, looking past her. And Augusta, who dislikes hearing anyone take the Lord's name in vain, barely made a face.

"What is it?" Ellis rushed to see and stood fixed in the doorway, her fingers fastened onto my shoulder. The small area in front of us contained the furnishings of a young girl's room, including a large rag doll in a rocking chair and an open book on the bed. In the narrow closet we found a limited array of clothing appropriate for a teenaged girl, and just about every space on the wall was covered with photographs of Dinah Tansey throughout most of the stages of her brief life.

TWENTY-THREE

"IT SEEMS TO BE SOME kind of shrine," I said, standing trans-fixed in the doorway. "How sad!"

"And creepy." Ellis walked over and looked closer at the book. "They've even left it open to mark the place as if she'll be back to finish reading it."

"What was she reading?" I asked, leaning over to see the title. I wasn't surprised to see Daphne du Maurier's *Rebecca*, which I had read a number of times during my teens.

"It's almost as if she never left," Ellis said, looking around.

"She didn't," I reminded her, "because she was never here. Dinah married Dexter Clark soon after high school before her parents even moved to Stone's Throw. She never saw this room."

So far Augusta had not spoken but I saw that she had stepped back from the doorway and now stood in the kitchen. The stones in her necklace, I noticed, were lusterless and dark. "I don't have a good feeling about this," she said. "I think we should leave right now."

"But we haven't even looked in here," I said, opening a drawer in the chest next to the bed. "If the locket is in this house, wouldn't this be the natural place to keep it?"

"Please, Augusta! We're so close. I'm sure we can find it." Ellis looked at the kitchen clock. "See, it's not even eight yet. Just give us a little more time."

The angel sighed. Her earlier confidence and enthusiasm seemed to have vanished into the night. "Very well, I'll be waiting out front, but do look quickly. However, I don't believe you'll be finding anything there."

"WELL, AUGUSTA WAS RIGHT…there's not much here," Ellis said, shutting a desk drawer a few minutes later. "I haven't seen anything but some old schoolwork, a couple of paperbacks, and a few letters."

I had found the dresser drawers to be almost empty as well except for a few pairs of stockings, underwear, and a modest bathing suit. "I guess this is what Dinah left behind when she ran off to marry that loser." I shoved the drawer back into place. "I can't understand what she saw in him. What a waste!"

While Ellis searched the closet, running her hands over shelves and crevices, I checked for a hiding place in the bedding, feeling under the mattress and pillow with no success. "Let's get out of here," I said finally. "This place is depressing."

Several pairs of shoes made a neat line across the closet floor and Ellis examined them one by one before carefully putting them back into place. "I'm with you," she said, and froze with her hand on the closet door. Someone was in the kitchen.

Heart thudding, I knelt behind the bed as close to the floor as I could get, but if one of the family was there, surely they would notice the door to the locked room was not only unlocked, but open.

Whoever was in there was now opening the refrigerator door and I heard the clanking of jars being shifted about. I dared to glance across the room at Ellis, who was attempting to flatten herself against the wall.

Something squeaked. An oven door? This was followed by a puzzling period of silence. I was working up the courage to make a dash for it when I heard another noise, one I couldn't identify, but it warned me the person was still there.

Ellis held a finger to her lips and began to move silently toward the door, hand out, as if she meant to close it quietly, when someone shouted, "Ah!"

I recognized that "ah" and it sounded even more heavenly than usual. Augusta! I jumped to my feet and joined her in the kitchen, where she stood at the counter holding something in a small plastic bag. "Ah!" she said again. "I thought I'd find it here!"

She had taken the top from the canister that held flour and the white powder lay scattered like snow on the countertop.

"What is it? Is it the locket?" Ellis reached for the bag. "It *is!* Won't Idonia be surprised when she sees it?"

But Augusta was already cleaning away the mess she had made and now she held out her hand for the locket. "We can't do that, Ellis. We have to put it back right away or they'll realize we've been here."

All this trouble for nothing! I thought. "So why look for it if we have to put it back?" I fumed. "At least let's open it and see what's inside. There must be a reason this is so important to somebody."

But the only thing we found inside was a yellowing photograph of a bridal couple and the engraved date of their marriage, just as we had been told. Augusta quickly buried the locket once more, replaced the top, and in an instant the countertop was gleaming. "Now that we know who took it, it will serve our purpose better to let the police discover it here," she said, quickly rinsing her hands at the sink.

Ellis frowned. "But we really don't, do we?"

"Don't what?" I asked.

"Know who took it," she said. "It could've been any of the Tanseys."

I watched as Augusta made sure the door to "Dinah's room" was locked, and one look told me she was wearing her "secret" face. "You know, don't you?" I asked. "You know who took the locket."

"Well, *who*? Don't keep us in suspense," Ellis said.

Augusta busied herself bundling up in her cape before

stepping out into the night. "I'd rather not say until I'm sure," she said.

I hurried after her. "But how did you know where to look? What made you think to check the flour canister?"

"Why, I read it in a mystery," she said.

WE HAD ONLY WALKED a few steps from the house when Augusta stopped suddenly in front of us, her hand lifted in warning.

"What is it?" I asked, untangling my sleeve from a briar.

The angel spoke quietly. "I don't think we're alone out here."

I listened. "I don't hear anything," I said. It was hard to see in the darkness and I hadn't seen or heard a car approaching.

"Oh, come on, Augusta. It's freezing out here!" Ellis grumbled. "I think we're all on edge, and it's getting late. Let's just hurry and get home."

We couldn't very well spend the night standing out here in the woods, I thought, and was relieved when Augusta finally moved on.

The three of us walked as quickly as we could but it was impossible to be quiet, at least for Ellis and me, as we seemed to step on every brittle twig in our path, and dry leaves rattled in our wake.

Was there someone else in the woods? Augusta wasn't the type to be alarmed for no reason. Had one or more of the Tanseys returned and were now waiting to confront us here in this lonely place?

I was soon able to make out the dark outline of the shed just ahead of us, and Ellis and I started to run to the safety of the car parked behind it. But again Augusta signaled us to stop.

And that was when I saw them. In the clearing beside the shed two figures waited as if they intended to block our way to the car. It was too dark to see their faces but they didn't appear to be trying to hide. It was almost as if they *wanted* us to see them.

Should we run? Try to escape? Terrified, I looked to Augusta for advice.

"Uh-oh!" she said.

Uh-oh? What kind of angelic response was that? Of course she didn't have to worry, I remembered. Whoever waited for us wouldn't be able to see *her*, which would leave them free to concentrate on Ellis and me.

One of them spoke. "You might as well come on out. We know you're there."

As soon as I heard the voice, the fear that had formed a huge icicle in my middle began to thaw—a little.

"I hope you have a good reason for being out here," Kemper Mungo said.

Someone shone a flashlight in our faces. "Miss Lucy Nan? Miss Ellis? This isn't a very good place for you ladies right now." Speaking softly but sternly, Police Lieutenant Ed Tillman, my son's boyhood friend, came out of the darkness to meet us. "I'm going to have to ask you to explain why you're here," he said.

"Fine, as long as we can do it someplace where it's warm," Ellis said.

I agreed. The wind had picked up and the athletic shoes I wore to sneak around in weren't doing a very good job of keeping my feet warm. Augusta, I noticed, had vanished altogether.

We wound up sharing a Thermos of coffee in the police cruiser parked off the road not too far away. Augusta was some-where close by. I sensed her presence and knew she'd never desert us even if she couldn't testify on our behalf in court. Ellis concentrated on relishing her steaming beverage and looked to me to take all the heat. And that was when I decided to tell the truth. Sort of.

"We went by to drop off some homemade candy but the

door was locked," I said. "I hated to leave it outside—it's divinity, you know, and moisture just ruins it, so I just let myself in—"

Ed Tillman frowned. "How?"

"With a key, of course. My cousin owns the place and sometimes asks me to look in to see if everything's all right—with the tenant's permission, of course."

Well, that was an out-and-out lie. I could just imagine Augusta flinching.

"But the Tanseys weren't at home?" I could barely see Ed's face, but there was a question in his voice.

I let that hang in the air for a minute. "I thought I might find Idonia's locket," I said finally.

Kemper cleared his throat. "In other words, you searched the house."

Ellis, seeing my dilemma, finally jumped in—and about time! "Just looked around a little, that's all," she said.

"You must have known you were breaking the law," Ed said. "And what made you think the Tanseys had Mrs. Culpepper's locket?"

I couldn't believe these two were as thickheaded as all that, but this wasn't the time to say so. "Who else would have taken it?" I asked. "That locket was given to the Tanseys' daughter, Dinah, when she became engaged. There's a picture on their piano of her wearing it."

The two men exchanged looks which I took to mean they *thought* they knew something we didn't.

"I don't suppose you found it," Ed Tillman said.

I let that one hang, too, until the silence got too much for them.

"Are you trying to tell us you *did*?" This from Kemper.

"Well, you did ask," Ellis reminded him. "What do you want us to say?"

Ed—or somebody—drew in his breath. "Then I'll have to

ask you to turn it over to us. That locket could be used as evi—"

"We don't have it," I told him.

"Then just where is it?" Ed was getting impatient.

Ellis finished her coffee and nudged me. "Should we tell them, Lucy Nan, or let them find it for themselves?"

I considered suggesting we make a game of it like I do with Teddy, letting them know when they're getting hot or cold, but my better instincts took over. "Oh, for heaven's sake, it's in the flour canister," I said.

"THEY NEVER WOULD'VE found it," Ellis said on the drive home.

Augusta spoke from the backseat. "Probably not. You did the right thing, Lucy Nan. Now it's their time to hit the ball."

I smiled to myself in the darkness. The ball was in their court, all right, if they would just pursue it. After a serious lecture on the dangers and repercussions of what we had just done, we were warned to stay on our own side of the fence, so to speak, and leave the detective work to the professionals.

"What do you think they were doing out there?" Ellis asked as we turned into my driveway on Heritage Avenue.

"I think they were on a stakeout," I said. "From what Weigelia tells me, Jeremiah seems to have cut and run. They must've been waiting for him to show up at home."

"I've read all about that," Augusta said. "It's called 'casing the joint.'"

Now that the police knew where to find the locket, I thought, the next step would be to obtain a search warrant, and it occurred to me we hadn't even told them about the locked room.

Ellis must have been thinking about it, too. "I was hoping we'd find at least some clue as to where Idonia might be," she said. "Tomorrow's the program of Lessons and Carols and she'd never miss that—not intentionally, anyway."

"Hey! It's not over till it's over," I said. "Maybe Nathan's heard from her by now." I didn't like the way this conversation was going.

"Isn't that a car parked over there by your hydrangea bush?" Augusta said as Ellis pulled up to the back steps.

I leaned forward to get a better look. Were the Stone's Throw police casing our joint, too? I had left the porch light burning and even with the headlights from Ellis's car, it was hard to distinguish one make from another. Julie wasn't due home for another couple of days and even in this poor light I would recognize her little red Honda.

"I think we'd better get out of here," Ellis said, and gunned the accelerator to back away, but Augusta leaned over to touch her on the shoulder. "Wait. It's all right," she said.

We watched as the driver's door of the strange car opened and a figure stepped into the light. "Where in the world have you been? I've been waiting out here for hours," Idonia said. "I thought you'd never get home!"

TWENTY-FOUR

"AND WE'D LIKE TO KNOW where *you've* been," I said, running to hug her. "Are you all right? We've been worried to death!"

Idonia practically shoved us up the steps. "First, I *have* to go to the bathroom, and then I'd really like something hot to drink. It's freezing out here."

"Does Nathan know where you are?" Ellis asked after Idonia's needs were taken care of. "He's been out of his mind wondering if you're okay."

Idonia waved that aside while she dunked an orange spice teabag in a cup of steaming water. "Oh, I left a message on his cell phone. He knows I'm all right."

"But does he know where you are?" I asked, and I was almost sure of the answer. If Idonia's son knew she was here he'd be in this kitchen with the rest of us.

"Well, you see…that's the thing…" We waited while she stirred sugar into her cup. "He'll have all these questions and it's late and I'm really tired." Idonia smiled coyly, which is *not*—I repeat, *not* her usual manner at all. "I'd rather not have to deal with Nathan until tomorrow."

Ellis was turning red in the face, which meant she was about two seconds away from giving Idonia Mae Culpepper a serious piece of her mind, but she'd have to get in line behind me. "Well, you're going to have to deal with us," I said. "Where on God's green earth have you been for the past two days?"

"Melrose felt uneasy about my staying here in town after

what happened at Bellawood, so he arranged for me to meet him at this lovely little inn this side of Raleigh," she said.

Ellis frowned at her across the table. "You've been with Melrose all this time?"

Idonia sipped her tea before speaking. "Oh, it was all very proper, you understand—separate rooms and all."

"I don't give a rat's ass if you and Melrose made out on the courthouse lawn!" I said. "Would it have taken too much of an effort to give at least one of us a call?"

Alarmed at the tone of my voice, Clementine scurried into the sitting room where I knew Augusta waited to calm her. If only she could calm me!

Idonia spoke serenely as if she were addressing a small child, one who isn't very bright. "But that would defeat the purpose, wouldn't it? The object, after all, was for me to remain out of sight until all this has been cleared up." She tucked a stray lock of red hair into place and cleared her throat. "Of course I in-sisted on returning for tomorrow's Christmas service, although Melrose was dead set against it. But I just told him, 'Melrose,' I said, 'I haven't missed taking part in our Christmas music pro-gram for over thirty years, and I don't intend to start now.'"

Idonia drained the rest of her tea and stood. "And now, if you don't mind putting me up for the night, I'd like to get some sleep. I was going to ask Nettie for that spare room upstairs but she must've already gone to bed as I couldn't get her to come to the door. You know, I wouldn't dare mention this to Nettie, but I believe she's getting quite deaf."

Ellis, who also stood, held up a hand. "Whoa!" she said. "Do you realize, Idonia, that the police are looking for Melrose DuBois?"

The woman seemed genuinely puzzled. "Now why would they do that?"

"Let me count the ways," I said, listing them on my fingers.

"First, he was seen at the church the night of Opal Henshaw's murder, and left town soon afterward—"

"Murder?" Idonia gasped.

"We're pretty sure it was deliberate," I said, continuing. "Also, he lied about that locket he gave you, which, if you'll remember, belonged to the Tanseys' daughter, Dinah, who was married to Opal's nephew Dexter Clark…"

"Remember him?" Ellis said. "Dexter was the fellow we found under the balcony at Willowbrook—deader than a door-nail. The police are kind of curious to find out how Melrose came by that fascinating piece of jewelry."

Idonia sat again. "I've asked him about that, and there's a perfectly good explanation, if you'll—"

"Idonia, if you know where Melrose is, I think you'd better tell us," I said.

She looked down at her hands in her lap. "You'll know soon enough. He plans to be at church in the morning…and Melrose didn't know anything about that locket, I promise!"

"But why the disappearing act?" Ellis asked. "And why isn't he with you now?"

Idonia shook her head and smiled. "He has his reasons. You'll see. And now, if you don't mind, I really need some sleep."

"Only if you make a phone call first," I told her, and Ellis and I stood on either side of her while she spoke with Nathan, who happened to be staying at Idonia's. I could hear Nathan Culpepper's stormy ranting from a few feet away.

"He wants to speak with you," Idonia said, handing me the phone, and I assured Nathan that his mother was safe with me and that I would deliver her to church in the morning. And then I laughed.

"What's so funny? What did he say?" Idonia asked.

"He wanted to know if I thought you were getting even with him for that time he played hooky in junior high," I said.

Idonia's eyes widened. "Nathan *played hooky* in junior high?"

ELLIS LEFT SOON AFTERWARD and Idonia was settled in the guest room for the night when I remembered there was something I meant to do. I looked at my watch. What time was it in Oregon? It didn't matter. I picked up the phone and called my brother, Joel, whom I hadn't seen in almost a year. He plans to come for a long visit soon after the holidays.

It was late when, after a long chat with Joel, I finally crawled into bed and I should've dropped right off to sleep, but the events of the day kept playing in my mind. Idonia was safely back, thank goodness; the local police were aware of where the missing locket was hidden, and it looked as if they would make an arrest soon. Or as soon as they could locate Jeremiah Tansey. Had it been Jeremiah who buried the locket in the flour canister? Augusta seemed to think she knew who had put it there, but she wasn't sharing her secrets.

When at last I drifted off to sleep I dreamed of a young woman I took to be Dinah Tansey, only the Dinah in my dream was even younger than the girl in the photograph. She lay across a bed in a room with yellow walls and white curtains at the window and she was crying. It wasn't at all like the room we had seen at the Tanseys' cottage except for the locked door. But in my dream the door was bolted from the inside.

"THERE'S SOMETHING I WANT to run past you when we get a chance," I whispered to Ellis in the choir room the next morning. With Idonia there I hadn't been able to discuss with Augusta what was on my mind, and we had to rush to the church after a hurried breakfast.

Ellis adjusted her stole and mine. "We have an hour break between services. Maybe we can sneak away to the parlor. Can it wait till then?"

I nodded. I guessed it would have to.

"Will Augusta be in the congregation this morning?" Ellis asked, checking to see if her music was in order.

"You might not see her, but she'll be there both times. You know how she loves Christmas music," I said. "And Idonia says Melrose is coming, too."

Ellis sniffed. "He'd better!"

But try as I would, I couldn't find Melrose DuBois among the people attending the Lessons and Carols program although I scanned every row while our minister read the scriptures, and again during the offertory until I felt my eyes would cross.

Idonia's son, Nathan, sat in the second row flanked by his wife and daughter and I don't believe he took his eyes off his mother for one second. I didn't blame him. Idonia had a nervous, distracted look as if she wanted to bolt at any minute. A few days ago she had been pleased when she heard Nathan would be bringing his family, and now, after hours of rehearsals, all she could think of was the absence of one Melrose DuBois. God help him if he didn't show up for the eleven o'clock service, I thought, because if the police didn't track him down, I would!

ELLIS CLOSED THE DOOR to the parlor behind us and, kicking off her shoes, curled up on one end of the sofa. "What's going on?" she asked. "Has Idonia heard any more from Melrose? She seems in a bad way—did you notice? I'll swear, if that little jerk doesn't show up for church this morning I'm going to wring his neck."

"Let's hope he's there at eleven," I said. "He'd better not be leading her on! I felt bad about leaving her there in the choir room. I know she wondered where we were going."

"Maybe some of Cissy's turtle bars will cheer her up," Ellis said.

Our choir director always baked her fabulous cookies made with chocolate, brown sugar, and pecans to go with the other goodies choir members brought to eat between Christmas services. Most of us, I've learned, will grab any chance to have a party and I hated missing this one, but I needed somebody to tell me I wasn't crazy.

"Ellis," I began, "I had the strangest dream last night. Have you ever wondered if Dinah Tansey might still be alive?"

"Lucy Nan Pilgrim, you are totally, absolutely, and undeniably crazy!" my friend said. "What makes you think a thing like that?"

I told her about my dream and reminded her that Dinah's family wasn't told of the girl's death until after she was buried. "What if she never died?"

Ellis frowned. "Then who's buried in her grave?"

"Maybe there isn't any grave. Maybe Dinah Tansey is the ghostly woman who haunts Willowbrook."

"Now wait a minute, Lucy Nan, let's don't get carried away. You aren't thinking she actually lives in that room we found? Dinah would be in her twenties now and the clothes we found, everything was for somebody much younger."

Someone passed by the door and Ellis waited to continue until the footsteps went away. "And why in the world would she do it? She'd have to be—well, you know—"

"Crazy," I said. "I wish there were some way we could find out for sure."

"I believe there is."

I looked up to see Augusta standing before us. "The music this morning was lovely," she said. "But if you want any of those refreshments, you'd better hurry. I'm afraid the others have already taken care of most of it."

"How?" I said.

Augusta glanced at herself in the mirror that hung over the sofa. Today she wore a garment of what looked like golden filigree over a deep green satin-like dress that swirled when she walked and brought out the turquoise depths in her eyes. "How what?" she asked.

Today I had little patience with her vanity. "How can we find out if Dinah Tansey Clark is really dead?"

"If what I've read is correct, they have to issue a death certificate when someone dies. If you can find out where she was supposed to have died, they should have one on record," she said.

"Augusta Goodnight, you're a genius!" I threw my arms around her and sensed her serenity like a balm. "But how are we going to learn that?"

"Preacher Dave would be the most likely source," Ellis said, "but if she really isn't dead and the family is keeping her there in secret, he certainly isn't going to tell us the truth."

"Soso," I said, remembering my conversations with Aunt Eula and her kin in the small Georgia town. "Dinah was a friend of the Shackelfords' daughter Carolyn. Maybe she kept up with her after she married. I'll call Aunt Eula as soon as we get home."

But I immediately shoved that to the back of my mind when we processed into the sanctuary for the second time that day and that scumball Melrose DuBois was nowhere in sight.

"I'm worried about Idonia," Jo Nell had confided when we met briefly in the ladies' room earlier. "First she disappears and now she looks like she's about to jump out of her skin. It's that Melrose again, isn't it?"

"He's supposed to show up at one of the services this morning," I explained. "Idonia said she had his word on it."

"Ha!" Jo Nell snorted, letting the door slam behind her.

Ben smiled up at me from an aisle seat and I smiled back remembering he would be taking me to lunch after church at one of those new steak restaurants out on the highway. Roger sat near the front with Jessica and Teddy, and Julie would soon be home for Christmas. If only things would work out for Idonia! How rude and inconsiderate of that pipsqueak Melrose to put a damper on our holidays!

Nathan Culpepper stationed himself by the choir room door as soon as the service was over and I remembered that he expected his mother to go back to Savannah with him for Christmas. I wasn't surprised to find Idonia waiting for me as I hung up my robe. "Lucy Nan, you've got to help me," she said. "I can't leave with Nathan today—I just can't! Something's happened to Melrose, I know it."

I could see that this was not the time or the place to try and convince her that Melrose DuBois might not be the knight in shining armor she thought him to be. Instead I sent frantic eye signals to Zee and Jo Nell who stood behind her putting their music in appropriate stacks according to Cissy's directions, and Jo Nell, bless her heart, came over and put her arm around Idonia.

"We're so glad to have you back," she said. "Don't you dare scare us like that again!" And Idonia, ever the one with the stiff upper lip, began to cry.

"Honey, he's not worth it," Zee said with tears in her own eyes. "If the man's going to make you unhappy like this, you're well rid of him."

"You don't understand. He's in trouble—bad trouble, and if we don't find him, it might be too late." Idonia accepted a tissue and used it accordingly.

"What kind of trouble?" Ellis asked. "I thought you said you knew where he was."

"I did yesterday. It's today I'm worried about. I'm afraid he's gotten in over his head." Idonia sank onto the nearest chair. "Melrose has good intentions—I know he does, but he has no idea who he's dealing with, or, I'm afraid, how to go about it."

"How to go about what?" I asked.

Idonia took another tissue and shook her head. "Detective work. He's been taking a correspondence course in how to become a private investigator, and he says he's on the trail of the person who drugged my punch and stole the dogwood locket.

Melrose thinks it's all tied up with the murder of that man you all found at Willowbrook and what happened to poor Opal Henshaw."

And Idonia Mae Culpepper began to cry anew.

TWENTY-FIVE

"PLEASE DON'T WORRY, Idonia," I found myself saying. "We'll work it out somehow. I think it's time to bring the police into this, and you're going to have to tell Nathan what's going on."

"Tell Nathan what?" Suddenly Nathan was standing beside us, and I saw Ben in the doorway behind him wondering, probably, what was taking me so long.

"Look, all of us have to eat lunch," I said. "Unless you have other plans, why not meet somewhere and discuss this calmly? Ben and I were thinking of Big Jake's out on the north end of town."

"I'm not hungry," Idonia said.

"Well, I am," Nathan told her, "and Big Jake's sounds just fine to me."

And so it was decided. Ellis had family coming for lunch, Claudia had already left for home, and Jo Nell was expecting some of her husband Paul's kin to drop by, but Zee and Nettie joined us at a table for eight, which included Sara and Millicent, Nathan's wife and daughter. Over two hours later when just about everyone else had left the restaurant and the busboy began pointedly sweeping under our feet, Nathan finally agreed to stay in Stone's Throw one more day to await news of the whimsical Melrose DuBois. Idonia, however, was to take her story to the local police.

"Lucy Nan, you will come with me, won't you?" she said when leaving the restaurant. "I mean, after all, you were at Bellawood when the locket was taken, and you said you saw Melrose at that mall in Georgia. Besides," she added, "those

Tanseys, who seem to be mixed up in all this, work for your family, don't they?"

Well, what could I say? If there was ever a time a friend needed support, this was it, and besides, I was dying to find out what had happened after we left the Tanseys' place the night before.

Ben, who would be leaving that afternoon to spend Christmas with his son Greer in Atlanta, kissed me briefly before we left in separate cars. Because Greer is in his last year of residency at Emory University Hospital, he wasn't able to get away, and Ben didn't want him to be without family, even though they might not have a chance to spend much time together. "See you in a few days," he whispered, as I drove away, and I grew warm at the thought. We had agreed to exchange gifts at a ski resort in North Carolina in early January, and the fact that neither of us knew how to ski didn't bother us a bit.

Earlier I had phoned Eula Shackelford in Soso and left a message for Carolyn to call me at my cell phone number, but as yet she hadn't returned my call.

I found a familiar vehicle in the parking lot behind the Stone's Throw police station and a familiar figure in it. I wasn't surprised when Ellis got out of her car to join me in mine. "Zee called and told me you all would be here," she said, "but you might as well just stay where you are because they won't let you in the room while they talk to Idonia."

"Then how am I supposed to give her comfort and support from out here?" I wailed, settling down to wait.

"I hope they don't arrest her for being an accomplice—or, what is it? An accessory after the fact," Augusta said from the backseat, startling both Ellis and me.

"Good grief, Augusta! You just about scared me to death," I said. "And that's not even funny."

"I didn't mean it to be," she said. "But I believe she'll be all right. Her son seems a solid sort, and I expect she'll be glad of his presence after all."

With eyes on the door where we hoped our friend would soon emerge, we settled in to make the best of the situation, and had been there only a few minutes when my cell phone rang.

Carolyn Shackelford Haney had a voice as rhythmic and full of humor as her mother's and I could hear a baby trying very hard to talk in the background. I told her I was looking for someone who had kept in touch with Dinah Tansey after her marriage to Dexter Clark, who might know where she died and was buried.

"It was somewhere in North Carolina," she said, "but I can't think of the name of the town. I kept several of her letters though, and if you'll wait just a minute, I'll go get them. I know Mama wouldn't throw them away."

I was going to tell her I would call her back, but she had already gone in search of the letters. A few minutes later I heard hurried footsteps approaching. "It was Asheboro," Carolyn said breathlessly. "I should've remembered because we drove through there looking at furniture once and I went to visit her grave."

"So you actually saw where she was buried?" I asked.

Carolyn didn't speak for a minute and when she did it was with emotion. "Dinah and I were friends since the fifth grade, but it was about a year after she died that I got a phone call from Dexter telling me what had happened. He cried, wanted to see me, to talk, I guess—seemed to be sorry…I don't know, but I did come. I came for Dinah. She was a gifted musician, you know. Played the piano and the flute. Dinah could've done something with her life. Instead she—" Her voice broke.

"That must have been a tragic experience losing a friend like that—and one so young," I said. "Carolyn, there's a reason I'm asking you this, but I need to know when Dinah died. Do you remember the date?"

"I sure do. It was April 17, 2002, the day my nephew was born. The little dickens was three weeks early."

I thought of the beautiful young girl dying too soon, and although it made me sad, it also made me furious. This could've happened to my own headstrong daughter, Julie. It might happen yet. "I'm so sorry," I said. "It seems like such a waste. What on earth do you suppose made her go off with somebody like Dexter Clark?"

Carolyn hesitated before she spoke. "I think she did it to get away from that house," she said.

But when I asked her what she meant, she wouldn't say any more.

"How do you know Dinah was really in that grave?" Ellis said when I repeated our conversation.

I hadn't thought to ask Carolyn if there had been a stone. "We'll have to wait until tomorrow and call about the death certificate," I said. "All the county offices will be closed on Sunday."

"No, we won't," Ellis reminded me. "Now that we know where and when Dinah was supposed to have died, we can access that on a computer."

Augusta sighed. "Glory be! I should've thought of that."

"I wish we had one with us," I said. Now that we were this close to learning the truth about Dinah's death, I couldn't bear to wait.

"What about your friend who works for the college?" Augusta asked. "Wouldn't she have one of those machines?"

"Claudia! Of course. I know she used to do a lot of freelance work from home," Ellis said. "Let's hope we can catch her before she goes off somewhere."

We were in luck. "Oh my gosh! Do you really think she might not have died? Wait a sec, let me turn off this food processor." Claudia, I learned, was in the middle of making clam dip for a family party. "I can look it up now if you can hold, or did you rather I call you back?"

I was going to tell her we'd wait when Ellis let out a shout, "Here she comes!" And I looked up to see Idonia coming out of the building with Nathan and his family.

At least they didn't arrest her, I thought. Not yet, anyway. "Idonia's just leaving the police station, and as far as I can tell, she's not in handcuffs," I told Claudia. "Just give me a call on my cell phone when you know something, okay?"

"Will do, if you'll fill me in on Idonia," she promised.

Nathan, I noticed, had a firm grip on his mother's arm and she signaled frantically for us to follow them as they left the station and turned in the direction of Idonia's house.

"I'll ride with you," Ellis said when I hesitated to follow. "We don't want to lose them."

Nathan's wife and daughter were leaving Idonia's as we drove up; they had things to do to get ready for Christmas, Nathan explained. He and his mother, he added, would be following them in the morning.

Augusta accompanied us inside, then disappeared, but I knew she was there listening. Like Ellis and me, she couldn't bear not to know what was going on.

Yawning, Nathan excused himself to take a short nap, as, he said pointedly, he didn't get much sleep the night before.

Good, I thought. Now Idonia can tell us what went on during her interrogation with the Stone's Throw police.

She didn't waste any time. "Bless his heart," she said as her son left the room. "I'm afraid he's a bit miffed with me."

"He'll get over it," I said. "What did the police have to say? They didn't tell you not to leave town, did they?"

Idonia sighed. "Oh, I wish! They really wanted me to tell them all about Melrose."

"And did you?" Ellis asked.

"I told them all I knew. Of course, I don't know where he is now. I wish I did!" Idonia went to the window and peered out at the empty street. "I'm afraid I was a little harsh on them, but Melrose is in trouble. I know he is, and they keep acting as if he's done something wrong!" She pulled herself up to her full stature and gave the curtains a jerk. "I told that simpleton Elmer Harris if he'd concentrate on finding the real killer instead of picking on innocent people, they would've cleared this up by now."

Idonia paced to the mantel and paused just long enough to adjust a candlestick. "And I'm not the only one who feels that way. Paulette Morgan—you know Paulette—dispatcher over at the police department—anyway, she told me Opal's brother was in there yesterday carryin' on something terrible about what happened to Opal. The man's no fool. He knows good and well it was murder."

I wasn't surprised. From what Terrance Banks had said when we spoke with him the day before, he was as determined to get to the bottom of this as we were.

"What else did they want to know?" I asked.

Idonia perched on the arm of a chair and spoke so softly I had to strain to hear her. "They asked where he got the locket."

I leaned forward. "Where did he get it?"

"From some booth at a flea market in Charlotte." Idonia flushed. "Oh, I know Melrose stretched the truth—okay, he told a whopper about it being a family heirloom and all, but he wanted it to be special, you see. He had no idea it had belonged to the Tanseys' daughter."

"And to Opal's family before that. I'm surprised Opal didn't mention it to him," Ellis said. "Didn't he show it to her?"

Idonia nodded. "Told him her grandmother or somebody like that—had had one just like it. She wanted to know where he got it, but of course he didn't want to admit it came from a flea market. Silly man! Didn't he know it wouldn't have mattered to me where it came from?"

Idonia turned away, I thought to hide her tears, but she stood and spoke with new resolve. "I want to speak with Al Evans. When Melrose disappeared after Opal died the police took a box of his belongings from the Spring Lamb. They turned it over to Al after they looked through it since he's his closest kin. I'd like to know what's in there."

Ellis grinned. "Lucy Nan thinks Al's been hiding Melrose. Thought they were in cahoots together."

"I did not!" I shot her a dirty look.

"Did, too! After Opal's funeral you wanted us to follow that poor man home. You know you did, Lucy Nan."

"Well…I thought he might know where Melrose was," I admitted.

"I wish he did," Idonia said, "but there might be something in the notes Melrose made that would give us an idea where to find him. I know he kept a notebook from that correspondence course he was taking. It's got to be in there."

I remembered what Idonia had said about Melrose taking a course in detective work and offered to bring her the box.

"I'll come with you," she said.

"Idonia, if Nathan wakes from his nap and finds you gone, I won't be responsible for what he might do," I told her. "If you'll call Al and tell him we're on the way, we'll be back before you can say, John Robinson."

"THAT'S JACK ROBINSON," Ellis said as we left. "You've been around Augusta too long."

I heard her laughter before Augusta appeared on the backseat. "I heard that," she said, "and who is this Robinson fellow anyway?"

My cell phone rang before I could answer but all I could hear was a football game in the background. "Brian, honey, turn that thing down!" Claudia hollered in my ear. "Sorry to be so late calling you back but my sister phoned right after I spoke with you, and I thought I'd never get away. You know how Gina is!"

I said I knew and what did she find out about Dinah Tansey?

"It was her all right. Died April 17, 2002. She was only nineteen, Lucy Nan. No wonder her mama looks so sad." And Claudia sounded close to tears herself.

"So Dinah's really dead," Ellis said when I told her. "Then who's been wearing those long dresses to try and frighten people at Willowbrook?"

And why? I wondered. And which of the family had created a shrine to Dinah's memory in a locked room?

TWENTY-SIX

IDONIA WAITED AT THE front door and Nathan was still asleep when we returned with the box of Melrose's belongings. "The police must not have found anything of interest in here or else they wouldn't have given it to Al," I said as Idonia set it on the dining room table and hastily pulled off the lid. "If there's a clue in there to all that's been happening, you'd think they would've followed up on it."

Idonia frowned as she examined a small composition book. "You'd think," she said.

Or maybe they had, I thought. The local law enforcement officials now knew everything we did and probably more about the two suspicious deaths, the whereabouts of the locket, and the disappearance of Melrose DuBois. Well, almost all, unless they'd also found the locked room.

It was obvious that Idonia wanted to sift through the box alone so Ellis and I made a tactful exit. "You will call if you think you've found something?" I said. "Promise you won't go running off somewhere again."

"Lucy Nan's right, Idonia," Ellis added. "If you find something that might lead to Melrose, for Pete's sake, let the police take care of it."

But Idonia was too busy reading to answer.

The call came about an hour later. I had dropped off Ellis at her place and Augusta had just plugged in the tree lights and was getting ready to light a fire in the living-room fireplace when Nathan Culpepper phoned.

"Is she there?" he demanded.

Although he didn't identify himself, I recognized his voice.

"Idonia's not here, Nathan. What happened?"

"I woke up about ten minutes ago and she was gone. God only knows where she went this time! I'm calling the police."

"Wait, Nathan!" I called, but I was already too late. All I heard was a dial tone. When I tried to call him back the line was busy.

"Idonia's going to have a hissy," I told Augusta. "She's given Nathan the slip again and he's already put the police on her trail." Not that she didn't deserve it. I would seriously consider taking her name off my Christmas card list if I hadn't already forgotten to mail them.

Augusta silently closed the fire screen and unplugged the tree lights. "Did he have any idea where she went?"

"He didn't give me time to ask him," I said, calling Idonia's number again. This time I got no answer. "She must've found something in Melrose's notebook…"

We started for the door at the same time.

"HOW ARE WE GOING TO get in?" I asked as I parked in front of Idonia's. Of course, Augusta could've opened the door, I remembered, but as it turned out, she didn't have to. Nathan had left the house unlocked. His car was not in the driveway and on checking, I saw that Idonia's garage was empty.

"I don't see the box," I said, seeing upon entering that the dining room table was bare.

"She probably took it in her room so she'd have more privacy," Augusta suggested, and there it was on the floor between the bed and the rocking chair. A composition book, the speckled black and white kind, lay open in the seat of the chair. Although Melrose had used a computer for the course he was taking, he apparently kept his notes in longhand.

I passed the book to Augusta while I phoned Ellis, only to find no one there. "Idonia has disappeared again, and Nathan and the police are looking for her," I said, leaving a recorded message. "We've found the notes Melrose left and I'm afraid she's gone to find him. I'm hoping the notes will help us know where to look. You can reach me on my cell phone."

Augusta sat in the chair and read silently while I looked over her shoulder.

"Now we know what he was doing at the church the night Opal Henshaw died," she said. "It says here he went there to talk with Dave Tansey since it seemed the problems all centered around that family."

"And that's what he was doing in Soso," I said. "He was there for more or less the same reason we were, but I wonder why he didn't want us to see him."

She looked up briefly. "Probably because he knew you would inevitably ask about the locket he gave Idonia."

Melrose had continued his investigation, it seemed, by attempting to trace the origin of the locket.

"Look here," Augusta said. "He bought it from a place that sells estate jewelry... a man named G. Wayne Gravitt..."

Melrose's notes were precisely written in letters as neat and rounded as Melrose himself. From them we learned that he had gone back to the flea market where he bought the locket and found it had been included in a collection of items purchased from a dealer. From what Melrose wrote, G. Wayne was reluctant to tell him the name of the person who sold them, but Melrose DuBois was not above bribery. He told the man he had seen a photograph of the locket with matching earrings and pretended interest in finding the earrings. It cost him a hundred dollars in the long run and he still didn't learn the name of the dealer. He was given instead a phone number. It only took seconds to find the listing under Tansey.

"I wonder why Melrose didn't take his notes with him," I said.

Augusta closed the notebook. "I suppose he had already found out what he needed to know."

I didn't have a clue how to get in touch with Nathan Culpepper, but I did know how to reach the Stone's Throw police. Ed Tillman, I was told, was off that day, and neither Kemper nor Captain Hardy was in, Paulette Morgan said. At that point I would've even agreed to speak with Chief Elmer Harris, but he had gone to Columbia to see his granddaughter in a Christmas pageant, I was told.

"I'm afraid Idonia has gone to the Tanseys thinking her friend Melrose is in some kind of danger," I told her, "and there's a good chance she might be in danger, too, so you need to get in touch with whoever's on duty *right now.* We—I'm going out there to see if I can find her, so please let them know where I am."

"You're going where?" Paulette asked.

"To the Tanseys out on Willowbrook Road—they know where it is, and if Nathan Culpepper calls, you can give him the same message."

"Will do," Paulette said. "Anything else?"

Isn't that enough? I thought as Augusta and I hurried to the car and headed for the Green Cottage on the outskirts of town. Paulette was dumb as a brick and the only reason she had that job was because her aunt was married to the chief's cousin, but surely she could remember a message as simple as that, I thought.

When we arrived the place seemed deserted and no one answered when I called their number on my cell phone. And then I remembered it was Sunday and the family would be at church for their Christmas program that night. I didn't know if the program was scheduled for late afternoon or evening, but I did know that the police had issued an APB for Jeremiah Tansey, so I would be surprised to find him here.

"It might be to our advantage if you turned the car toward the road in case anyone shows up," Augusta advised. "Meanwhile, I'll check the house to see if Idonia's there."

"Don't forget the locked room!" I called, but she had already disappeared inside. I let the engine idle and watched the road ahead until my eyes ached, feeling as if I were experiencing déjà vu from our adventures of the night before. The Tanseys had left a light burning in the living room, but except for that, darkness surrounded me and I was relieved when Augusta slipped in beside me. "No one's there," she said.

"Did you look in the locked room?" I asked.

"I looked everywhere," she said. "And, Lucy Nan, I've been thinking about that room since you told me what Dinah's friend Carolyn said." Augusta touched my arm. "I believe there was something very wrong in this family."

I had been thinking the same thing. Dinah married Dexter Clark…*to get away from that house*, Carolyn had said. I told Augusta about the dream I had about the young girl crying. "Only her door was locked from the *inside*," I said. "Dear God, do you think her brother, or even her *father*—"

"I think we'd better get to Willowbrook as fast as possible," Augusta said. "I just hope we're not too late."

THE SHORT DRIVE to Willowbrook took only a few minutes but it seemed much longer and I had the door open as soon as we stopped. I saw Idonia's car parked out front about the same time I heard her scream.

"Wait!" Augusta said, and I felt her hand on my shoulder in an attempt to hold me back, but I was already running toward the house. A couple of the boards that were nailed over the entrance had been pried off and I heard someone crying inside. It sounded like Idonia.

"Let me go! I know he's here somewhere and you'd better not have hurt him!" she yelled. "Melrose, where are you?" This was followed by the sound of a scuffle taking place. I stood at the door listening to see if I could tell where it was coming from and wondering what to do when Idonia screamed again, and although the night was cold, I felt as if a fire burned inside me. I had to try and stop whatever was happening, but how? I

stepped through the opening and into the entrance hall but it
was so dark I couldn't see a thing, and almost jumped through
the ceiling when someone touched my arm.

"You'll need this but don't turn it on yet," Augusta said,
pressing a flashlight into my hand. Linking arms we made our
way toward the noise, muffled now. It seemed to be coming
from upstairs and I had started up when I heard someone pound-
ing on the wall somewhere toward the rear of the house.

"Idonia! Idonia, I'm coming!" a man shouted. His voice
sounded far away.

"Melrose?" I paused on the stairs. "It's Lucy Nan. Is that
you?"

"Oh, Lucy Nan, thank God! They've locked me in this place
down here and I can't get out. You've got to get the police!"

"They're on the way," I said, although I knew no such thing,
and hoped they wouldn't hear me upstairs. I had been in such
a hurry to find Idonia, I had left my cell phone in the car. Had
Paulette Morgan relayed my message?

All was quiet upstairs until somebody cursed—a man.
"You'll not get away with this!" Idonia said. At least she was
still alive.

I froze when I heard the sound of a car pull up in front of
the house. *Oh, please, let it be the police!*

"Lucy Nan, what on earth's going on in here?" Ellis said,
shining a light in my face.

I hurried down to shush her and almost stumbled in the
darkness on the bottom step. "For God's sake, be quiet!" I
whispered. "Somebody's got Idonia upstairs and they've locked
Melrose in the basement."

I felt Ellis stiffen beside me as Idonia cried out again. Below
us, Melrose, or I thought it was Melrose, banged and clattered
about as if he meant to send the old house crashing down on
top of us.

Ellis grabbed a splintered board from the front door and
stepped in front of me. "Come on!" she said, shining her light

on the stairs. I was about to follow when the light came to rest on a pair of shoes. The shoes had feet in them.

"Run!" Idonia shouted, but it was too late.

"Jeremiah Tansey!" Ellis muttered under her breath.

"Looks like a party down here," Jeremiah said. "You didn't tell me you were going to invite your friends, but since you're here, let's all go into the living room—*now!*"

I switched on my light to see him shove Idonia in front of him with one hand while he held a gun in the other. Idonia's hands were tied in front of her and she had trouble maneuvering the stairs, although Jeremiah appeared to be accustomed to making his way around the house in the dark. He didn't seem to have noticed Ellis was holding the board. If she could just get close enough, I thought—

"Whatever that is you have in your hands, drop it right now!" he commanded as he herded us into what was once the drawing room, and Ellis did as she was told. "Now what in hell am I going to do with you?" Forcing us into a corner, he waved the gun about, mocking us. "First the old guy comes poking about, and now you!"

It occurred to me then that Augusta was no longer with us but I knew she would find a way to help if she could—and the sooner the better. If we all rushed him at once, I thought, he probably wouldn't be able to take aim. But if he did, I would surely be the one he hit. Still, I was contemplating such a move when a figure entered from the room behind him, the yellow gleam of her flashlight bouncing on each of us in turn. "Well, Jeremiah, what now?" Louella Tansey said.

"Thank heavens you're here!" I said. Surely he wouldn't shoot us in front of his mother. But why was she just standing there?

"What's all that racket about in the basement? Sounds like a wild man down there? And what are all these people here for?" Louella said.

"He has a gun, Louella," I shouted, "and he's locked—" But

Louella Tansey didn't seem the least bit concerned. I couldn't see her face in the darkness but her voice didn't sound at all like the mousy woman we knew. "Be quiet!" she said.

"As you can see, I have a little problem here," Jeremiah said. "I had the old man tied up down there but he must've gotten loose somehow." He gave Idonia a shove and she would've fallen if Ellis hadn't steadied her. "Then this one comes crashing in—pulled half the boards off the front door and came in here hollering for the old guy—and now these two! What am I supposed to do with them now?"

"Put them down there with that other one, I reckon," his mother said. "But we'll have to hurry, Jeremiah. The police have been here looking for you. We can't stay here any longer."

"And then what? Somebody's sure to find them, and you know they'll tell," he said.

His mother didn't answer, but her silence lay like a suffocating shroud around us.

If we could only delay them! "You were the one who killed Dexter Clark," I said to Jeremiah. "Why?"

"I'll tell you why," his mother answered. "Dexter was afraid to come to our house, afraid he might see Dave or me. My husband never forgave him because of what happened to Dinah. But Dexter got religion, it seems, and wanted to return the locket—"

"So we'd have something of hers to keep, he said," Jeremiah added. "When he called, I told him I'd meet him here. Hell, I didn't mean to kill him!"

"It was an accident," Louella added, with unmistakable impatience in her voice, "but nobody would've believed it."

"We had a slight disagreement," Jeremiah said.

Ellis spoke from behind me. "And you pushed him from the balcony?"

"We fought. He fell." Jeremiah's account sounded almost as if he were explaining away a broken lamp. "He was going to—"

"That's enough, son!" Louella spoke sharply.

I threaded my arm through Idonia's. If we had to run, I would try to pull her along. "Why are you doing this?" I asked. "What are you hiding here that you don't want anybody to see?" If I was going to be locked away—or worse—I wanted to know the reason why.

I didn't get one. "Come on, better get 'em on up there," Louella said, heading for the stairs.

Up there? I thought they were taking us to the basement. "I'm not going," I said, hanging back.

"I'm not either!" Ellis spoke beside me.

With a sudden jerk, Jeremiah wrenched Idonia away from me. "I don't think you'd like to see me shoot your friend here right in front of you."

"He means what he says," Louella said, stepping in front of us. "Get up the stairs, all of you."

"Where's Augusta?" Ellis whispered as we climbed the stairs ahead of them.

"She's here. Don't worry," I said.

"Shut up!" Jeremiah gave us a push from behind. "You know, with a little help, this old place would go up in a minute," he muttered aside to his mother.

If Augusta was going to help us, she'd better hurry, I thought. And that was when I heard footsteps above us—or was that just wishful thinking? But Ellis heard it, too. Her hand tightened on my arm, and behind us, Idonia gave an encouraging gasp.

Melrose DuBois stood at the top of the stairs with something that looked a whole lot like a gun and he pointed it at Jeremiah Tansey. "If you don't drop that gun right now, I'll shoot you where you stand," he said in a voice as solid and steady as the heart-of-pine stairs beneath us.

TWENTY-SEVEN

"MELROSE! WHERE DID YOU come from?" Idonia would have run to him if we hadn't held her back.

"Idonia, honey! Are you all right?" he said, then added to Jeremiah, "I'd drop that gun *now* if I were you. I'm about mad enough right now to shoot you anyhow."

"Where did you get that gun?" Jeremiah asked, hesitating. But Ellis had had enough of Jeremiah Tansey. His gun clattered to the floor below as she gave him a push that sent him sprawling backward, his head banging on the treads.

"Oh no! You've killed him! Jeremiah, baby, are you all right?" His mother ran to gather him into her arms, and holding to the railing, I stepped quickly around them and made my way down the stairs to retrieve the gun he had dropped.

ELLIS USED HER CELL PHONE to call the police while the rest of us kept an eye on the two Tanseys. Jeremiah had managed to pull himself into a sitting position and now sat on the bottom step with his head in his hands while Louella hovered over him.

"Why didn't they send somebody out here the first time I called?" I asked.

"Because Paulette sent them out to Winternook," she said. "You know, that retirement community on the way to Columbia. "Told them Idonia was in big trouble out there."

And I'm not sure, but it sounded like a giggle came from Idonia Mae Culpepper.

"How did you manage to get upstairs all the way from the basement?" I asked Melrose.

"There's a narrow stairway that goes all the way up from there. I found the door to it down there while I was trying to feel my way out, but it was so dark, I couldn't see where it came out. That's where I was when I heard you, but I wasn't sure where I was."

"So how did you see the exit in the dark?" Idonia wanted to know.

"After I heard all that was going on, I was determined to try again," Melrose said. "I felt my way up on my hands and knees until I couldn't go any farther, but I knew there had to be an opening somewhere…and then the strangest thing happened. The door just started to open by itself. It was behind a bookcase in that big old room upstairs at the very back of the house. The bookcase just swung out, and let me tell you, I got out of there in a hurry!"

"You must've touched something," Idonia suggested. "A lever or a button or something."

"But I didn't!" Melrose insisted. "It just happened. And you know, this is a funny thing, too, but it smelled just like strawberries up there."

I couldn't see Ellis's face in the dim light, but I knew she was smiling, too. "But where did you get the gun?" I asked.

"There's a room down there you can't see from the other part of the basement and that's where he had me tied up until I managed to work loose. The door to it appears to be just another part of the wall, and it looks like it's been that way forever. That's where the stairs come out and that's where I found the gun along with enough stuff to stock a store," he said. "You wouldn't believe all the things down there: computers, televisions, jewelry, even a motorcycle. And guns—several guns. That one wasn't loaded, of course."

A motorcycle. According to Weigelia, Kemper had said that when Dexter Clark disappeared he had been riding a motorcycle.

Melrose put his coat around Idonia when she began to shiver

and encouraged us all to go out to the car and turn on the heater, but Idonia didn't want to leave him with the Tanseys and neither did Ellis nor I. I could barely stand to look at Louella Tansey crouching beside her son. After all the terrible things he'd done, she still excused him, though she knew he was responsible for Dexter Clark's death and had probably sold the locket that had belonged to his sister. Of course it had to have been Louella who hid the locket in the flour canister, I thought. We should have known right away it wouldn't occur to a man to put it there.

Idonia sighed. "Surely that locket wasn't worth all this!" She directed her question to Louella who continued to fret over her son. "What was so important about that locket that one of you drugged my drink to get it back?"

"And it very nearly killed her!" Melrose added in a voice trembling with rage.

Jeremiah struggled to stand but a shouted warning from Melrose sent him back to his seat on the stairs. "Look," he said, "I only meant for it to make her sleepy. You've got to believe me! I didn't know it would—"

"Stop it, Jeremiah!" Louella said. "Can't you see my son is delirious? He has a head injury and doesn't know what he's saying. Why, he might even have a con—"

"Oh, shut up!" Jeremiah shoved his mother's hands aside. "It was your idea and you know it."

"And just whose idea was it to sell your sister's locket?" Louella snapped. "Of all the stupid notions, Jeremiah! Of course we had to get it back."

"The locket was your only connection to Dexter Clark—the only real link with your sister," Ellis said. "And when Opal Henshaw noticed that photograph of Dinah on your piano, she signed her death warrant."

"It wouldn't have been long," I said, "before Opal put two and two together and realized Dinah's husband was her nephew, Dexter Clark."

I assumed it was the police when I heard footsteps approaching outside a few minutes later, so I was surprised to see Preacher Dave Tansey standing in the doorway with a lantern in his hand. It was the kind you use for camping and gave out a warm yellow light.

"I saw all the cars over here and thought I'd better check it out," he began. And then he saw Jeremiah. "You!" he said. "I thought I told you to clear out of here. I suppose you know the police are looking for you. They say you killed the Clark fellow, and probably Opal Henshaw, too. And you might as well have killed your sister. Well, it's going to end, and it's going to end now."

Dave Tansey set his lantern on the floor and raised a rifle to his shoulder, pointing it at his son.

"No!" Louella threw herself on Jeremiah. "No! Don't hurt him! Please don't hurt him."

Jeremiah didn't speak but stared defiantly at his father as I was sure he had done many times before.

"Get out of the way, Louella. I don't want to kill you, too, although you deserve it for covering up for him all these years. If it hadn't been for the two of you, our Dinah would still be with us. I—I had no idea what was going on until I found her diary, and God help me, I read it. Did you know she left a diary?" His voice broke with a sob.

"But I didn't know. I didn't!" Louella reached out to him. "Not until it was too late. Our Dinah's gone…Jeremiah, he's all we have left!"

"Preacher Dave! Think what you're doing," I said. "This is against everything you believe in."

"Let the police take care of him," Ellis begged. "Don't ruin your life this way."

"It's already ruined," he said. "It's too late."

"No, it's not!" Idonia chimed in. "He's not worth it. Think of your congregation. They need you."

Still, he didn't lower the rifle but held it steady, ignoring our pleas and those of his sobbing wife. I looked at Melrose, who now held the gun Jeremiah had dropped, and waited for him to speak, to intercede, but Melrose only drew Idonia closer. Maybe he didn't care if Preacher Dave shot Jeremiah or not. Finally he stepped away from us. "Preacher, that's not a good idea. You're going to regret this. Now, listen—"

I jumped when I heard the clear, deadly click as Dave Tansey cocked his rifle. He meant to kill his son and there was nothing we could do about it. Melrose stood with the gun hanging loosely by his side. He was not going to fire on Dave Tansey and I didn't blame him, but what Dave was about to do was worse than being shot.

"I can't bear to think of what you did," Preacher Dave said to Jeremiah, and his voice was so full of heartbreak it made me cry.

"Please, Daddy, no! I'm sorry, I'm sorry!" Jeremiah sobbed.

I felt as if we were part of a freeze-frame in a movie: the gaunt man with the rifle and the pleading son; the hysterical woman, the dark old house, the soft glow of the lantern, and the rest of us, stiff with dread. And then suddenly, Preacher Dave stepped back and lowered the rifle, and his face seemed to glow as brightly as the lantern at his feet. "Forgive me," he said, and turned and walked away.

"I CAN'T BELIEVE she's really gone and done it," Nettie said. It was almost a week after Christmas and The Thursdays who gathered around my kitchen table didn't even pretend they were there to discuss a book.

"And she didn't even invite us to the wedding," Jo Nell said. "Looks like she'd want one of us to stand up with her."

"Nathan and his family were there," I said. "She said she didn't want a big wedding this time." Idonia and Melrose had been married in a tiny chapel the day before and were now honeymooning on a cruise ship in the Bahamas.

Ellis stroked Clementine's big head. "Sneaky thing didn't tell us she and Melrose got their license and blood tests when they were staying at that inn near Raleigh."

"And we were all frantic thinking she'd been snatched by the evil Melrose," Zee said, laughing.

Claudia smiled. "But he really did turn out to be her knight in shining armor, didn't he?"

"Sure did," Ellis said. "He had all of us believing that gun was loaded."

Since that frightening night at Willowbrook we had learned that Jeremiah Tansey, with his mother's knowledge, had been running a fencing operation dealing in stolen goods, which were stored in a hidden room in the basement at Willowbrook. When Dexter Clark met Jeremiah there to return Dinah's locket, he'd arrived when Jeremiah was unloading some of his plunder and threatened to tell his father. The two fought and Dexter fell or was pushed from the decaying balcony. He dropped the locket before he fell and Jeremiah, hoping to keep the meeting and the locket a secret from his parents, sold it, along with stolen estate valuables, to G. Wayne Gravitt, who asked no questions, and that's where Melrose came into the story.

Nettie folded a paper Christmas napkin in accordion pleats. "So it was Jeremiah who drugged Idonia's punch. But how did he manage to do it?" she asked.

"When the police finally arrived at Willowbrook that night they found a tape player hooked up to a microphone that could be controlled by a remote, along with a dress and wig in that hidden room in the basement, and the music he played was probably an old tape of Dinah's. Jeremiah was slender enough to easily fit into the dress. From a distance, no one could tell the difference," I told her.

"So he wore those to slip in and drug Idonia's punch," Jo Nell said. "But I don't understand how."

"Jeremiah's small," I explained, "and wearing the dress and

wig he could walk right past that bunch at Bellawood, then go upstairs, and slip something in Idonia's punch. He and Louella didn't want that locket traced back to them as it would connect him to Dexter Clark's death. It must've been a shock when Melrose bought it and Idonia turned up wearing it."

"Remember when Idonia carried on so about being followed the night we went caroling?" Ellis said. "I wonder if that was Louella."

"Maybe. Those two were determined to get that locket back," I said. "It could just as easily have been Jeremiah."

"Was he the one who pushed Opal from the balcony?" Zee asked.

"The police seem to think Louella moved the swag and Jeremiah did the pushing, but I don't think they know for sure," I said.

"If only Opal hadn't noticed that locket in the photograph and told Louella about an identical one in her own family," Claudia said.

"That was before most people knew the body at Willowbrook had been identified as Dexter," Ellis added. "Unfortunately for Opal, the police seemed to want that kept quiet. And, too, Opal had seen the locket Melrose bought for Idonia. She was bound to wonder how he came by it when she heard of Dexter's death."

"If Opal Henshaw hadn't been so hell-bent on delivering that fruitcake, she'd be alive today," Zee said. "I always knew that stuff was deadly!"

"She was only trying to do the right thing," I said, shaking my head. "And look where it got her."

Nettie sighed. "Poor Dexter! It's a shame he waited until Dinah's death to change for the better."

"Well, it won't help to dwell on that now," Jo Nell reminded her. "Are Cudin' Vance and his fiancée still planning to renovate the old home place?" she asked. "If I were those two I think I'd just find a nice little house in the suburbs."

I laughed. "The last I heard they were still interested, but Vance says they'll probably have to do it in stages, so if they start from the basement up we might not live to see it!"

Ellis got up and poured coffee all around. "I feel bad about Preacher Dave. It makes me sad to think of what he must have been through. His son and his wife are both in jail for murder, or accessory to murder. And can you believe that mealy-mouthed Louella? I wonder how long she knew that degenerate Jeremiah was abusing his own sister and still did nothing about it."

"That must be why Preacher kept Dinah's things in that locked room," Ellis said. "It really was a shrine of sorts. I expect he spent a lot of time in there just thinking of what could've been, and can you imagine how he felt when he found that diary? That's probably what drove him to what he almost did."

"I'm glad to hear his congregation has been supportive," Zee said. "They even helped move him into a small house next to the church out there. I guess your cousin will have to find another caretaker for Willowbrook."

"Pete Whittaker told me Dave Tansey had spoken to him about forming a group with other churches in the area to reach out to abused children," I said. "I'm sure something good will come of that."

"I wonder what stopped him from shooting Jeremiah," Claudia said. "From what you all told me, he came close to killing his own son."

Nettie stirred sugar into her coffee. "Somebody told me Preacher Dave said he sensed somebody standing right behind him, and felt such goodness surrounding him he just couldn't pull the trigger. Kind of a wild tale if you ask me. I don't know whether to believe that or not."

I looked up to find Augusta standing in the doorway and smiled.

"Believe it," I said.

Some of Stone's Throw's Favorites

Ellis's Hot Clam Dip

One 8-ounce package cream cheese
½ pint sour cream
One 7 ½-ounce can minced clams
Drained juice of 1 lemon
Dash red pepper, Texas Pete (or Tabasco), and
Worcestershire sauce
Salt to taste

Cream the cheese and sour cream together and add the other ingredients. Heat in chafing dish until hot and bubbly, and serve with crackers or chips.

Serves about 6–8 (easily doubled).

Claudia's Marinated Mushrooms

1 pound fresh mushrooms, washed, or two or three 6-ounce cans whole mushrooms
1 onion, sliced
2/3 cup tarragon vinegar
½ cup olive oil
1 medium clove garlic, minced
1 tablespoon sugar
1½ teaspoons salt
Dash freshly ground black pepper
Dash pepper sauce

Put the mushrooms and onion in a jar or tightly covered container.

Combine remaining ingredients and pour over them. Refrigerate until ready to serve.

—In memory of Meredith Camann—

Augusta's Spicy Meat Pies

Pastry:

    2 cups all-purpose flour plus more to cover surface

    1 teaspoon baking powder

    1 teaspoon salt

    2/3 cup shortening

    4 tablespoons ice water, more if needed

Sift dry ingredients together, blend in shortening with a fork or pastry blender, and add ice water a little at a time. Knead on a floured surface to form a ball.

Filling:

    2 teaspoons vegetable oil

    1 small onion, finely chopped

    1 large clove garlic, minced

    1/4 teaspoon ground cinnamon

    ½ teaspoon ground red pepper (cayenne)

    ¼ pound ground lean beef

    ¼ teaspoon salt

    3 tablespoons golden raisins, chopped

    3 tablespoons pimiento-stuffed olives, chopped

    1 cup canned diced tomatoes with juice

    1 egg

Heat the oil in a skillet and add the onion and seasonings. Add the beef. Cook until the beef begins to brown and stir in the raisins, olives, and tomatoes. Cook about 10 minutes until almost all the liquid evaporates. Remove from the heat.

Preheat the oven to 425 degrees.

Roll out the pastry—thin for pie crusts. Cut as many rounds as possible using a glass or 3-inch cutter. Put about 1 or 2 teaspoons of the filling in each round, fold over, and crimp the edges. Brush the tops with 2 tablespoons water beaten with the egg. Bake about 12 minutes on an ungreased cookie sheet until golden brown. Serve warm. (These are kind of troublesome but very good.)

(Easily doubled.)

Martin Shackelford's Good-and-Easy Biscuits

1¾ cups self-rising flour plus more to cover surface
1 cup whipping cream

Preheat the oven to 425 degrees.

Mix the dough and roll out on a floured surface. Cut with a biscuit cutter and bake in the preheated oven about 10 to 12 minutes. Serve hot.

Anna's Cream Cheese and Apple Salad

One 3-ounce package lemon gelatin
(Anna usually adds about ½ 3-ounce package more)
One 8-ounce package cream cheese, softened
One 20-ounce can crushed pineapple, drained (reserve juice)
1/3 cup sugar
2 cups tart apples, peeled and chopped
1 cup pecans, chopped
One 8-ounce container frozen whipped topping, thawed
Lettuce (optional)

Cream the dry gelatin and cream cheese together. Combine the reserved pineapple juice and sugar in a saucepan and bring to a boil. Add to the gelatin mix and stir until dissolved. Add the apples and pecans. Cool, then fold in the whipped topping and spoon into a 9x13-inch ungreased pan. Chill for 6 hours or overnight. Cut into squares and serve on lettuce, if desired.

Cousin Jo Nell's "Joyed-It" Jam Cake

1 cup butter
1½ cups sugar
3 eggs

1 teaspoon baking soda
1 cup buttermilk
3 cups flour
1 teaspoon each allspice, cloves, cinnamon, and nutmeg
1 cup seedless blackberry jam
1 pinch powdered ginger
Glaze (optional)

Preheat the oven to 300 degrees. Grease and flour a tube pan, put wax paper cut to fit in the bottom of the pan.

Cream the butter; add the sugar and eggs. Add the baking soda to the buttermilk and add to the egg mixture. Sift the flour and sift again with the spices. Add the flour mixture gradually to the butter mixture. Add the jam last. Bake for 1 hour and 20 minutes. This is good with a glaze made of the juice and grated rind of one orange, mixed with sifted confectioner's sugar. You don't want to get it too runny so measure a little at a time. It's also good just plain.

Mattie Durham's Charleston Squares

1 stick (½ cup) butter or margarine
1 cup sugar
2 eggs plus 1 egg yolk
2 cups all-purpose flour
1 teaspoon baking powder

½ teaspoon salt
1 teaspoon pure almond extract
1 teaspoon pure vanilla extract
1 egg white
½ cup firmly packed brown sugar
½ teaspoon vanilla extract
½ cup chopped nuts (pecans or almonds are good)
1 4-oz. bottle maraschino cherries, chopped and drained

Preheat the oven to 350 degrees.

Cream the butter and sugar. Add the eggs and egg yolk, one at a time, mixing well. Sift together the flour, baking powder, and salt and add to the creamed mixture. Add the almond and 1 teaspoon of the vanilla extracts. Spread the batter in the prepared pan. Beat the egg white and add the brown sugar and the remaining ½ teaspoon vanilla. Spread over the batter and sprinkle with the nuts and cherries. Bake for about 30 minutes. Cool and cut into squares. These are delicious and great for parties.

Aunt Eula's Lemonade Cake

One (3-ounce) package lemon Jell-O
¾ cup boiling water
1½ cups granulated sugar
¾ cup oil
4 eggs

2½ cups plain flour
2½ teaspoons baking powder
1 teaspoon salt
2 tablespoons freshly squeezed lemon juice
1 tablespoon grated lemon rind
1 tablespoon lemon extract
1 6-ounce can frozen lemonade
¾ cup powdered sugar, sifted

Preheat the oven to 350 degrees. Prepare a greased and floured 10-inch tube or Bundt pan.

Dissolve the Jell-O in the boiling water and set aside to cool. Mix the sugar and oil and add the eggs one at a time, beating well after each addition. In a separate bowl, mix the sifted flour, baking powder, and salt. Add to the egg mixture alternately with the gelatin mixture, beginning and ending with the flour. Beat thoroughly after each addition. Stir in the lemon juice, lemon rind, and lemon extract. Pour into the prepared pan and bake for 1 hour. While the cake is baking, thaw the lemonade and stir in the powdered sugar. Beat until smooth. Punch holes in top of cake while it's still warm in the pan and pour the lemonade mixture over it a little at a time. Let cool in the pan before removing. If you like lemon, you'll love this.

Cissy's Turtle Bars

Crust:
2 cups flour
1 cup firmly packed brown sugar
½ cup butter, softened
1 cup whole pecan halves

Caramel layer:
½ cup firmly packed brown sugar
½ cup butter
12 ounces milk chocolate chips

Preheat the oven to 350 degrees.

Combine the flour, brown sugar, and butter for the crust, mix well and pat firmly into an ungreased 9x13-inch pan. Sprinkle the pecans evenly over the unbaked crust. Prepare the caramel layer by combining the brown sugar and butter in a heavy sauce pan. Cook over medium heat, stirring constantly, until the mixture begins to boil. Boil ½ to 1 minute, stirring the whole time. Pour over the pecans and crust. Bake for 18 to 22 minutes or until the crust is light golden brown. Remove from the oven and immediately sprinkle with chocolate chips. Allow to melt and then swirl. Cool and cut into bars.

Makes 3 to 4 dozen.

REQUEST YOUR FREE BOOKS!

2 FREE NOVELS
PLUS 2 FREE GIFTS!

MYSTERY **WORLDWIDE LIBRARY** ®

Your Partner in Crime

WWLI0